Rethinking Law as Process

Rethinking Law as Process: Creativity, Novelty, Change draws on insights from 'process philosophy' in order to rethink the nature of legal decision-making. While there have been significant developments in the application of 'process' thought across a number of disciplines, little notice has been taken of Whiteheadian metaphysics in law. Nevertheless, process thought offers significant opportunities for serious inquiry into the nature of legal reasoning and the practical application of law. Focusing on the practices of organising, rather than their effects, an increased processual awareness re-orients understanding away from the mechanistic and rationalist assumptions of Newtonian thought, and towards the interminable ontological quest to arrest or to classify the essentially undivided flow of human experience. Drawing together insights from a number of different fields, James MacLean argues that it is because our inherited conceptual framework is tied to a 'static' way of thinking that every attempt to offer justifying reasons for legal decisions appears at best to register only at the level of explanation. *Rethinking Law as Process* resolves this problem, and so provides a more adequate description of the nature of law and legal decision-making, by repositioning law within a thoroughly processual world-view, in which there is only the continuous effort to refine and to redefine the continuous flux of legal understanding.

James MacLean is Lecturer in Law at the University of Southampton, where he teaches legal reasoning and legal theory. He is co-editor of *The Universal and the Particular in Legal Reasoning*, a collection of essays on the work of the late Professor Sir Neil MacCormick.

Rethinking Law as Process

Creativity, Novelty, Change

James MacLean

Routledge
Taylor & Francis Group

a GlassHouse book

First published 2012
by Routledge
2 Park Square, Milton Park, Abingdon, Oxon OX14 4RN

Simultaneously published in the USA and Canada
by Routledge
711 Third Avenue, New York, NY 10017

A GlassHouse Book

Routledge is an imprint of the Taylor & Francis Group, an informa business

British Library Cataloguing in Publication Data
A catalogue record for this book is available from the British Library

Library of Congress Cataloging in Publication Data
MacLean, James.
    Rethinking law as process : creativity, novelty, change / James MacLean.
      p. cm.
    Includes bibliographical references.
    1. Law--Philosophy. 2. Law--Methodology. 3. Process philosophy. I. Title.
    K213.M33 2011
    340'.1--dc22

                2010052902

ISBN13: 978-0-415-57540-9 (hbk)
ISBN13: 978-1-136-69777-7 (ebk)

Typeset in Times New Roman
by Taylor & Francis Books

For Diana

Contents

Acknowledgements

I have a number of significant debts to acknowledge; in particular, to Zenon Bańkowski and Emilios Christodoulidis for their immense assistance, encouragement and involvement through many lengthy discussions, all of which have helped to bring this work to completion. My early research for this project began when I undertook doctoral research at the University of Edinburgh and I would like to acknowledge the assistance provided then through an award from the Arts and Humanities Research Council. My thanks, also, to John Bell and Claudio Michelon whose comments on an earlier draft have proved invaluable. Finally, I would like to acknowledge the help and encouragement that I received from the late Professor Sir Neil MacCormick through his careful and thoughtful responses to some of the ideas presented in this work.

List of abbreviations

ITL   Institutional Theory of Law
CLS   Critical Legal Studies

Introduction

Two things always bothered me when I was a boy. First of all, I puzzled interminably over my inability to catch a single moment, to identify anything that I could really call 'the present'. I had been taught in school that time could be divided up into past, present and future and that these three related to each other in particular ways, but I had great difficulty understanding how this relation worked. I could see what the teacher meant when she said that the past was 'what was over': it was like the road already travelled, similar to the long stretch of grey tarmac that I could see out of the back window of my father's car as he drove along. The future, too, I could understand: it was like the road ahead, perhaps less clear because as yet untraveled but able to be anticipated nonetheless. But what of the present? How was *that* to be understood? Was it the road beneath? My problem was that because the car was always moving I couldn't fix on anything that I could identify as 'the road beneath'. Of course, I tried to anticipate the road ahead as it appeared to move towards me (made a little easier by the way it was structured with a series of telegraph poles), but every time I tried to say 'now' it immediately became 'then', and I could see my 'now' out of the rear window. So what was the 'present'? Was it that part of the road that I could see immediately behind, that we'd just passed over? It couldn't be: that was 'past'. Every time I tried to think of this I became very confused. It seemed like everything was changing just a little too quickly for me. Nothing was standing still.

The second illustration takes place the day I came home from school after being told for the first time about fractions and dividing. I remember sitting down in a chair, puzzled, repeatedly drawing my finger down slowly to the arm of the chair and thinking all the time: 'If I bring my finger down to the armrest I can touch it. I know this because if I continue to press then my finger gets sore and it makes a mark on the armrest'. Yet the teacher had only just finished telling us about fractions, and she had explained how, if you keep on halving something, you will always have something left to half that can itself be halved, and so on. 'So', I asked myself, 'am I not always, at some point, halving the distance between my finger and the armrest? How, then, can the two ever meet?' At that early age I could find no way out of this: I concluded that either there must be something wrong with the halving rule, or my finger must never actually touch the surface of the chair. Yet when I tried it with a bowl of water, my finger definitely got wet!

In thinking about law, I am continually drawn back to this childhood puzzle, for traditional approaches to the meaning and practice of law appear beset by this problem, forever stumbling on the same difficulty. In seeking to address the events and circumstances of human experience by means of *legal representations* of these events, law abstracts from and 'freezes' what is essentially a continuously moving and changing flow, progressing by way of *a series of static representations* of this experience, a collection of 'snapshots' of an otherwise ever-changing reality. But, of course, as we know, reality is not static; it only conveniently appears that way. Even the mountains that give the impression of standing firm forever do actually change over time (as, indeed, advances in photography and technology, which supposedly 'speed up' time, demonstrate consistently).

This connects with my other puzzle, for if law is, as it is commonly supposed to be, a way of understanding reality that involves abstraction for the purposes of representation, a reduction to role and rule achieved through the application of general rules to particular concrete facts, events and circumstances, then how does it not come up against exactly the same problem as my childhood experiment with the application of the halving rule to the continuous action of my finger towards the arm of the chair? If, in my earlier experiment, the difficulty with the application of the universal rule to the particular facts is that it always results in a 'gap', then why should this be any different for law, since law also seeks to achieve its purposes through the application of universal rules to particular facts, events and circumstances? Moreover, if this is so, then how is this crossing of the gap achieved in law, and, if not by legal means, what does this tell us about the legal decision-making process and about law in general?

This question of the relationship between universals and particulars against the backdrop of an understanding of reality as constituted by continuous change is really what is at the heart of this investigation. Here, I attempt to examine legal reasoning from a 'process' point of view, beginning with an understanding of reality that necessitates a reversal of the normal ontological prioritising of stability over change, asking what it might mean to represent law in these terms. Identifying a way of looking at law and legal reasoning that centres on the relation of particulars to universals, I focus on the problem of finding justifying reasons for legal decisions in hard cases. The difficulties involved in attempting to articulate the legal decision-making experience in this way are well documented in the contemporary literature, being variously described as 'the particularity void', 'the aporia', 'the phronetic gap'. In order to deal with this, some theories of practical judgement have been developed that are inherently particular while alternative theories that give more weight to the role of universals, rules and principles, are also advanced to validate the decision-making process. Between these limits, of particularism and universalism, yet more theories attempt to find a sort of *via media*, reworking the understanding of the particular/universal relationship; still others claim that although justifying reasons are offered to characterise decisions as legal the reasons that would ground their justification cannot be found or given in law.

What unites all of these approaches is a desire to take seriously the matter of justification in legal decision-making and in doing so each may be seen to articulate one or another understanding of the particular/universal relationship. But there is a difficulty. Prevalent as these theoretical approaches are, every time an attempt is made to account for legal decisions, they somehow appear to effect an escape. Every attempt to offer *justifying* reasons for legal decisions appears at best to register only at the level of *explanation*. Why? I suggest that perhaps part of the problem may be that our inherited conceptual framework is tied to a 'static' way of thinking that is now outmoded. We try to understand by objectifying reality, analysing what we objectify. But reality is not static; it only conveniently appears that way. It is not, in fact, composed of simply locatable, separate 'entities' but is more akin to a continuous flux, where things merge into each other and the essential qualities seem to be more correctly describable in terms of relatedness than separateness. So any articulation of the problem of finding justifying reasons for decisions conceived in static terms may be misconceived in law. In other words, a decision cannot be 'caught' because once a decision is made, it is gone: it is momentous, and all that we observe of it is its trace.

In this sense, law can never deliver the reasons to justify a decision, since it is always 'catching up'. In that sense, law is always the observation of the trace left behind, the multiplicity of points through which the movement has passed, rather than the experienced unity of the action. The application of universal rules might reduce indefinitely the distance that must be bridged to cross the 'particularity void' but, like the repeated application of a halving rule, without closing the gap. Understood thus, some gap always remains, the distance represented by the question concerning the appropriateness of *that* universal continuing into *these* particulars.

So, one of the questions I am grappling with is: in what sense, if at all, can this 'gap' be closed? How, given the difficulties mentioned, does a judge acquire knowledge of any particular set of circumstances and link this to rule-like generalisations to formulate a decision? How do the universal and the particular meet? My contention is that judges do not simply use, instrumentally, already existing propositional knowledge, but they also draw upon the reservoir of their own factual knowledge and upon a collective knowledge of which they may or may not be wholly aware, and create new knowledge. In this way, to use the same terminology, the gap *is* closed, but not in the obvious way of bringing together the two extremes or bridging the distance between them: rather, through experience and through participation in a 'community of practice', judges develop a 'sense' of what is going on, of what is at stake, a legal skill that over time becomes instrumentalised. It allows them to reflect on things as they are going on: a skilful intuition that they develop and use as an extension of themselves to focus on the issue at hand. This is what accounts for the moment of decision, and the closing of the gap, and is one reason why it is so important that decisions must then be justified by providing reasons for the decision. But this intuitive, insightful aspect of legal decision-making reflects a knowledge that cannot be told, one that is difficult to put into words let alone be put in the form of propositional statements. In this latter sense, in terms of social practices, legal knowledge has a narrative structure, to complement its institutional propositional form. And what all of this points to, I suggest, is the fact that we need to revise our understanding of what is going on here. The supposedly unreflective practice of applying general rules to particular cases must somehow be transformed into a reflective one. The skill of legal decision-making needs to be augmented by an understanding of what judges are doing when they practise that skill. Since *what* we know and *how* we know are recursively linked then we need to begin to think more seriously about how we think about things. Thus, I argue in favour of the importance of creative personal understanding – a method of decision-making obtained or employed by judges using the exploration of possibilities rather than by following set rules; that is, heuristic knowledge. And what this implies is an activity that is as much about changing understandings as about changed procedure. It must involve the embracing and articulation of a vision and a definition of a new institutional reality and the ability and expertise to control information imaginatively.

So while my contention is that reality is properly understood only when it is perceived as dynamic, and not static, my task has been to try to provide a thoroughgoing processual account of the nature of legal reasoning to meet this; that is, an account that sees everything in terms of process *all the way down*. In attempting to articulate such a view, I suggest that repositioning law within a processual world-view allows a better understanding of the dynamic between institutions and practices and provides a more adequate description of the nature of law and legal reasoning; in particular, how a legal decision is created, maintained and employed within the decision-making system.

There is an overriding conviction identifiably present throughout. Since reality must always be infinitely more than our ideas about it then it is important always to be critical of abstractions, not interpreting the whole of reality by way of only some of its aspects but trying to remain faithful to the totality of our experience, helping to show the limitations of our way of thinking and identify what is being ignored. In this way, not only will we understand how the different forms of abstractions that we make relate to each other, but our critical approach may also help to resolve conflicts of interpretations. This means a continuous effort to refine understanding and an implicit acceptance that there can be no final knowledge: there is only progress in the process of discovering the limitations of past understandings and moving beyond them. The book is presented in the following way.

Part I begins by revisiting a recent controversial case involving a pair of ischiopagus conjoined twins, the questions surrounding their legal separation and the issues arising from that, and identifies a way of looking at law and legal decision-making that centres on the relation between universals and particulars. Explaining how attempts to understand law in these terms encourages a dualism that results in a shortfall between lived experience and that which can be accounted for by legal representation, a number of different approaches to legal decision-making are considered to show how certain influential schools and strands of theories of legal reasoning have attempted to address this. I engage with a number of influential theories of legal reasoning, including the 'institutional' school of Neil MacCormick (and Ota Weinberger); the natural law approach of Michael Detmold; American Legal Realism, as updated by certain varieties of Critical Legal Studies; Bernard Jackson's 'narrative structure' approach; and the 'discursive turn' that considers institutional discourse as a special case of practical discourse.

Part II outlines an alternative approach, derived from the Whiteheadian tradition of process thought. Building on recent developments in organisation studies, these chapters demonstrate how, while much of contemporary legal theory is effectively the expression of a continuing concern to bridge the gap that opens up in law between theory and practice, these should not be thought of as two separate but connectable areas; rather, as outlining a mutually constitutive process of becoming, interpenetrating and interrelating. Employing Henri Bergson's notion of 'creative evolution' and Gilles Deleuze's metaphor of 'rhizomic' communication, together with Michael Polanyi's notion of 'tacit' knowledge, this approach is viewed alongside Edward Levi's familiar account of legal reasoning.

Part III focuses on the position of judge as institutional actor and decision-maker to describe how the different types of institutional knowledge that exist in law interact with each other and can be seen to be founded on different features of the legal institutional context. Building upon the constructionist approach developed and deployed within the context of organisation studies to illustrate the links between individual knowledge, organisational knowledge and human action undertaken within organised contexts, these chapters explore the relations between institutions and practices, propositional knowledge and narrative knowledge, within the formal legal context. This is explored further through ideas associated with chaos theory and complexity.

Part IV brings the preceding argument towards a conclusion by demonstrating how the judge's role in managing the tensions that arise here may be seen to suggest an alternative process-theoretical understanding of the nature of law and legal reasoning, emphasising creative potential, novel adventure and continuous change. This paves the way for a creative reconstruction of law according to the conceptual categories of process thought, offering a description of how a discrete instance of legal judgement is created and maintained within the decision-making process.

Part I

Legal decision-making and legal reasoning

Chapter 1

Locating the problem in law

The conjoined twins case, Re A

The conjoined twins Jodie and Mary were born in August 2000 to Michelangelo and Rina Attard who lived on the Maltese island of Gozo but had arrived at St Mary's Hospital, Manchester, seeking medical assistance unavailable in their home country. Joined at the pelvis, the twins had mainly separate vital organs. Their circulatory system, however, was shared, being joined at the main artery through which Jodie's heart supplied oxygenated blood to both babies. Critically, Mary's heart and lungs did not work and her brain function was significantly impaired; indeed, had she been born a singleton she would not have survived birth and could not have been resuscitated. After examination by the doctors various options were established, with widely varying consequences: leaving the twins conjoined would result in the death of both; performing surgery to separate them would preserve Jodie's life but prematurely end Mary's; separating only in an emergency would diminish significantly the likelihood of a successful outcome for Jodie. Crucially, although both parents were keen to take advantage of the best medical assistance available they opposed surgery, arguing that they could not accept or contemplate that one of their children should die to enable the other one to survive.

In many jurisdictions that would have been the end of the matter, and an operation to separate the twins would never have taken place since the parents' wishes would have prevailed. But the Manchester medical experts felt they could not simply stand by while both babies died; especially, since in their opinion they could certainly save one of them. So, unable to secure the necessary parental consent for the operation, the hospital applied to the High Court for a declaration that surgery to separate the twins would be lawful.

In the High Court, with no legal precedent to guide and with very little time available to form a carefully reasoned and researched judgement, Justice Johnson decided to allow the separation. Unhappy with this decision, the parents appealed; however, in the Appellate Court all their appeals were dismissed, each of the judges, though for vastly differing reasons, finding in favour of lawful separation. In November 2000, surgery to separate the conjoined twins, Jodie and Mary, was performed at St Mary's Hospital, Manchester, England. As expected, Jodie survived, but Mary died.

No doubt, many people would agree that the 'least worst' option was to perform the surgery to separate the twins, to save one at the cost of the other; somewhat less would have sought to impose that view on parents who resolutely chose the alternate view, refusing to kill one to save the other; few indeed would argue to enforce that solution in a situation where parental responsibility was deemed paramount and where the particular parental choice in question had already been declared legitimate. Yet this was effectively the solution which prevailed in *Re A (Children) (Conjoined Twins: Surgical Separation)* [2000] 4 All E.R. 961. So how did the presiding judges in this case reason that the twins not only could and should but must be separated?

Having first established that under the Children Act 1989 the court had authority to override a decision by the parents that was not in the best interests of their child, Lord Justice Ward went on to question where, in relation to the proposed surgery, each of the twins' best interests lay. In respect of Jodie, this seemed obvious: separation would offer infinitely greater benefit to her than letting her die; but what about Mary? Could surgery be in her best interest? He suggested that the operation could only be in Mary's best interests if, and only if, it were carried out either to save her life or to ensure improvement or prevent deterioration in her physical or mental health. However, since the only perceivable gain for Mary was the dignity of an independent existence which would be short-lived at best, and result in her demise, then the operation could not be seen to be in her best interests.

Constructing the problem in this way immediately gave rise to a further problem; namely, since the interests of Jodie were in conflict with the interests of Mary, how were those interests to be balanced? (*Re A* at 1004). And, since established law dealt only with the interests of a single child, not comparatively with the interests of two, whose interests were paramount? Lord Justice Ward responded by arguing that although Mary had always been 'designated for death' the consequences for Jodie of not acting were extremely grave, since Mary 'sucks the lifeblood out of Jodie'. In these particular circumstances, the best course of action was to sanction the operation that would provide the only viable twin, Jodie, with the best chance of life; it was not the court's business to engage in a comparative exercise over the worth of each life. Even so, the separation of Jodie from Mary would still involve clamping the main shared artery, severing the twins at the pelvis and donating to Jodie the whole of the shared single bladder, sex organs and anus; in other words, killing Mary. As a result, a deeper legal conflict, between these medical and family law issues and others from a criminal law perspective, began to emerge.

In a nutshell, this was a typical catch-22 situation. On the one hand, in carrying out the operation to separate the twins the doctors would have the intention to kill Mary, which even if it did not imply any desire for Mary's death would, nonetheless, be murder; on the other hand, failing to carry out the operation might just as easily attract an allegation of the murder of Jodie since both the doctors and Jodie's parents could be seen to be under a duty to save her life. Each of the judges responded in a different way. Lord Justice Ward considered two criminal law defences: a version of *self-defence* and *necessity*. Engaging the full drama of the courtroom representation of the twins' dilemma, suggested that Mary was effectively killing Jodie: 'If Jodie could speak', he proclaimed, 'she would surely protest "stop it, Mary, you're killing me"'. Besides, he felt that there were significant factors present here that could bring into operation the defence of necessity; therefore, the doctors and the court must, in this case, choose the lesser of two evils, allowing Jodie to live by killing Mary. But could one of the twins be sacrificed to save the other? Lord Justice Brooke certainly thought so. For him, it was not a question of choosing Mary to die but of asking whether Jodie must also die with her. Lord Justice Walker, on the other hand, argued that what was at stake here was *not* the question of valuing one life over another; actually, not separating the twins would violate *both* girls' rights.

Giving judgement, Lord Justice Ward outlined the court's responsibilities:

> This court is a court of law, not of morals, and our task has been to find, and our duty is then to apply the relevant principles of law to the situation before us – a situation which is quite unique.
>
> (*Re A* at 968)

In conclusion, he felt it necessary

> to restate the unique circumstances for which this case is authority. They are that it must be impossible to preserve the life of X without bringing about the death of Y, that Y by his or her very continued existence will inevitably bring about the death of X within a short period of time, and that X is capable of living an independent life but Y is incapable under any circumstances (including all forms of medical intervention) of viable independent existence …

This is, he repeated, 'a very unique case' (*Re A* at 1018).

Arguably none of the vastly differing responses of the judges provides a satisfactory solution to the problems encountered in this difficult case; however, there are much more serious matters than the effectiveness of the Lord Justices' arguments at issue here. On one reading at least, what we are concerned with here is not a question about the legitimacy of surgery to separate conjoined twins when the procedure results in the death of one of the twins but the legitimacy of performing such an operation *over the legitimate wishes of the parents*. Looked at in this way it is clear from the beginning that two very different versions of events, and accounts of the situation, run in parallel here: there is an impossible tension between, on the one hand, the parents' real life experience of and concern over the plight of their daughters, and, on the other, its medical and legal institutional representation. Moreover, it is equally clear that this tension exists because these two versions of events actually belong to two quite different worlds. The objective events and circumstances to which they refer and from which they derive their meaning are really quite different 'entities' in each, and, to put it succinctly, *ne'er the twain shall meet*. So how do the judges deal with this tension?

In the first place, even though the court had established that it could, legitimately, override a parental decision to consent, or refuse consent, to medical treatment for their child, there was no conclusive authority supporting the court balancing the interests of the two children. This meant that the court was attempting to reason in an area where no law applied directly. It was uncharted territory, a paradigm example of what Herbert Hart has famously described as an area of 'open texture'. Lord Justice Ward, describing the dilemma facing the court as, on the one hand, a choice between the 'lesser of two evils' and, on the other hand, a legal and moral obligation not to kill, concluded that parents 'placed on the horns of such a terrible dilemma' must simply 'choose the lesser of their inevitable loss'. Yet surely this is simply to beg the question in favour of the judges' preferred option. Furthermore, concluding because it was in the best interests of Jodie that the operation should proceed but not in the best interests of Mary to be killed by the operation that then, in view of this conflict of interests, 'there was no other way of dealing with it than by choosing the lesser of two evils and so finding the least detrimental alternative', merely 'affirms one limb of the moral dilemma, ignores the other, and begs the moral question as to which is "the lesser of the two evils"' (Gillon 2001: 3). Is there no other way of dealing with this dilemma? What about the parents' argument that *not killing* an innocent baby *is* 'the lesser of the two evils', *despite* the fact that the baby would die in a few months and *even if* the killing would save the other baby's life? Except, that argument has already been ruled out under the guise of fairness in decision-making. Lord Justice Ward has secured this with his declaration that because the court is a legal authority the case must be decided on the basis of settled legal principles and not moral, ethical, or religious values. Ultimately, faced with an impossible dilemma, and unable or unwilling to avoid a decision on the merits, the court abandoned its stated position of moral neutrality, bridging the gap that it perceived to exist between the facts and the law with its own moral values. Since law alone could not cross the gap the court felt compelled to resort to a utilitarian calculus that betrayed its avowedly deontological approach.

However, this case demanded far more than a simple assessment of the best interests of each twin. Choosing to decide in this way also meant that a decision had to be made about whose best interests should prevail. In addressing this question, the court felt that it was best placed to provide a suitable answer. But why is the assumption so readily embraced that such a dispassionate, disinterested observer is the one best placed to decide what is in a child's best interests? What overriding reasons are there to suggest that three persons who neither knew nor loved either child were automatically better qualified to make this choice than their parents? Was the decision in *Re A* a responsible application of legal principle that captured the ethical dilemma, or a failure of the ethical and legal imagination? (Bratton and Chetwynd 2004: 280).

According to Emilios Christodoulidis (2004), writing in a different context, cases such as this, involving limit situations, are not exceptions that can be ignored for their infrequency of arising; rather, they expose the characteristics of the observed institution that ordinary cases leave intact and overlooked. He questions the legitimacy of the courtroom as a forum that provides the procedural means to accommodate and resolve disputes and wrongdoing. On this analysis, what we find in *Re A* is nothing less than the expression of an impossible dialogue, a non-engagement with the protestations of the parents that really amounts to a banning of the statement of their objections. In this sense, the further (prior) question that emerges is not whether the parents' decision was the only correct one, or even if it was well founded, but why it was not and could not be put in law.

This problem is one which arises as a result of the way that we think about law. In electing to confront the twins' dilemma by resort to the legal institutional realm, the Court is effectively shifting the debate into an arena where the choice of language used always-already selects and prescribes the context within which events are to be recognized. In this sense, the official language of the court establishes itself as a privileged vocabulary, determining the context and the form in which claims are to be made. The consequence of this imposition of the institutional upon the experiential is the collapse of the parents' objection through its removal from its living context and its realignment under the terms, conditions and relations of the legal context. On one view at least, what is being engaged with here in the courtroom setting is not the living reality of conjoinment as experienced by Jodie and Mary and their parents, Michaelangelo and Rina Attard, but the highly abstract legal representation of that situation and its construction as a legal issue conceived and presented in pairs of oppositional terms – a conflict of doctrines, principles and values: a conflict of rights between two individual right-bearers, between Mary the aggressor and Jodie the innocent victim; a choice between two distinct alternatives, the lesser of two evils. On that view, the substitution of context is witnessed from the parents' perspective by the double suggestion of a conflict that *never actually is*: first, between the parents (whose 'legitimate' view is somehow construed as not being in the 'best interests' of the twins and from whose care the twins are thus portrayed as being in need of protection) and the twins and, second, between one twin (whose actions, however passive are killing, 'draining the life-blood', from her sister) and the other.

Understood in these terms, there appears to be no way at all for the parents' objection to be heard *in its own terms*. Within the legal institutional setting, the judges effectively control the criteria of what counts as legal and the court's setting and arrangements work together to construct a context that will cater for the judicial as legal but not the living experience of the parents, who are thereby deprived of any means to articulate their claim other than as *extra*-legal. In thus removing any possibility of dispute over the constitution of meaning as a stake of the debate the judges establish the innocence of the legal mode of expression, and, in positing this mode as universal, draw irresistibly both the parents and the twins within the circumference of its jurisdiction.

Through such devices and steps any suggestion of incompatibility between the two discourses and languages apparently disappears and the task becomes straightforward, uncomplicated and clear: choose the lesser of two evils. In this way, too, any threat to the legitimacy of the court's decision is removed and the judge can affirm the autonomy of the parents as addressor and addressee of their own prescriptions, since *any* '[p]arents ... placed on the horns of such a terrible dilemma simply ha[ve] to choose the lesser of their inevitable loss ... ' If the parents might still wish to argue '*we* cannot' then they will simply be met with the reply, 'yes, *you* can; for the *we* and the *you* have been universalised, are now the same, and this is fair'.

In this way, the unique living experience of parents and twins is confronted by the court and universalised in law, but not without a cost: the silencing of every one of their objections before they can be raised, achieved through the imposition that if they must be raised then they can only be raised in terms that register in the court's legal context. The crucial point here is that, in this sense, the parents' objections (and the interests of the twins) cannot really be said to register at all, or, if they do, it is under some other category and, in that sense, they cannot be said to register *in their own terms*; therefore, they find no representation in law.

According to Christodoulidis, the only response that might be able to provide any normative justification for the passing of a sentence on a citizen is that which includes the citizen in the creation of that norm from which the sentencing originates, giving her a voice during the processes of deliberation as to whether the norm applies to her. He cites Klaus Gunther's 'sense of appropriateness', Jurgen Habermas' 'discourse theory' and Robert Alexy's 'theory of legal argumentation' to suggest how such a response might be constructed. But, for Christodoulidis, even such an apparently credible normative underpinning of legal procedures must ultimately fail under the weight of its own aspirations, because any objection can only be understood as logically cutting across the coincidence of addressor and addressee, 'we' and 'us' (Christodoulidis 2004: 10). Indeed, presented thus, there appears to be nothing within law that can account for or redeem the subsequent displacement that continues to invoke in their absence those who are spoken about, usurping the right to speak *in their name* after any possibility of their speaking for themselves has been tactically withdrawn.

If we accept this conclusion, then we must also include within it the Attards' objection on behalf of their daughters. We can see exactly how this happens in *Re A*: first, the right of the parents to make health care decisions on behalf of their children is removed; then, the court, assuming the mantle of guardian of 'best interests', speaks *for* them. Ultimately, the parents' objection must be understood as an objection to the invocation of the 'we', but the legal institutional context in which they must legitimate their claim operates to deny them both the opportunity and the means with which to make it; that is, their dissensus immediately puts them on the side of those not seeking the twins' best interests. Trapped under the terms of this inclusion that simultaneously excludes, they are unable either to step back or to object. In this way, the path opens up for Lord Justice Ward to speak and he does so in dramatic terms. But his appeal to Mary and to Jodie, as it were speaking for them, becomes simply another desperate attempt to legitimate the Court's law as *their* law: Mary 'sucks the life blood out of Jodie ... [Her] parasitic living will be the cause of Jodie's ceasing to live. If Jodie could speak, she would surely protest, "Stop it, Mary, you're killing me"' (*Re A* at 1010).

Of course, it is quite incorrect to describe Mary's physical relationship to Jodie in these terms (she was not actually engaged in any threatening activity towards Jodie) and for Christodoulidis this is nothing more than ideology operating at a deep level, where the possibility of raising an objection is always-already undercut and the objector is always invisible except as an outsider. Here, with the objection that cannot be heard, we have come to the limits of legal possibility: '"The objection that cannot be raised" is not merely ... side-lined in official discourse [but] the very possibility of raising it, in the courtroom, is structurally removed' (Christodoulidis 2004: 180).

In this way, the silencing of the parents' (and, by extension, the twins') voice is achieved with what appears to be little more than pretence: in the name of reflexivity and representation we find curtailment and exclusion. In effect, it is really an act of violence on the free flow and expression of opinions and arguments – all that could be contested is not actually contested – and the result is a critical shortfall that looks difficult to calculate and impossible to remedy. It appears like an impossible passage, an unbridgeable gap.

Chapter 2

Justifying legal decisions in hard cases

Different approaches

Neil MacCormick's universalisability thesis

It is 'an important aspect of the rule of law', writes Neil MacCormick, 'that courts and judges take seriously the established rules of the institutional normative order'. Precisely because of this the whole business of the justification of legal decisions will 'focus on a syllogistic element, showing what rule is being applied, and how' (MacCormick 2006: 5). According to MacCormick, Ward LJ's final ruling in *Re A* demonstrates clearly that this case must be understood:

> as a type-case, as a universally stated situation ... [I]t is not some ineffable particular feature of this Jodie interacting with this Mary that justifies the decision but certain statable aspects of the relationship between them in the context of a particular practical dilemma.
>
> (MacCormick 2006: 16)

Thus, while it might indeed be true that 'particular reasons must always exist for particular decisions', the real issue is 'the significance of the justifying relationship between reason and decision, and whether or not this involves the universalizability of grounds of decision' (MacCormick 2006: 3). Ultimately, '[t]here is ... no justification without universalization ... For particular facts – or particular motives – to be *justifying reasons* they have to be subsumable under a relevant principle of action universally stated' (MacCormick 2006: 21).

With this updated account, MacCormick both confirms and expands the model of legal reasoning he first presented in detailed form in 1978. There, building upon H.L.A. Hart's linguistic criteria of 'open texture', and his analysis of reasoning in hard cases, he suggested a process of legal decision-making made up of several stages: universalisability; consequences; coherence; consistency. Unlike Hart, MacCormick did not suggest that a judge enjoys an almost unfettered discretion in decision-making in hard cases; rather, he outlined a theory about the constraints that govern the exercise of judicial discretion when hard cases occur. Nonetheless, like Hart, MacCormick regarded open texture as an attractive feature, allowing the law an opportunity for advancement. His theory can be stated briefly. First, the principle of universalisability entails that the way a decision is made in a hard case must also hold for decisions in every such case in the future (one must treat like as like; both backward-looking and forward-looking) and involves generalisation as a first step towards identifying the relevant general category. Second, an assessment of the consequences of generalising allows one to balance universalisability, fixing the genus through a subjective judgement of value and permitting a choice between two or more possible rulings to disclose a likely rule. Next, the requirement of coherence operates to ensure that the chosen rule can be subsumed under some principle of generality already present in settled law, that it is not simply an exercise in creative interpretation but the rule is grounded in some general principle of law, the existence of which may be described as being like part of the 'glue' that holds law together; in other words, that what is presented is really only a making explicit of some principle already implicit in law such that the relevant rule may be seen as correctly subsumed under it (MacCormick 1978: 44). Finally, 'consistency' tests the non-contradictoriness of this rule in relation to other explicitly formulated legal norms within the legal system.

This fuller account of legal decision-making emerges as consistent with the account of law as 'institutional fact' that MacCormick developed under the idea of an Institutional Theory of Law (ITL) in association with Ota Weinberger. Within that 'institutional' theory of law, MacCormick (1986) claimed to provide an ontological basis for the analysis of all social action, including law. There, they adopted the theory of institutional facts as set out by G.E.M Anscombe (1958) and John Searle (1969), drawing on their observations that there are some entities that seem to exist in the world independent of our frameworks of thought, will and judgement, which they call 'brute facts', and others which appear not to exist in this way; for example, a goal in a football match. We cannot point to any physical thing or event and say that it, bare and simple, is a goal, and yet we do, nonetheless, talk intelligibly about a goal. Searle called these facts 'institutional facts', since they 'are indeed facts; but their existence, unlike the existence of brute facts, presupposes the existence of certain human institutions' (Searle 1969: 51).

Institutional facts, then, are explicable given these overarching institutions and exist within their systemic framework. They might be tied to specific physical acts or events but they are not identical with these physical events. Much depends on Searle's distinction between regulative rules and constitutive rules. Whereas a constitutive rule might define what constitutes a goal, a regulative rule would specify what one does next after a goal has been scored. The objects that together make up the physical setting for the football match assume a new form of existence in them being interpreted in terms of these constitutive and regulative rules.

MacCormick develops Searle's distinction to suggest that legal 'institutional facts' (such as the temporal existence of a contract between two persons) exist within the frame of reference of certain organised activities that we may term 'institutions' (for example, the institution of Contract that precedes any particular instantiation of it). In this regard, three features structure our use of these concepts: institutive rules, which lay down 'the conditions which are essential to the existence of an instance of each such institution'; consequential rules, which detail the consequences that arise as a result of the establishing of an instance of an institution, and terminative rules, which outline the provisions regarding termination of instances of institutions. But there is a difference between the institution *per se* and instances of it:

> The existence of an institution as such is relative to a given legal system, and depends upon whether or not that system contains an appropriate set of institutive, consequential and terminative rules. If it does, then the occurrence of given events or the performance of given acts has by virtue of the rules the effect of bringing into being an instance of the institution.
>
> (MacCormick 1978: 66)

So we can envisage such institutions as being 'structured by legal rules' (MacCormick 1988: 76), and:

> [t]his way of conceptualising the matter ... makes clear the diachronic quality ... of our legal arrangements, by virtue of the way it separates or 'individuates' institutive and terminative rules ... 'Instances of institutions' exist in the eye of the law ... from the moment of an institutive event until the occurrence of a terminative event.

And this, in turn:

> makes clear the way in which ... 'momentary legal information' connects logically with 'diachronic legal information'. Diachronic information concerns standing arrangements ... [from which] one can derive by deduction the momentary consequential duties, liberties and powers one has in respect of the given arrangement.
>
> (MacCormick 1988: 79)

Momentary legal information is normative: 'it tells us what ought to or must, be or be done ... what can or cannot validly be achieved ... [I]t is choice guiding' on the basis of some 'underpinning value' without which 'the information would lose its practical or normative quality'. But '[s]etting up legal arrangements will help us achieve valued states of affairs only to the extent that we have a reason to suppose that their normative consequences will be mirrored in actual behavioural outcomes', and 'it is not worth much if arrangements we make can largely be ignored'. Consequently, some degree of '[r]elative immunity from arbitrary change is in effect a necessary condition for legal arrangements and legal institutions to have the diachronic quality which ... is one of their characteristic features' (MacCormick 1988: 79–80). Inasmuch as legal reasoning is deductive, then the model towards which this tends is 'predicate logic', so that 'institutional facts could almost be re-named as "normative predicates"' (MacCormick 1988: 81).

To explain how all of this relates to the practical decision-making setting, MacCormick recounts two familiar stories, the shrewd and penetrating judgement of King Solomon in 1 Kings 3: 16–28, in respect of the competing claims of two women to motherhood of a single child, and the death of Cleopatra. He begins this analysis by juxtaposing the Solomonic judgement and the decision of the Court of Appeal in *Re A*: 'the phenomenon of conjoined twins ... can [easily] pose issues quite as awful as the king's sword' (MacCormick 2006: 15). For instance, imagine that before some contemporary tribunal we have established the rule that 'children should be under the custody of their natural mothers' and, together with this, we have also developed some 'reliable evidentiary (DNA) test'. In this event, we will immediately have translated Solomon's skilful achievement into 'a routine practice', albeit that 'the real world will always be capable of throwing up surprises'. However, the point is that as soon as the application of law is problematised in this way then the issues raised must be addressed and then the most immediate issue becomes that of how to do this (MacCormick 2006: 5).

Suppose we were to regard King Solomon's method as a model for our judgement, offers MacCormick. On this basis, we might also consider it right to posit some form of instinctive or intuitive awareness that will enable us to latch on to the particulars of the instant case to indicate the response that the rules fail to provide and, in that situation, our answer in the present case might well be thought of as providing a precedent for future cases. But a precedent can only ever be an *analogy* for a new decision: no two sets of events are ever exactly the same. In these circumstances, our intuition might also tell us that it would be right to have a rule and to treat the instant case as a rule-case. Nonetheless, unusual and unexpected cases will still appear and force us to ask whether our rule permits a different interpretation or if all of the facts are classified correctly. In this way, we are now beginning to 'problematize the rule's applicability to the case in hand', understanding it as 'a case of first impression' and directing our intuitive judgement once more towards its unique particularity. Within such a scenario, quips MacCormick, every judge will require 'to be possessed of some small share of Solomon's wisdom'! (MacCormick 2006: 6).

In effect, every judge will face two choices: either she must regard the instant case as a rule-case or she must concede that it presents something new. But the point is that no matter how routine the case, the judge's decision will always be a particular decision. It is not simply a question of universals but of *particulars and universals*; that is, of 'particular persons ... that ... instantiate certain universals' (MacCormick 2006: 9). In this sense, the reasons that a judge gives to justify her decision will always be grounded in the particular case, but what an intuitionist approach would do is help a judge to discover her intuitive capacity to determine the features of a decision that make it right. In that sense, a good decision-making procedure would be one that:

> maximized opportunities [for] careful attention to all points of a problem situation, and that gave decision-making tasks to appropriate persons ... endowed both with adequate attentiveness to detail and with a fair-minded readiness to make no decision till in possession of all relevant reasons in any particular case.
>
> (MacCormick 2006: 10)

But does such intuition exist? MacCormick suggests that Adam Smith's model of the ideal, fully informed, impartial spectator may provide the best example of how to go beyond our immediate reaction to a situation towards one that represents a 'rationalized response to the whole of a situation in all its particularity'. But he also notes that any fully developed moral agent who is 'capable of giving allegiance to moral rules ... derived from generalizing responses to recurring types of cases' will inevitably also belong to a community, the members of which offer allegiance to such rules. In that case, any such 'fully refined moral capacity' could exist only as a result of 'a more unrefined attachment to rules of a heteronomous character' so that deciding according to rules is not inconsistent with deciding in some 'deeper way that confronts the whole complexity of real-life situations'. Thus, it would be wrong to overemphasize the particularistic aspects of decision-making, especially when rationalized according to Smith (MacCormick 2006: 12–13).

MacCormick finds clear evidence of this procedure in the Solomonic judgement: first, Solomon infers that one of the women is 'the mother'; then, he delivers his judgement, '"Give her the child ... [because] she is the mother ... "' We have to understand, he argues, that in the procedure followed here the '"because" nexus is all-important'. Not only does the sword-drama expose the 'true mother' but it also reveals how being the true mother becomes the reason for awarding the child. Moreover, since this mother relation is identified as a 'because-reason' here, in this case, then it also becomes a 'because-reason' for any future cases. What this amounts to, he suggests, is merely another way of saying that reasons must be universalisable, which is precisely why Lord Justice Ward, in his closing remarks, determines that *Re A*, however unique, must be regarded as a type-case. It is precisely this element of universalisability that, together with the requirements of 'consistency over time' and 'an overall coherence of values and principles', provides the foundations for the whole rationality of a system of precedents (MacCormick 2006: 13–14).

Causes are always particular, says MacCormick, and, inasmuch as we are able to discern 'sets of like cause-and-effect series, we may be able to establish inductive generalizations from them'. However, just because:

> ... one particular has been shown to cause another particular would be no proof that anything else has ever caused, is now causing or will ever again cause any other thing ... At the level of ... observation of particulars, we never observe anything. We may see the snake biting, we may see the queen dying. But we do not see this bite causing this death. And if we did ... , that would be no ground at all for supposing that every such bite will be a cause of death.
>
> (MacCormick 2006: 18)

Therefore, the relationship between particulars and generalisations is one of 'potential falsification' and any 'explanatory hypothesis' will need to 'be capable of forming a consistent part of a coherent general theory'. In other words:

> what enables us to conceptualise the death of Cleopatra is that the particular fact of the snake biting belongs as minor premise in an argument of which the major premise is a hypothesis culled from the snake-venom theory and the conclusion is the death
>
> (MacCormick 2006: 19)

Merely to affirm that reasons for actions are particular and factual does not prove that the connection is not a 'relevant universal'; on the contrary, to justify an act is to demonstrate that 'upon any objective view of the matter, the act ought to have been done ... given the character of the act and the circumstances of the case'. Just so, for any reason to be a justifying reason it must indicate 'the generic nature of the act and the generic circumstances of action' and, as soon as these are provided, 'an implicit principle – universal in terms – is revealed'. In this way, justifying reasons are 'conceptually distinct' from both explanatory and motivating reasons:

> There is no justification without universalization; motivation needs no universalization; but explanation requires generalization. For particular facts – or particular motives – to be *justifying reasons* they have to be subsumable under a relevant principle of action universally stated.
>
> (MacCormick 2006: 21)

On one level, 'this is irrefutable', concedes Christodoulidis. However, 'it is a level that concerns the delivery of explanation rather than the making of decisions' and as soon as we recognise the importance of the distinction between these two levels this 'throws the issue of "particularity" wide open' once more. Of course, the decision will depend upon particulars, and it will address questions of appropriateness as well as justify the use of universal categories, but the *justification of the application* cannot draw its reasons from "universalizability" but from the appropriateness of extending the universal ... into *this* set of particulars' and that 'is a judgement that cannot be carried in the universal category but requires attentiveness to the particular' (Christodoulidis 2006: 98).

In this sense, law can never deliver the reasons to justify a decision. It always comes too late to inform the moment of its occurrence. In this sense, in the terms stated previously, law is always the observation of a trace left behind, a multiplicity of points through which a movement has passed, rather than the experienced unity of an action itself. Universalisation may reduce indefinitely the distance that must be bridged but, like the repeated application of a halving rule, without closing the gap: some gap always remains, the distance represented by the question concerning the appropriateness of *that* universal continuing into *these* particulars. In fairness to MacCormick, however, universalism is really only seen as doing part of the work here, even if the greater part, and particularism, as in the form of the appeal to consequences, actually concludes the task. At this point, there is always the possibility that the judge will deem the circumstances of the case to present a 'new problem'. But in the context of decision-making in a hard case, when the rules appear to have run out and the judge is faced with what appears as a new problem, how, given the prior commitment to universalisation, will she recognise the problem as a new one? What provides the cue for her recognising the *in*appropriateness of applying the universal rule here? How can some particulars that do not register in law as instances of a general rule register as exceptions to it? Given a prior commitment to universalisation, how is it possible that any case might be recognised as not always-already instantiating some general rule?

If the pull to universalise is grounded in a prior commitment to select from among a variety of possibilities only those features that identify a case as always already instantiating a rule then, by definition, choosing some means not choosing others. The issue then is whether those characteristics that are not chosen thereby become invisible in such a way that their exclusion also prevents their reappearance later on, their subsequent registering as significant within the system. Are we not simply brought back once more to a question over the limits of legal possibility?

Michael Detmold's 'Particularity Void': the moment of *in*decision

According to Michael Detmold there are particular situations, practical questions, which universal reasoning cannot answer. For him, part of the meaning of universality, that the rule is always applied when the conditions of its application are met, presents us with a problem. It is not that we cannot use a rule when deciding a case but that rules are not self-applying. There is a gap between a rule and its application, which he calls the 'particularity void'. What he means is that there is a difference between asking whether a rule is reasonable and whether it is reasonable to apply it. In other words, it is in particulars and not in universals that actions must be grounded, so that an assessment has to be made each time a decision is made whether the conditions of application are met. In this way, a judge cannot evade responsibility for her decisions by hiding behind the rules. She cannot meaningfully say that she sentences someone to death and at the same that she does not support the death penalty, since she must decide each time whether it is the right thing to do and also think that it is the right thing to do. In this sense, the particularity void, as he calls it, becomes the place where *I* must take responsibility for *my* decisions.

For Detmold, legal reasoning is practical insofar as it is 'reasoning towards a decision for or against action' and his primary concern is with a 'judge's practical reasoning towards the action of giving judgment' (Detmold 1989: 436), what he calls '[t]he particularity of adjudication'. He gives the example of someone seeking to acquire judicial office through examination:

> I am given a problem to solve consisting of facts A B and C. I work it out and ... [m]y conclusion is universal: *a* defendant in circumstances A B and C must pay damages. But am I right? I check my reasoning and conclude I am right. I finish the exam, content. But ... I go to my books after the exam to make sure. Yes ... I am sure. I am now sure that I have the answer to the (universal) question ...
>
> (Detmold 1989: 455)

Nonetheless, this is still not 'a practical answer', argues Detmold. It will become practical only when it becomes particular. But is this merely a matter of waiting for a suitable particular to come along that accords this universal judgement?

In due course I am appointed, he continues, and my first case replicates the case of my exam. As I sit alone in my chambers contemplating judgement, why does my will not unleash itself? It is not that I doubt my conclusion: 'I remember my reasoning very clearly'. But 'I now have a radically different problem', he explains, one 'which universal (hypothetical) reasoning does not solve'. Indeed, 'the whole problem is that no reasoning can solve it. It is particular'. It is something of which 'nothing can be said (anything I *say* will be universal)' (Detmold 1989: 456). How might we account for this?

We can take this further, Detmold suggests, by looking at the confrontation between Pierre and Davoût in Tolstoy's *War and Peace*. A 'moment of indecision' saves Pierre from being shot as a spy on Davout's orders. Davout, holding his rifle, looks towards Pierre; he hesitates and does not fire. At this moment, according to Tolstoy, many things pass through Davout's mind:

> Davout looked up and gazed intently at him. For some seconds they looked at one another, and that look saved Pierre. Apart from conditions of war and law [ABC] that look established human relations between the two men. At that moment an immense number of things passed dimly through both their minds, and they realised they were both children of humanity and were brothers.
>
> (Detmold 1989: 457)

At first, this appears very like universalist reasoning and indeed Tolstoy seems to suggest as much. But for Detmold both the hesitation and the action are deeply significant:

> Davout, at the moment of practicality entered the unanswering void of particularity, the realm of love, about which only mystical, poetic things can be said ... ; or nothing ... Judges enter this realm every day (if only they knew).
>
> (Detmold 1989: 455–57)

In this sense, he claims, those theorists who seek to find through 'the progressive refinement of the categories of law according to experience' a means by which to settle these issues are mistaken; in fact, no matter how:

> highly defined A B and C are ... [the] problem [is] exactly the same ... A judgment in respect of A B and C ... cannot cross the void ... [I]t can justify *a* judgment ... a theoretical/hypothetical ... right up to the void. But the final rationality of practical judgement seems in doubt ...
>
> (Detmold 1989: 458)

Detmold notes how Neil MacCormick has attempted 'to reassert that rationality against ... particularity' through a reconsideration of the idea of justification. But, for Detmold:

> th[is] act of justification is incapable of solving the problem for it immediately raises the question, why justify? and the answer, like that to the original question, will be ultimately particular, not universal; so it will have its own particularity void.
>
> (Detmold 1989: 459)

Even MacCormick's attempt to derive the desired universality along the lines of Adam Smith's postulate of the ideal spectator does not successfully evade criticism, since 'anyone's question is anyone's void'. Ultimately, what

MacCormick and Smith both fail to demonstrate, he argues, is 'how the impartial spectator's judgment is not also incorrigibly particular'. In fact, we find 'two questions of universalization' involved in practical reasoning: on the one hand, 'whether I am to be universalized to all moral agents judging p' and, on the other, 'whether p is universal or incorrigibly particular'. Moreover, 'it is p which opens the particularity void and casts doubt on the truth of all practical judgments, subjective or objective' (Detmold 1989: 459). We need to investigate further, he claims, this question of whether 'the negotiation of the particularity void depends upon the particular in respect of which my action is contemplated speaking for himself'. Although reason brought Davoût to an 'acceptance of the norm: execute all Russian spies', nonetheless, a 'void of reason ... stood between this norm and the particular Pierre'. Davoût might just as well have responded: 'it is reasonable to execute the enemies of France, but why should *I* do it?' So, we find 'a second particularity void: ... one for subject as well as object' and, in the end, 'particularity holds out'. Ultimately, what this suggests is 'a category leap: the particularity void cannot be crossed by reason' (Detmold 1989: 464–65).

More recently, Detmold has elaborated further on the problems of particularity in adjudication identifying two problems, which he characterises as the 'in-tray' and the 'out-tray': the 'in-tray' is the matter of what it is that informs a decision, how it will be justified and the extent to which the informing thing is particular or universal; the 'out-tray' is the making of the decision and deciding to whom or to what it applies, the particular or the universal. According to Detmold, all practical judgements are of the out-tray and are radically particular: even though there are clear difficulties with the notion of deciding something about another person's life, still the common law seeks to address itself to history, an always radically particular history, judging that history. In other words, it is always a particular person and a particular history that form the basis of the law's judgement (Detmold 2006: 83–94).

On this view, the gap that we recognised earlier in *Re A* may be seen to have at least two aspects: first, in terms of the potential asymmetry between addressor and addressee; second, in terms of the void between determination and application. In general, judges only tend to make law conservatively, says Detmold, but 'the fullness of law as practical reason is achieved when the law that judges apply is law that has crossed the citizen subject void; when law is in a true sense the citizen's law, when law is common law' (Detmold 1989: 467).

American legal realism and the critical legal studies movement

'American Legal Realism was the most important indigenous jurisprudential movement in the United States during the 20th twentieth century' (Leiter 2003: 50). Indeed:

> [c]urrent debates about legal reasoning are best understood as attempts to answer the central question that the realists left unresolved: How can we engage in normative legal argument without either reverting to the formalism of the past or reducing all claims to the raw demands of political interest groups?
>
> (Singer 1988: 468)

Essentially, the legal realists argued on three fronts as to why rules alone cannot decide cases and are of limited use in predicting the way that a court will decide: first, legal rules resist any form of mechanical application because they are inherently vague and ambiguous; second, this vagueness and ambiguity means that any case can be read in a number of different ways; third, the resulting indeterminacy of abstract legal concepts leads to a manipulability of precedent through a blurring of the distinction between holding and dictum (*ratio* and *obiter*). Effectively, a judge could redefine the holdings in precedent cases to reveal alternative or multiple rules of law capable of governing the outcome in the case before her in different ways.

This challenge drew several concessions from Hart. First, although 'there is no single method of determining the rule for which a given authoritative precedent is authority', nonetheless 'in the vast majority of cases, there is very little doubt. The headnote is usually correct enough'. But of course this says nothing more than that one particular choice of rule is usually to be preferred over others. It does little to counter, and nothing to defeat, the essential realist objection. Second, while 'there is no authoritative or uniquely correct formulation of any rule to be extracted', nonetheless 'there is often very general agreement, when the bearing of a precedent on a later case is in issue, that a given formulation is adequate' (Hart 1961: 131). But, as Andrew Altman notes:

> Hart seems to be saying here that lawyers may disagree on the precise formulation of a rule but still agree on the correct outcome of a case and so be able to accept, for the purposes of the case, a formulation which, in the given instance, straddles the different versions of the rule. This claim may very well be accurate, but it fails to defeat the realist indeterminacy claims for two reasons. It assumes that the problem of being able to extract conflicting rules from the same line of precedents has been resolved ... Second, even if there is general agreement on the outcome of a case and on some rough statement of the governing rule ... [i]t does not follow that the law determines the outcome. Agreement on the outcome and on the statement of the rule used to justify the outcome may both be the result of some more fundamental political choice which is agreed upon. Indeed this is exactly what the realist analysis would suggest ... Realism is not committed to denying broad agreement. It is

simply committed to the view that the agreement cannot be explained by
the determinacy of law.

(Altman 1986: 210–11)

Hart's third and final concession here is to concede that although the courts
regularly expand or contract the legal rules created under the operation of
the doctrine of precedent, the doctrine of precedent has, nonetheless, fashioned 'a body of rules of which a vast number, of both major and minor
importance, are as determinate as any statutory rule' (1961: 132). But this, as
Altman correctly suggests:

> misses the crucial realist point regarding the availability of competing
> rules: let each legal rule be as precise as is humanly possible, the realists
> insist that the legal system contains competing rules which will be
> available for a judge to choose in almost any litigated case. The claims
> made by Hart ... all systematically fail to deal with this crucial realist
> point.
>
> (Altman 1986: 211)

In a nutshell, the legal realists' argument strives for the substitution of
formalism with a more pragmatic attitude towards law in general, one that 'treats
law as made, not found'. Understood thus, law is inextricably related to and
bound up with human experience, tied to social, political and ethical
circumstances and conditions, rather than formal logic:

> Legal principles are not inherent in some universal, timeless logical
> system; they are social constructs, designed by people in specific histor-
> ical and social contexts for specific purposes to achieve specific ends.
> Law and legal reasoning are a part of the way we create our form of
> social life.
>
> (Singer 1988: 474)

But if legal realism began as a pragmatic movement in law, concerned with
the elimination of certain types of persuasive argument from the legal tool-
box, it did not, in the end, produce a viable substitute vocabulary to replace
these. Nonetheless, the legacy of realism persists, pervading contemporary
disagreements and controversies over the nature of legal reasoning and the
relation of law to society.

The Critical Legal Studies (CLS) movements that emerged simultaneously
in America and Britain towards the end of the 1970s may not as yet
have provided that single substitute vocabulary, but most of these critical
theorists do attempt to connect with normative legal argument without any
reliance on formalism. Several common themes, found generally in CLS literature, reflect this realist dependence and inspiration. For example, as well

as claims about the indeterminacy of legal rules, the incommensurability of legal decision-making and the inherent contradictions within law and legal materials generally, CLS writers have argued for a deeper awareness of the ways in which politics and law interrelate and how different political, social and economic interests and structures condition and are served by law.

If, on the one hand, the realists stress the importance of competing legal rules, the CLS emphasis, on the other hand, is on competing (and irreconcilable) legal principles and ideals. Against liberal scholars such as Ronald Dworkin, CLS scholars argue that there can be no such thing as a 'principled decision making', whereby legal decisions are understood as the outcome of a process of reasoning that can be reconstructed in terms of rational, articulate and comprehensible principles. Rather, as Altman observes, 'the law is a patchwork quilt ... of irreconcilably opposed ideologies'. That is to say, 'the spectrum of ideological controversy in politics is reproduced in law ... [T]he law is a mirror which faithfully reflects the fragmentation of our political culture' (Altman 1986: 222).

The origin and development of a critical viewpoint can be traced within Greek tragedy. Martha Nussbaum (1986) notes how the tragedies depict the contradictions and tensions experienced by a person being pulled simultaneously in two directions. Of course, the discovery of a coherent and consistent belief system solves this moral dilemma in one sense: if we know what justice demands then we can act accordingly. But the tragedies as a whole oppose such rational reconstruction of a moral problem to relieve the tension. As Nussbaum notes, the person who can 'feel no opposing claim, no pull, no reluctance' and who 'goes ahead with eagerness, even passion ... has failed to see and respond to his conflict as it is' (Nussbaum 1986: 39). By contrast:

> [a] proper response ... would begin with the acknowledgement that this is not simply a hard case of discovering truth; it is a case where the agent will have to do wrong.
>
> Such a response would continue with a vivid imagining of both sides of the dilemma, in a conscientious attempt to see the many relevant features of the case as truly and distinctly as possible. For even if the agent comes to the dilemma with good general principles, the case does not present itself with labels written on it, indicating its salient features. To pick these out, he must interpret it ...
>
> (Nussbaum 1986: 50)

'What is at stake in this debate about moral argument?' asks Joseph Singer. On the one hand, '[f]rom the standpoint of the liberal theorists, the critical theorists have sought to undermine, fundamentally, the possibility of legitimate, normative argument' (1988: 538). On the other hand:

from the standpoint of the critical theorists, the liberal theorists have tried to create a new kind of formalism. Their procedures for decision-making conceal the underlying value choices that decisionmakers must confront directly and honestly if they are to make legitimate social decisions ...

(Singer 1988: 539)

Can this gap be bridged? To do this, Singer argues:

we need to develop a language capable of both expressing and disciplining our normative commitments ... We should not attempt to achieve the definitive recipe for justice, but to engage in a democratic process of mutual persuasion in light of our disparate visions ... We must talk with each other about our competing visions of the good society if we want to achieve justice.

(Singer 1988: 543)

As Edwin Garlan (1941) observes:

Viewed only as an abstract structure, justice is distorted; it is equally distorted when seen not in process but simply in flux. Though justice ideally may be one, yet, as empirically known, it is at best a collective unity, composed of rights, interests, claims, pressures, and values which are both integrated, independent, and, even in some cases, in competition

(Garlan 1941: 52)

All of which brings to mind Benjamin Cardozo's observation: 'Is it possible that in rationalizing we have been hampered by [an] illusion? We have sought for a formula consistent with a steady advance through a continuum. The continuum does not exist'. What Cadozo is asserting, Garlan suggests, is that:

every new case is always more or less a shot in the dark and a matter of adjustment, there are no ultimate principles from which can be derived other principles which in turn measure justice and injustice in particular situations. Decisions reflect the pull of many values and standards and a decision comes to rest usually between two poles. Centers of energy exist, of attraction and repulsion. A landing place is found between them. We make these landing places for ourselves through the methods of the judicial process.

Just so:

[j]ustice, empirically viewed, assumes the appearance of a collective concept open at both ends with a membership list of rights and pressures

that is constantly changing. Law is not, nor ought it to be, ever completely sure of the character of any one member. Membership therein is always on good behaviour. Old members sometimes stay long after they have served their usefulness and the grounds which made them members have long departed. New members fail of admittance frequently because of cliques of old members who oppose them. But membership is never absolute, neither in time nor in authority. No member is a member except in the perspective and context which made it a member. This is the character of justice in its empirical content as we meet it in the courts.

(Garlan 1941: 52–53)

Bernard Jackson's 'narrative structure' approach

'One characteristic of the formalism traditionally associated with positivism', writes Bernard Jackson, 'is its elision, in practice, of the difference between decision making and the justification of decisions' (Jackson 2009). According to Jackson, MacCormick's attempt to integrate an account of intuition within his theory of justification rests on the assumption of a *dualist* model: on the one hand we have *rationality* and syllogism but, on the other, a form of *emotivism* that intervenes to save the justificatory process from collapse when something appears to have gone wrong. Instead, Jackson proposes 'a unitary model' where the same processes would operate in all cases, easy and hard, albeit with different outcomes.

Jackson argues that one of the problems with MacCormick's approach is that he assumes that law is in principle calculable and what is significant about the syllogism is the ease with which it allows a separation to be made between the analysis of law (major premise) and that of the facts (minor premise). To demonstrate the shortcomings of this, Jackson provides a well-known example:

> All persons who blaspheme the gods are liable to be executed.
> Socrates has blasphemed the gods.
> Therefore Socrates is liable to be executed.

(Jackson 1988: 37)

For this to work, he claims, a number of links will need to be established; in particular, we will need to show that Socrates actually said something, that what he said is blasphemy and that the rule as stated covers the case. However, there is a conflict between the temporal aspect of the past tense in the minor premise that appears in the process of adjudication and the atemporality of the major premise enacted in legislation, which presents a problem in terms of the value we attach to the prospectivity of laws in terms of the Rule of Law. On the one hand, if the rule has been enacted before the events to which it refers occur then adjudication is impossible, for a rule can refer only to acts that precede it; alternatively, if a rule is enacted after those events then this will result in a retrospective application of the rule. Both of these situations entail a denial of the Rule of Law.

How then, can a judge, in deciding a case, link together this atemporal law with the temporal events and activities that fall to be decided under it? According to Jackson, when we assert that a rule covers a case what we are actually saying is that it *refers* to that case. But reference is not inevitable or automatic; rather, it is something that we do with a rule to bridge the gap that opens up between legislation and adjudication, between the meaning of a rule and its application. In other words, the confirmation that a rule applies in a particular case occurs only at the point of deciding that case and, for MacCormick, the way that we do this is in and through the deductive syllogism. For Jackson, however, the prospectivity of the Rule of Law and the atemporality of the deductive syllogism reveal an internal consistency that is problematic: every reconstruction of judicial decision-making according to the syllogism appears to run counter to the Rule of Law. Therefore, because the syllogism can never establish the necessary correspondence upon which its use is based, we must surrender either our adherence to the prospectivity of legal norms or their referential character. The rule simply cannot be made to cover or pick out the instant case.

Jackson's response to all of this is to propose an alternative theory of truth, based not on correspondence but on coherence. For him, there is no such thing as a direct access to reality but reality is filtered through the frameworks that we impose on it: 'our only access to the outside reality, our only way of making sense of it, is mediated through significatory systems' (1991: 179). So, although MacCormick goes on to argue for a limited use of the concept of narrative coherence as a tool sufficient to bridge the correspondence gap, ultimately:

> this form of correspondence claim falls foul of exactly the same objections as ... traditional correspondence theory. We have no unmediated access to actual experiences of everyday life or the outside world, with which our narrativised accounts can be said to correspond.
>
> (1991: 183)

Similarly, MacCormick's attempt to rescue the lost temporality of the Rule of Law by suggesting that matching the premises in a normative syllogism is not a problem of reference but of sense: any identification of 'the sense of the predicate of the major premiss with the sense intended by the legislator ... is based on a correspondence claim' and, without unmediated access to the original sense of the words, the temporal gap cannot be closed (1991:

187–88). For Jackson, the real point is that in decision-making both premises are reduced to the level of 'narrative structures'. Meaning is constructed through relations within systems of signification and none of this requires any necessary correspondence with the outside world.

Two levels of discourse are posited, deep and surface. Located at the deep level are those elementary structures of signification that comprise the minimum conditions for any discourse to have meaning. At this level, sense is constructed by the interplay of two axes, the syntagmatic and the paradigmatic: the former relates to the surface structure of a text, our natural tendency to construct sense in narrative terms or sequence; the latter relates to those sets of signifiers that underlie the content of a text, the substitutable elements within a sequence. We can think of this as the difference between positioning and substitution where we apply conventional closure rules in order to privilege binary oppositions and construct sense in a socially contingent way:

> I call this the 'narrativization of pragmatics', and have illustrated it within the legal context by distinguishing between 'the story *in* the trial' (the factual issues which the trial is called upon to decide) and 'the story *of* the trial' (the narrative or narratives of how the various participants behave within the trial, and how successfully they perform their respective tasks of persuasion).
>
> (Jackson 2009)

Jackson presents an analysis of four English cases to demonstrate how decision-making can be understood to reflect the '*tacit social evaluation*' of the case (Jackson 1988: 101–6) and to demonstrate that there is really no conceptual distinction between fact and law: while the former is a truth claim constructed within language in respect of real-life circumstances or events, the latter is a claim constructed within language in relation to the normative significance of certain types of behaviour with an averment that this rule is valid. Thus, both truth and validity are qualifications about the status of propositions offered in discourse. How they are received depends upon who makes them, in what circumstances, on what authority and through what forms of speech and language. This essentially Greimassian view of narrative is required, claims Jackson:

> in order to bridge the gap between 'the deep structures of signification' … and socially-constructed typifications of behaviour, which represent substantive narratives … [I]n assessing the plausibility of a particular narrative, we make *comparisons* with the typifications which are socially constructed, but within an existing semiotic constraint: the narratives are recognizable as such in so far as they are generated by a single grammar. But once we have the grammar, we can construct an

infinite number of new narratives, and can judge their relative similarity to existing typifications ...

(1990: 47–48)

Narratives provide us with the limits within which to negotiate the construction of sense. Very often we see only what we expect to see but sense construction means comparing the empirical data received through observation with our 'internalised narrative expectations' and interpreting these data with respect to those internalised narratives:

> There is a prior level of narrative expectation brought to the reading even of laws: their words evoke typical narratives or 'standard cases' ... How far the rule extends then becomes a matter not of linguistic analysis alone, but rather linguistic analysis influenced by the criterion of narrative similarity: how similar is a proposed extension to the typical narratives evoked by the rule? When interpretation is located within the institutional setting of courtroom adjudication, the same cognitive processes still apply: the perception of cases as 'hard' or 'easy', as well as their resolution, may be analysed in terms of perceived relative similarity to already internalised legal narratives. What differs is the pragmatic context, the interaction of the 'stories of the trial', including the communicative behaviour of those involved in debating the legal issues ... Legal norms thus take behaviour whose meaning is based on internalised social narratives and apply to it one of the modalities available within legal discourse.
>
> (Jackson 2009)

Thus, while MacCormick espouses a normative theory of justification, Jackson understands it as 'communicative fact'. His concern is to 'distinguish the different modes in which [justification] may be communicated and the different communicative contexts in which it may operate'. Law, in practice, does not exist on a single narrative level but must 'be conceived in terms of the interaction of a multiplicity of narrative/discursive structures' (Jackson 1988: 226). That is to say, a court's judgement 'may comprise within it a combination of discourses, corresponding to the different audiences which the judge ... is addressing' and 'the doctrinal audience is not the only audience of judicial discourse' (Jackson 1992: 214).

Jürgen Habermas' discourse theory

We can take this question over the possibility of closing the gap between facts and norms a little further by looking at discourse theory. For Jürgen Habermas, the answer to the question of how a judgement is reached in respect of the issues arising for determination in a case is found through anticipating the response that participants in a democratic discourse would have made if they had considered these. Effectively, for Habermas, this involves positing a temporal continuity between legislation and adjudication, between the creation of norms (or rules) and their application, that operates retrospectively, allowing us to posit a link that enables us to conceive of a decision as having been achieved through a process of communication, a transfer of knowledge between these two poles without corruption or diminution. In other words, what this suggests is a relationship between two discourses – justification and application – such that the decisions reached in one (adjudication) are already provided for in the other (legislation) in such a way that nothing significantly novel may enter the process of their communication from one pole to the other.

In order to give legitimacy to law making, Habermas draws upon and adapts the Kantian principle of universalisability to formulate his 'discourse principle': '[j]ust those action norms are valid to which all possibly affected persons could agree as participants in rational discourses' (Habermas 1998: 107). For Habermas, vis-à-vis Kant, the 'We' that is constituted as the addressor of the law is thus actually and simultaneously (not counter-factually) the same 'we' that finds itself addressed by the law. In this way, a correspondence is communicatively achieved, enabling a 'democracy principle' to achieve legitimacy through institutionalisation of the discourse principle: '[t]he discourse principle is intended to assume the shape of a principle of democracy only by way of legal institutionalization' (Habermas 1998: 121–22). In this way, law acquires its strongest basis for legitimacy: a law is valid and justified 'if and only if equal consideration is given to the interests of all those who are possibly involved' (Habermas 1998: 108). Thus, 'only those statutes may claim legitimacy that can meet with the assent of all citizens in a discursive process of legislation that in turn has been legally constituted' (Habermas 1998: 110). Nonetheless, the question arises: in what sense, if at all, can any particular, determinate fact circumstance be held to have been in the contemplation of those who agree upon any law? Statutes are, by and large, general in outlook. In what sense, then, can an abstract legal norm be understood to cover any particular fact? Or, to put this in the form of our earlier question, in what sense can the gap be closed?

Klaus Günther (1989) argues that a 'perfect' norm would include, from its inception, all possible future instances of its application, which will mean that 'participants of a discourse would be certain that there will be no situation where observance of a norm will violate a universalized interest' (Günther 1989: 156). In this sense, far from being entirely general and abstract what is being suggested is that a perfect norm is perfectly particular since, in each case, 'every particular situation can be anticipated by everyone' (Günther 1993: 33). But do such perfect norms exist? Indeed, to put the question another way, is it possible that any finite mind could hold in contemplation in this way the infinite possibilities for instantiation of such norms? If not, does that not open up the same gap once more? And, if so, how then can this gap be closed?

Günther suggests, and Habermas agrees, that a distinction must be made between two discourses: justification and application discourses. Thus, although, on the one hand, novel and unexpected cases may arise, which were not foreseeable and are thus unaccounted for in the justification discourse, yet on the other hand, these can be accounted for within the application discourse. According to Günther, although the norms created in the legislation discourse are indeterminate, and pick out only a limited series of typical fact circumstances (so that several norms will appear as relevant), nonetheless, in the application discourse, all the salient features of a situation are considered together and a decision is made that the application of a particular norm is appropriate to cover the situation.

For both Habermas and Günther, what this amounts to is the relatively straightforward application of a relevant norm, whose substantive content remains essentially unchanged throughout the process, albeit that it has achieved additional specification through an appropriate application in a novel case: 'we apply a valid norm as if we could have foreseen this situation under the conditions of unlimited knowledge and time' (Günther 1989: 163). Everything hinges on this sense of *appropriateness*. So, for example, an action taken in adjudication (application discourse) is appropriate if it could have been foreseen in legislation (justification discourse), which is, of course, just another way of positing 'the perfect norm' indirectly, through reconstructive observation. Effectively, what this amounts to is a way of deriving the full, universally approved content of a norm from a consideration of the contingent, concrete fact circumstances of an individual case and positing the latter as having been always-already, *a priori* included in the former. In this way, appropriateness does all the work of distinguishing between and reconnecting these to discourses, allowing us to envisage a whole system of such 'perfect norms', entirely coherent and consistent with each other. In this way, for discourse theory, the gap between fact and norm is closed but only at the expense of excluding creativity, novelty and change.

Zenon Bańkowski's 'inside outside' distinction: occupying 'the middle'

Zenon Bańkowski observes how Günther, following Habermas, has:

posit[ed] two different discourses. One is the justification discourse where norms are justified and where criteria of universalisability are [used] ... The second is the application discourse which decides whether or not a particular justified norm is to be applied. The criteria used here are different ... [A] distinction has been made between the criteria used to justify the norm and those used to apply it ... opening up a gap in the seamless, universalising rationality of legal doctrine.

(Bańkowski 2003: 2–3)

For Bańkowski this separation is not entirely helpful and he attempts instead to conceptualise a more dynamic form of legal reasoning and legal process. He begins with those 'two opposed and irreconcilable positions' represented in this way of thinking:

> On the one hand the law is static, locked into its universalising criteria and becoming a form of ... legalism. On the other hand, it becomes so open to other criteria that there appears to be no law left; just the contingent decisions of judges. My attempt is to show that law should be seen as the articulation of two systems, the doctrinal and universalising system which has its own internal world and the more arbitrary and contingent application system which is sensitive to the outside ... [O]ne system instantiated in the articulation of the two.
>
> (Bańkowski 2003: 3)

On this basis, Bańkowski begins to articulate what he refers to as an 'Outside Inside' distinction, something that 'emerge[s] from the fluctuating negotiations at the border posts of identities', where the outside, what is not law, is introduced to 'leaven and change the law'. In contrast to Detmold, for whom the moment of particularity 'cannot be covered by any criteria and is forever ... mystical', Bańkowski seeks to 'adduce some criteria and capacities' and to 'get a little more concrete' about judicial reasoning. He suggests that we begin by 'paying attention to the particularity of the situation', considering in the first instance 'whether or not the inside needs to be readjusted with the outside' (Bańkowski 2003: 10). But he warns that we must be careful not to understand this as some kind of independent 'sociological thesis as to what sort of extra legal factors influence the law'; rather, what we have is 'a theoretical thesis about how the law is open to the "outside" ... [as] part of the nature of the process of law and thus "inside" ... ' (Bańkowski 2003: 2–3). So what we have, in effect, is a new way of conceptualising the legal task:

> the attempt to overcome a dichotomous mode of thinking based on the polarisation of seemingly opposite principles ... It goes on to explore a new construction of the space within and between ... in which two terms co-exist with paradox but without logical contradiction.
>
> (Bańkowski 2003: 34–35)

Following Gillian Rose (1992), Bańkowski sees this 'middle' place as a 'tension-laden space', one that is so difficult to maintain that we attempt to 'theorise it away'. But this only results in the to and fro of a 'false and distorting polarisation', where we find ourselves drawn 'on the one hand to the soulless force of instrumental rationality and, on the other, to the always frustrated search for immediacy' (Bańkowski 2003: 35). Precisely because of this struggle between extremes, we understand the middle as a space to be protected, where concepts are held apart without collapsing into 'an unreflective mass'. In this sense, the middle is always 'an ambiguous place', where law not only defines the power we possess already but also, at the same time, becomes the precursor of anxiety. We can see this, he suggests, in Martha Nussbaum's reading of *Antigone*. Nussbaum (2001) explains how both Creon and Antigone make 'the same moral mistake', attempting to escape from the tension and anxiety of the middle by denying conflict. This, Bańkowski asserts, is the condition of modernity, an endless attempt 'to seek a "comfort zone" – either by the soulless application of universalism … or by recognizing the "violence" behind the law and going over to the nihilism of love'. But how do we refrain from giving ourselves over to one or the other polarity? (Bańkowski 2003: 36).

According to Bańkowski, we do this by 'suspending the ethical', refraining from seeing everything as always-already 'an incarnation of the universal' and 'us[ing] that anxiety creatively'. The starting point for this is 'the distinction that Günther makes between justification and application'. According to Günther, when we justify a norm we use universalistic criteria but when we apply that norm we attend to the particularities of the case; that is, first we decide what the law means and then we decide whether and how that law applies in a particular case. In the former part, the criteria are universalistic, says Bańkowski, and in the latter more particular. But this still leaves unanswered the question of how exactly we decide on the particularities of the case and, here, even Günther appears to quash the distinction between justification and application, for 'the idea … that the judgement must fit and be coherent with all similar instances … at least on one of the ways that he interprets it … is just another version of the justification criterion' (Bańkowski 2003: 37–40).

However, if we think of the middle in terms of what Detmold calls the particularity void, then we can take the argument a little further, says Bańkowski. For Detmold, there is a difference between deciding whether a rule is reasonable and whether it is reasonable to apply it; thus, Davoût does not shoot Pierre as a Russian spy, despite his orders. What this suggests is that the problem must be recast as one of 'recognition and discernment': recognition is 'what emerges from a held tension between particular and universal … a means of discerning the path ahead' (Bańkowski 2003: 42).

What all of this means, says Bańkowski, is that the law may be seen both as something that 'forms individuals' and also as something which the individual, once formed, is able to 'deploy in new and original ways in the diverse situations': that is, the individual, in turn 'becomes a lawmaker'. This subsequent 'encounter between the law and the particular situation' is what marks out the conditions for the emergence of 'the singular'. Here, 'the particular is neither simply subsumed beneath the law ... nor is the law abandoned'; rather, the emergence of singularity depends upon the 'ability to recognise the particular instance as both consistent with and different from previous instances'. In this way, we recognise our understanding as 'contingent and limited, continually subject to the revision and rearticulation afforded by fresh encounter'. There is 'no final judgement; I can always be wrong' (Bańkowski 2003: 43). However, notwithstanding this, '[I] have to engage and take responsibility'. This is what gives to law its indeterminate character, 'the fact that in the encounter we enter the place where we have to decide whether to apply it or not' and that there we must 'take responsibility'. Contra Detmold, for Bańkowski 'the "particularity void" is not mystical' at all, it is simply 'a statement of the fact that we have to start from the particular situation' and we should not let the rules make us forget this: 'Davoût does not start from the rule "Spies are to be shot"'; rather, 'paying attention to his encounter with Pierre, he sees his affliction and does not shoot him, in a sense recreating the law as "All men are brothers and not to be shot"'. What is important is our 'paying attention to the story ... But this attention will always be something done within the context of the law. The encounter is a journey which we cannot prejudge although we have a context within which to understand' (Bańkowski 2003: 44–45).

Bańkowski notes how Bernard Jackson also appears to affirm that 'it is attention to the *stories* of the cases which leads to an understanding of the result, rather than the rules [bestowing on them] a pre-ordained meaning' (Bańkowski 2003: 48). For example, it makes a difference to whether and how we apply the law if we are talking about the sale of jewels to a jeweller, who might be expected to encounter at least some fraud in the course of business or if we are talking about a private transaction with two old ladies. What this tells us, claims Bańkowski, is that 'getting immersed' in the details of a story, reading it from the inside out, is critically important. This is what 'drives the judgement on'. Looking at things from the perspective of the middle will help us to realise that, although the rule is necessary, it is the encounter with the facts of the case that will determine whether or not the principle will be applied: '[i]t will be in that act that the law is suspended and recreated anew on the model that we saw of the encounter between Davoût and Pierre' (Bańkowski 2003: 49).

Perhaps we can understand better this idea of 'suspending the ethical', Bańkowski suggests, if we think of legal reasoning as a form of:

> operating in a sphere which is barred by a thick almost opaque curtain. You sometimes see dimly other things that might be important through it. You lift the curtain to look but the curtain is extremely heavy ... You

have to drop it and remain on the side you were or move to the new side.

(Bańkowski 2001: 174)

But how do we know *when* to look beyond? And when we do, how do we balance the reasons while holding the curtain? What informs our decision whether to remain on one side or move to the other? Bańkowski's answer is that we must go back again to the story:

> The key is to pay attention, to let the story speak for itself and not be too quick to apply closure by imposing a principle or pattern on it. This is the sense behind these mystical post-modern utterances like 'deferring the undeferrable'; of 'saying what cannot be said'; 'listening to what cannot be heard' … [It] is the ability to listen; to know when to stop because you know what is before you is a case of x; to know when to continue listening because you see difference. A common mistake is to jump to a conclusion before the story has a chance to reveal itself … The trick is to explore the story until you know that it is appropriate to stop and make a decision … when to move beyond; when not to apply a pattern … [I]n this way one can understand what I mean by living as though there was no outside. We cannot go actively seeking the outside because that would … negate the point of the routinised activity. It is the anomaly and the interruption that sensitises us to the need for action but we spot it by paying attention *from the inside*.

(Bańkowski 2001: 180–81)

But how could we recognise any anomaly? How, for example, would the fact that an injustice was likely to be done by the application of a certain rule pierce the exclusionary curtain privileging that rule in order to make its presence known? It cannot be that this would happen automatically, for the whole point of law is to reduce such complexity and facilitate predictability of results in decision-making by the application of rules. This is an important question, since the exclusionary nature of legal reasons would seem to exclude such substantive considerations.

Exploring exclusionary reasons

The idea of an exclusionary reason was first introduced by Joseph Raz (1975). Adapting a distinction from Hart (1961), Raz distinguished between first- and second-order reasons. Essentially, a first-order reason is a *reason to perform an act*, a reason balanced against other first-order reasons according to relative weight. A second-order reason is *a reason to act for a reason*, which may be positive (a reason to act on the basis of the weightiest first-order reason) or negative (a reason not to act for a reason). It is this negative second-order reason that Raz terms exclusionary, since it provides a reason for not acting on the basis of a reason that is conclusive (there is no need or possibility of inquiring behind it). Conflict between a first-order reason and a second-order reason that excludes it is unlike the conflict between two first-order reasons: where two first-order reasons compete the actor weighs up the balance of reasons and acts accordingly; where a first-order reason conflicts with a valid exclusionary reason the actor may well be acting against the balance of first-order reasons but the action of the exclusionary reason is better described not in terms of the balance of first-order reasons but as taking that reason out of the balance of first-order reasons altogether, without affecting its weight as a reason. This is the crucial difference between exclusionary and first-order reasons: a weightier first-order reason will override a weaker first-order reason but a valid exclusionary reason will exclude from consideration all those first-order reasons to which it has reference whatever their strength. Clearly, to function properly, exclusionary reasons must be exempt from the need for re-examination with a view to revision on those occasions to which they apply. But this raises the question of whether this exemption operates on every occasion or if exclusionary reasons may sometimes yield to waive the exclusion of disregarded reasons. What, then, is the possibility, having entrenched a reason at the exclusionary level, of opening it up for revision?

Patrick Atiyah (1986) uses the example of marriage to show how formal reasoning operates much on the model of Raz's theory of exclusionary reasons. If a reason is there then it provides us with a reason not to question but simply to act: we don't think about it, we just do it! In marriage, for example, the reasons underlying patterns of interaction between lovers become entrenched into rules informing the marital relationship. As a result, substantive reasons for action become temporarily frozen into formal (exclusionary) rules. This facilitates decision-making; that is, since the rules are there we don't ask, but just apply them. However, if, or rather when, the rules fail to reflect their underlying substantive reasons we can, says Atiyah, revise them, by going behind the rules and starting to look at the substantive reasons once more. But what gives us the reason to do this?

Frederick Schauer (1991) agrees with Raz that rules should be understood as entrenched generalisations. Rules ensure that the presence of certain operative facts always triggers certain prescribed consequences. So we follow a rule because it is the rule and we do so regardless of any underlying justification. However, Schauer makes a distinction between the idea of exclusion and the force of exclusion to allow that, on occasion, one may look at the first-order reason to determine if it is to control in that particular case:

> Insofar as it is possible for an exclusionary reason to tell an agent to
> look just quickly, if possible, at the excluded first-order reason to see if

this is one of those cases in which the exclusion of that factor should be disregarded ...

(Schauer 1991: 91)

Inasmuch as one is, in this way, always looking at first order reasons, and looking just quickly rather than taking careful consideration, this might not necessarily be regarded as negating the idea of exclusionary reasons.

But the question still remains: how is it possible that a 'signal that revision is needed [could] be received at the exclusionary level given that first-order reasons no longer resound at that level, by the very nature of a reason as exclusionary'? 'Revisability', argues Christodoulidis, 'has been cut off from the concerns that informed the entrenchment of a reason as exclusionary in the first place'. It has been 'removed from the concerns that might have occasioned it' (Christodoulidis 1999: 231). On this basis, suspensions are not only improbable, they are impossible:

[L]aw stands impotent before the particular ... It has to address the complexity that confronts it by reducing that complexity and of course it can neither address nor redress its own complexity deficit that results from this. It is that deficit and the blindspot that accompanies it that forces law to miss the particular. At the same time, there can be no legal judgement over the appropriateness of the application of law. There can be no decision within a context as to the appropriateness of the context.

(Christodoulidis 2000: 189)

Christodoulidis argues that if we want to find a way to incorporate respect for the particular into our thinking then we must look not to law but to ethics. Ethical reason is 'reflexive', he argues, and so it can 'accommodate complexity'. It 'allows for the comprehension of the "other" not as classification in terms of abstract categorisation, but as inseparable from "his" invocation'. In other words, it has more flexibility and freedom in the encounter because 'while it fixes the terms of that encounter ... it keeps open the question of their revisability *as appropriate to the encounter rather than as appropriate to a certain function ...* ' Christodoulidis points to what he calls 'a disjunctive between the reductive and the reflexive', arguing that while 'the reductive works to immunise ... the reflexive remains [open] to ... contingency, the admission that a determination could be otherwise' (Christodoulidis 2000: 189).

We see an example of how he employs this distinction in his 'Reply' to Roberto Unger's law-as-politics thesis, where he underscores his contention that although law may be 'shaken from within' this surprise cannot carry through to upset the 'constitutive assumptions' underlying law's institutional identity. He sees what Unger (1996) calls law's 'institutional imagination' as, on the one hand, both limited and limiting, as a result of the forcing and entrenching of reductions on 'the "plastic" world of political possibilities' (Christodoulidis 1996: 383). To challenge those reductions would be tantamount to dispensing with law altogether (Christodoulidis 1996: 378–79). On the other hand, reductions, while limiting, are also empowering:

> Legal institutionalisation is the entrenchment of certain reductions on the possibilities of communication ... to the exclusion of other possibilities ... Institutional imagination is indeed a reduction *achievement* ... to be assessed in the light of the possibilities it offers people to communicate successfully ... in a world that is making it all the more urgent but at the same time all the more unlikely that such communication and the action that depends on it ... will be carried out with success.
>
> (Christodoulidis 1996: 384)

Luhmann, as Christodoulidis notes, both draws upon and then creatively diverges from what Talcott Parsons describes as a situation of 'double contingency' (Parsons and Shils 1951: 105). For Luhmann, the possibility for the interrelating of human behaviour rests on the question of whether and how the complexity of this double indeterminacy can be reduced. One way is through the 'fixing of a context', through its 'structuring into frameworks that have the form of "expectations of expectations"'. Communication becomes possible 'through reductions ... premised on system selectivity ... ' (Christodoulidis 1996: 385). Law achieves constancy through a narrowing of 'the expectability of expectations', he says, and 'by abstracting from the "concrete" parties involved ... : *it allows people to encounter each other as role players, ... as legal actors*' (Christodoulidis 1996: 386). Thus, '[l]aw provides a context to settle contingencies ... at the expense of other contexts'. In other words, contra Unger, there can be no negotiation of these roles. But this means that systems, as 'institutionalised versions of society' are 'relatively stable and delineated'. They 'reproduce themselves by projecting *expectations*', permitting the system to 'react, modify [its] expectations and evolve' (Christodoulidis 1996: 387).

Still, legal expectations are always reductions from 'possible expectations' and this always includes a certain '*immunisation* from challenge'. That is to say, law, as an achievement, is always achieved at 'a cost': some contingencies are admitted and others precluded, the latter being unable, thereafter, to register as expectations. In this way, with conflicts perceived as order and conflicting elements silenced, the 'system is neither static nor insensitive to change' but must continually 'vary the expectations it projects'. It '"learns" and *evolves*' by means of conflict, without which it would atrophy and die. 'In a nutshell', says Christodoulidis, 'the evolution of a system is structural variation; and what can vary depends on what already exists' (Christodoulidis 1996: 387–88).

Of course, all of this has 'major consequences', he warns. In this way, 'already existing structural assumptions [are brought] into play as preconditions to all attempts to push for change'. Since the only way that a 'claim for change may register is if it manages to surprise projections of expectations', and 'we can only see what we know how to look for', then, '[f] or a challenge to register ... the system's memory has to be tapped'. Thus, law 'controls the context against which informative surprises may be articulated' (Christodoulidis 1996: 388). In other words, any challenge that is 'to register in law will only make a difference in the evolution of the system on the basis of its *alignment* to already existing reductions ... against a background of settled meaning' (Christodoulidis 1996: 390–91). Now, this radically circumscribes the possibilities for change, he argues, since '[c]hallenges *to* the structure can only be accommodated *by* the structure as demands to draw new internal distinctions and boundaries ... This assimilation of the extraordinary to the ordinary ... places a wooden hand on the possibility to politicise and contest'. The point is, he argues, that 'Unger's formulation ... is misleading because it refers to what is *not* selected ... what remains an environment to the system ... And that is the crux of institutionalisation, of the drawing of the legal system's boundary' (Christodoulidis 1996: 391). Consequently, 'structural reductions cannot be employed and defied at once ... [A]t the first-order level ... where complexity is reduced and the world becomes legally observable, the reduction cannot but remain a blindspot ... There can be no structure-defying structures [because] the institution cannot see its blindspot and shake it off' (Christodoulidis 1996: 393).

To bring this all back to the question of what possibilities for radical change in understanding are present in the encounter between Pierre and Davout, an 'instance of "merciful" legal judgement cannot account for the emergence of a context that names it as "an application of x norm", as "an instance of x commonality", *a posteriori*' (Christodoulidis 1999: 224), says Christodoulidis. 'Norms that inform legal judgement ... must ... *pre-exist their application*' (Christodoulidis 1999: 223). So, in the encounter between Davout and Pierre, any emergence of 'known commonality' as the criterion for judgement can occur only at the expense of law: '[t]o law the particularity of the affective encounter is invisible, the particularity could not have pierced the legal terms of its exclusion' (Christodoulidis 1999: 224).

Precisely because, in law, particularity is abstracted, more-or-less fixed and reduced to role and rule, this involves a reduction to an exclusionary language that both prevents visibility of the particular and is unyielding to considerations of appropriateness; otherwise, law's exclusionary reasons would have to give way to substantive ones, which is impossible due to the limits of revisability of exclusionary reasons. Thus, for Christodoulidis, while the particular can be meaningfully invoked it cannot be addressed in legal judgement; that is, law cannot cross the particularity void.

Of course, Christodoulidis is certainly correct to insist that '*universalization is only justification a posteriori*'. Can it ever be anything else? Experience is always experience of the past as it is presented to us in perception and, even at the most, will be experience of the immediate past. So the statement, that it 'comes too late to guide the decision of the judge', while correct, may not necessarily be understood to negate the understanding of justification as, for example, MacCormick uses it. Indeed, in the sense in which we normally understand the reasons given in a judge's judgement as justifying her decision, surely this simply operates to affirm a necessary relationship between her decision and its subsequent justification; that is, as Charles Hartshorne puts it 'memory of E is not memory of something like E ... but of E itself' (Hartshorne 1970: 60).

Likewise, Bańkowski's objection that MacCormick's emphasis on the knowing subject and her reasoning seems inevitably to downplay particularity is also, in a sense, correct. The point is made well by Nigel Simmonds (1993). Simmonds claims that all talk of the particular is misguided since the particular is itself a very abstract description, the 'most abstract of all abstractions'. So, for him, there is really no such thing as the particular, merely different sets of descriptions: all talk of particulars as captured by categories means that particulars are always subject to further description. The real particular, if there is one, always 'slips beneath every description, and escapes every act of judgement' (Simmonds 1993: 66). Correspondingly, for Bańkowski, the more universal that one gets in description then the more abstract the reasoning becomes and thus also the more removed from the actual event, person or thing to which one is referring.

The point is that no description, however reflective, will ever yield a real, irreducible particular. All attempts to capture or describe the particular will, to some extent, be abstractions from reality, from process. What we are really talking about, it seems, is not so much real particularity or the objective reality of the universal but, as Hartshorne puts it, 'the objective reality of the *distinction* between universal and particular'. For in the attempt to simply locate it, the real particular disappears, and, given that it is sensible to suppose coincidence among the contrasts universal-particular and possible-actual, 'no possibility is literally particular, no universal is literally actual ... but only seems so' (Hartshorne 1970: 61).

With '[c]ommon sense', writes Hartshorne, one 'tends to think of a particular animal or physical thing as the extreme contrary of the abstract or general'. However:

> a particular person or thing, enduring and changing through time, is really a kind of low-level universal, compared to the momentary states or events in which alone the individual is fully concrete or actual ... The supposition that the indivisible units of concrete reality are single substances rather than single states or events has produced endless confusion.

> (Hartshorne 1970: 73)

But '[i]f the extreme of concreteness tends to be missed by ordinary speech, so does the extreme of abstractness'. Therefore, the real task of the legal philosopher is more correctly described in terms of an engagement with endless refinement of the abstractions that she uses, criticising them, attempting to put into words 'what can be said *universally* about the most concrete levels of reality' (Hartshorne 1970: 73–74). Scott Veitch comes closer to this when he writes that:

> [p]articulars and universals are relative, not just to each other, but to a complex and varied range of institutional settings ... Are there any particulars? Are there any universals? It may well be that while there are undoubtedly universal forms, universal and particular in practical reasoning (including legal reasoning) are no more than relative forms of abstraction or of generalization – more or less useful tools, stakes in a debate ... always deployable, not categorical. This is arguably what Adam Smith's model of moral reasoning ... grasped so well. What it saw less clearly ... was that the basic *elements* that he claimed make up this low level particularity ... may themselves be results, *effects rather than causes*, of other processes ...
>
> (Veitch 2006: 153–54)

We can see then how theories of legal reasoning usually proceed on the basis of an assumption that rule definition is different from rule application, whether this is thought of as problematic, as in Detmold, or not, as with MacCormick. Here, legal knowledge is believed to engage with an explicit, precise and coherent representation of social reality and the real challenge for decision-makers is to facilitate the transition or transmission of rules from creation to application without diminution or corruption; in other words, the aim is to maintain the correspondence of law to fact, theory to practice, allowing the dominant rule-definition/rule-application relationship to be founded or confirmed. Such an understanding of the method of applying law is widely held to be the natural and transparent mode of operation of the legal system.

In this way, we can also see how traditional thinking about the nature of legal knowledge and the practice of law is generally assumed to proceed on the basis of a simple correspondence between the production of norms, or rules, and their implementation. In this sense, it is in terms of its functional value as a commodity (Lyotard 1984), its meaning and relevance for the legal institutional system, that information is held to be significant. Indeed, it is the assumption about the correctness of this way of thinking that underlies, for example, Detmold's notion of the 'particularity void' as a troublesome gap between rule-determination and rule-application. Nonetheless, it should be obvious that any 'gap' as such can only emerge if we focus first on the abstracted 'ends' of the processes of creating, communicating and applying legal knowledge ahead of any analysis of the nature of such knowledge; any 'bridging' of this gap can proceed only on the basis of an assumption about the possibility of transferring knowledge between those abstracted ends.

Such a view itself presupposes an understanding of reality as composed of essentially static, immobile and discrete 'things'. Understood thus, legal knowledge is considered as the substantial flow of information from point A through point B to point C, and so on, which means that any conception of knowledge as a continuous process that 'goes beyond the simple determination and application of the criterion of truth' (Lyotard 1984: 18) seems to have disappeared altogether. Nonetheless, as I will argue, legal knowledge should not be understood merely in terms of an informational commodity whose progressive development can be charted as from points A to B to C; rather, it is properly to be understood more in terms of what happens in between, the undefined, indeterminate and limitless processes from which these points are but momentary abstractions, frozen from time.

Employing a process metaphysics, informed by the work of Alfred North Whitehead, Henri Bergson and Gilles Deleuze, I will argue that such an ontology of being involves a counterfeit movement, that terms like rule and fact, universal and particular, theory and practice are really only momentary snapshots of reality, images extracted from an otherwise heterogeneous continuity and movement, merely convenient labels that we utilise to describe and illustrate interpenetration by means of side-by-side representation. Thus, I will argue that we cannot say that rules as universals are applied to facts as particulars; neither can we say that legal practitioners somehow reflect upon theory to justify the application of their decisions as if these activities were essentially separate entities. Indeed, such a view only prevents us from seeing the extent to which rule and fact, universal and particular, already actually interpenetrate one another. In fact, on a Bergsonian view, judges reflecting on their decisions for the purpose of giving justifying reasons for their decisions are really only institutional actors giving linguistic expression to a past experience within the terms of an already ordered institutional code. That is why although their justifying reasons may deliver a symbolic representation of experience, an account of it, they do not inform the actual, lived moment of that experience.

Part II

Developing an alternative approach: the importance of process

Chapter 3

Alfred North Whitehead's philosophy of organism

Introduction

Much of contemporary legal theory is effectively the expression of a continuing concern to bridge this gap that opens up in legal decision-making between living reality and legal representation, two supposedly separate and distinct but connectable domains, most obvious in respect of hard cases such as *Re A* where the interface between the so-called theoretical and the practical is revealed as problematic but nonetheless true of other cases where the anomalies are not so obvious or so easily recognised. Such an understanding of the legal task plainly has its roots in a Parmenidean-inspired universe, in particular in the teachings of Democritus of the Eleatic school; that is, with the understanding of an entitative conception of reality in which the ultimate building blocks of reality are atomic entities, basic and undividable, whose relative motions and relationship to each other are regulated and apprehended through the use of general predictable laws. Clearly, only on the basis of such an understanding as composed of fixed, or fixable, and relatively constant entities can we make any further assumption about the accuracy of their linguistic and conceptual representation within a correspondence theory of truth. The counter view to this Parmenidean theory of essentially unchanging reality has its roots in the tales of Heraclitus. Unlike Parmenides, Heraclitus contended that 'everything is in flux, and nothing is at rest' (Popper 1989: 44), so that rather than it being this outward appearance of stability which most truly represents reality, reality is more accurately thought of as a world of continuous but imperceptible change.

The proposal offered here is that although the minutiae of legal decision-making and the relations between them are often thought of in terms as separate but connectable and essentially stable elements in the ongoing process of law they should not be thought of as 'simply locatable', or isolatable, elements whose forms and functions can be abstracted to imply separate fixed points with connections and correspondences between them. Rather, they should be thought of as outlining a mutually constitutive process of becoming, not reducible to each other or to anything else; that is, inter-penetrating and interrelated. But how might we begin, and where should we look to, to develop further such a view of law? According to Alfred North Whitehead (1938):

> creative activity ... is the process of eliciting into actual being factors in the universe which antecedent to that process exist only in the mode of unrealised potentialities ... [I]n conceiving ... an occasion of experience, we must discriminate the actualised data presented by the antecedent world, the non-actualised potentialities which lie ready to promote their fusion into a new unity of experience, and the immediacy of self enjoyment which belongs to the creative fusion of those data with those potentialities. This is the doctrine of the creative advance whereby it belongs to the essence of the universe, that it passes into a future.
>
> (Whitehead 1938: 206–7)

Whitehead's early philosophical interest

In his early writings, Whitehead's concern was mainly with the problems of modern science and, in particular, with the breakdown of Newtonian cosmology. 'Newtonian physics', he observed, 'is based upon the independent individuality of each bit of matter ... fully describable apart from any reference to any other portion of matter ... [and] adequately described without any reference to past or future[,] ... conceived fully and adequately as wholly constituted within the present moment' (Whitehead 1933: 200–1). But this concept of the ultimate facts as 'simply located particles' is inconsistent with the notions of 'velocity, acceleration, momentum, and kinetic energy, which certainly are essential physical qualities', proving that 'there is a fatal contradiction inherent in the Newtonian cosmology' (1938: 199). In providing a different conception, 'we must ... include the notion of a state of change' (Whitehead 1919: 2).

So, in place of the concept of simply located particles of matter, Whitehead attempted to formulate a conception of the ultimate facts consistent with experience and free from the contradictions of the older theory. His proposal was that 'the ultimate facts of nature in terms of which all physical and biological explanation must be expressed, are events connected by their spatio-temporal relations' (Whitehead 1919: 4). On this basis, taking 'event' as the ultimate fact, he included 'a state of change' as an intrinsic feature of the ultimate facts and, in recognising that events extend over each other, was able to account for their essential relatedness. However, 'sense-awareness also yields to us other factors ... which are not events ... with a definite implication in events ... ' (Whitehead 1920: 15). Clarifying his concepts and working out the relations between events, and between events and objects, Whitehead now entertains problems and issues essentially different from the strictly scientific ones that characterised his early work. Philosophical considerations take centre stage and issue in a comprehensive metaphysical enquiry; in particular, 'the idea that the relation of extension has a unique pre-eminence' gives way to 'the true doctrine, that "process" is the fundamental idea. ... Extension is a derivative from process, and is required by it' (Whitehead 1919: 202). Believing that a more complete account of the 'complex essences' of events as derivative from their interconnections is discovered through emphasising the 'prehensive', rather than the 'separative', character of space-time, Whitehead ascribes to events the essential feature of 'unity'. 'The event is the unit of things real' (Whitehead 1925: 189). Yet, 'this abstract word cannot be sufficient to characterise what the fact of the reality of an event is in itself' (Whitehead 1925: 116). Thus, what began as a fairly abstract theory of 'events' put forward to replace the older theory of simply located matter now becomes a much more complex, and concrete, investigation into the ultimate nature of reality: 'The final problem is to conceive a complete fact [παντελης]'; not being as such, but being in the sense of a fully existing entity, a particular concrete thing (Whitehead 1933: 203).

The formative elements of a philosophy of process

In contrast to traditional philosophy, then, Whitehead conceives of individual entities as a series of moments of experience rather than masses of static substance. Within each moment, an entity is influenced by others, creates its own identity and propels itself into further experiences. Reality, then, is this process of creative advance in which many past events are integrated in the events of the present and, in turn, are taken up by future events. Events particularise ultimate creative power; the world is the realisation of a selection of creative potentials. Process thought is an attempt to elucidate the developmental nature of reality, of 'becoming' rather than sheer existence or 'being': it seeks unity-in-diversity, the 'many-becoming-one', in a sequence of integrations at every level and moment of existence.

For Whitehead, reality is composed of complex combinations of actual energy events. These units of becoming, or 'occasions of experience', may be described as dipolar: that is, Whitehead describes each as having a *physical* pole, which is the repeat of past occasions of experience in the present unit of becoming, and a *mental* pole, which represents the element of subjectivity that enables each occasion of experience, in the process of becoming, to entertain novel possibilities and exercise some determination over the shape it will take. The basic idea is the Heraclitean one, that all things are in flux, and that there is no 'unchanging subject of change', for the primary feature of existence is not 'substance' or 'being', but 'process' or 'becoming'. Being is the final outcome of each process of becoming, the result of it instantly 'perishing' as the next stage of becoming commences. However, with the perishing of each moment comes the possibility of the present and the advance into the future; everything is in this process of becoming, moving from the past through the present into the future.

This process of becoming of each 'actual-occasion' of experience White-head terms 'concrescence'. It consists as follows: first, at the physical pole, there is the passive reception of data (or 'physical prehension' of prior occa-sions of experience); next, at the mental pole, an entertaining of novel pos-sibilities (or 'conceptual prehensions'); finally, a reconciliation of the initial desire to conform to the past and the subsequent desire to achieve new pos-sibility. So, each actual occasion of experience takes on a new form and immediately perishes, to be replaced by a succeeding occasion in *its* first phase: passively receiving data and attempting to maintain the same aim of immediately preceding occasions; entertaining novel possibilities; achieving reconciliation and 'choosing' the form it will take (i.e. determining its 'sub-jective aim' or 'guiding principle'). Finally, to account for where and how these novel possibilities arise, that are 'felt' or 'grasped' through conceptual prehensions, Whitehead develops the concept of 'eternal objects', the pure potentials of the universe that forever remain constant (in the same way that 'blue-*ness*' remains unchanged even though the different things that we refer to as 'blue' change). Thus, logically, each actual occasion prehends all occa-sions of experience antecedent to itself: 'the many become one and are increased by one' (Whitehead 1933: 32).

It is to be noted that prehension, in Whitehead's terms, does not equate to rational or conscious activity. It is more properly understood as a sort of selective filter, providing emphasis or de-emphasis. Equally, not *all* past occa-sions and present possibilities may be absorbed in the integration of physical and conceptual prehensions in the process of concrescence: as well as 'posi-tive' prehensions, there are 'negative' ones, excluding certain past occasions of experience and certain possibilities from the process of concrescence; more-over, organic, unlike inorganic, forms of life exhibit modes of behaviour that suggest creative impulses that go beyond a mere physical prehension of the past.

So, in each present occasion of experience, past occasions are synthesised with conceptual prehensions into a subjective aim before being returned to the realm of data to be prehended by future occasions. In this passing from 'subject' to 'object', each occasion achieves an 'objective immortality', an existence that all future occasions prehend and with which they must grap-ple. But, while all prior occasions of experience internally determine the present occasion in this way, nonetheless, each present occasion is free to come to its own 'satisfaction'; that is, as well as feeling a desire to conform to the past each also contains its own lure to novel adventure.

How then can we make sense of our commonly expressed experience that 'things' change over time? Accepting, on the one hand, the implication that this scheme seems to suggest (that the ultimate metaphysical truth is atomism), Whitehead, on the other hand, appears to evade the same charge by developing a notion of 'societies' or groupings of occasions of experience that together exhibit some sort of enduring order or pattern that is reproduced in each occasion in society. As long as this commonality remains, a society, or a 'society of societies', unlike an occasion of experience, may change over time. Subject to evolution in this way, they too can never really be defined until their existence is totally in the past.

'Between order and chaos': on the development of human civilisation

We can appreciate the thrust of Whitehead's scheme by looking at what he says on the development of human civilisation. This tension between the physical and mental poles in an occasion of experience is the tension between order and chaos, a tension between conformity to the past and creativity in the future. Here, chaos is inevitable, for progress demands the forsaking of present perfections for greater possible perfections and without the advance into novelty there is no possibility of achieving higher perfections. Whitehead describes two types of advance into novelty, 'the discovery of novel pattern' and 'the gathering of detail within assigned pattern' (Whitehead 1938: 80). The first of these he describes as 'the condition for excellence'; the second, as 'stifling the freshness of living' (Whitehead 1929: 338). These are illustrated by reference to the Hellenic mentality of ancient Greece and the Hellenistic mentality of the later Alexandrian and medieval scholastic tradition, respectively. Hellenism was an advance of the first type, beyond known modes of perfection; Hellenistic scholarship was an advance of the second type; that is, within a given state of perfection, exploring new ways to achieve this perfection.

Significantly, this latter form generates only a minor form of chaos, while harmony among the occasions is overwhelming. Eventually, though, the various possibilities for advance within a mode of perfection play themselves out and, at that point, repetition begins to produce a gradual lowering of vivid appreciation – convention dominates, suppressing adventure. Precisely at this point, adventure of the former type, the search for new perfections, becomes essential; there must be a 'leap of imagination ... beyond the safe limits of the epoch, and beyond the safe limits of learned rules of taste' (Whitehead 1933: 360). A sense of discord occurs, until the contrasts can be resolved into new and larger patterns of harmony. Nothing can prevent this advance into novelty: there is no moment when the process halts or when being can be understood independently of becoming. And there is no end state, 'no perfection which is the infinitude of all perfections' (Whitehead 1933: 330).

Of course, bad choices can be made as well as good ones, so a civilisation must possess other qualities such as Truth, Beauty and Peace, the highest goal being Beauty: '[t]he teleology of the universe is directed to the production of Beauty' (Whitehead 1933: 341). Beauty is the internal conformation of the various items of experience with each other, that is, the perfection of harmony. Thus, an advancing civilisation must integrate in each present occasion three conditions: the infusion of pattern; the stability of pattern; the modification of pattern. What is required is 'order entering upon novelty; so that the massiveness of order does not degenerate into mere repetition; and so that the novelty is always reflected upon a background of system ... But the two elements must not really be disjoined ... In either alternative of excess, whether the past be lost, or be dominant, the present is enfeebled. This is only an application of Aristotle's doctrine of the "golden mean"' (Whitehead 1929: 339).

But how does this scheme coordinate other features, such as morality? Whitehead sees morality as an aspect of beauty, it 'consists in the aim at the ideal, and at its slowest it concerns the prevention of relapse to lower levels ... '. In other words, 'stagnation is the deadly foe of morality' (Whitehead 1933: 346). But there can be no universal moral ideals; moral codes are relative to social circumstance, useless when unduly rigid, most useful when they retain a provisional quality that remains sensitive to novel conduct that aims at higher perfections. Here, what is of greatest importance in any social system is the promotion of value experience among individual human beings, 'a social mingling of liberty and compulsion' (Whitehead 1933: 71).

Whitehead's analysis of the phases of concrescence

> The creative advance of the world is the becoming, the perishing, and the objective immortalities of those things which jointly constitute stubborn fact.
>
> (Whitehead 1929: xiv)

Whitehead maintains that although each actual entity is in fact undivided, rational analysis can understand it as a process:

> [t]he analysis of an actual entity is only intellectual ... only objective. Each actual entity is a cell with atomic unity. But in analysis it can only be understood as a process; it can only be felt as a process, that is to say, as in passage. The actual entity is divisible; but is in fact undivided. The divisibility can thus only refer to its objectifications in which it transcends itself. But such transcendence is self-revelation.
>
> (Whitehead 1929: 227)

We can summarise the basic elements of Whitehead's theory for the simplest case in the following way. Every actual entity, being dipolar, has both a physical pole (where it experiences other actual entities) and a mental pole (where it experiences possibilities and values). In the simplest case, an occasion's concrescence (or process of becoming) consists of three phases:

(a) The first phase constitutes the physical pole, the phase of physical prehensions, involving:

(i) something to be received (the objective datum for the concrescence);

(ii) the act of receiving or inheriting the objective datum (referred to as physical feeling);

(iii) the way that the objective datum is received (the subjective form of physical feeling);

(iv) the conformation of feeling (at least in the simplest case), since the subjective form of the physical feeling is the same as the form in the datum.

(b) The second phase constitutes the mental pole, the phase of conceptual prehensions, involving:

(i) the receiving or grasping of forms of definiteness (which are abstract potentials, or mere possibilities), also known as eternal objects;

(ii) the act of grasping eternal objects (conceptual feeling);

(iii) the way that eternal objects are received (the subjective form of conceptual feeling); that is, a valuation of the worth of the various possibilities open to it;

(iv) the determination of the relative worth of possibilities (the subjective aim of the concrescence). It is the desire to form the subjective aim (the concrescing subject's appetition to make something of and for itself in the present) that drives the process of becoming. The initial subjective aim guides the process of valuations towards the production of the final subjective aim.

(c) The third phase is the phase of simple comparative feelings: the integration of second-phase conceptual feelings (and their valuations) with first-phase physical feelings. Here, the actual occasion in the process of concrescence makes a 'decision' about which eternal object it will present in itself, integrating it with its physical prehension and thus terminating the process of becoming. The actual entity becomes what it is – its subjectivity of becoming passing or 'perishing' immediately into the objectivity of being – and propels itself into the future as an objective datum to be taken account of by new concrescing subjects. In the simplest case, where only minimal or negligible novelty is introduced, this third phase forms what Whitehead terms a 'physical purpose', which accounts for the persistence of physical order in the universe.

It will be clear that, even in the simplest case, subjects 'are not simply what the past allows them to be. There is always some measure of self-creation' (Hosinski 1993: 91).

Having summarised the basic elements of Whitehead's theory of concrescence for the simplest case, we are in a position to understand what he says about those more complex, 'higher-grade', occasions and his description of the supplemental phases to the process of concrescence. In higher-grade occasions, the concrescence does not terminate with the integration of conceptual and physical prehensions; instead, it produces a further datum, called a 'metaphysical proposition'. A metaphysical proposition can be understood as formed by the application of a predicate (a possible form of definiteness), derived from an occasion's conceptual prehensions, to a subject, the actual entity (or entities) grasped in its physical prehensions. Whitehead calls this integrated prehension or feeling a 'propositional feeling'. Such a proposition *lures* the concrescing occasion towards feeling *it*. The proposition merely presents a possibility that may be acted upon; its purpose is to influence the concrescence, not to express truth or falsehood. In higher-grade occasions, as the concrescing occasion 'feels' the metaphysical proposition, and reacts to it, the third phase of concrescence grows more complex, becoming 'prolonged' into sub-phases. Consciousness, or capability for language, is only a sufficient and not a necessary condition for the prehending or feeling of metaphysical propositions.

Plainly, in everyday life, we often act without conscious forethought, allowing propositions to influence or lure us into action that we might otherwise not have chosen, or which we later regret. Even when we consciously reflect upon possibilities, we often act without exercising rational judgement. Here, propositions attract us through value. We can see this in our aesthetic appreciation of, for example, Hamlet's famous soliloquy. As Whitehead puts it, we react to the proposition 'To be or not to be … ' not on the basis of 'a judgment concerning truth or falsehood but simply as a lure for feeling' (Whitehead 1929: 185). Such a proposition is purely theoretical but it draws us into Hamlet's imaginary life, and from there to a deeper appreciation of the tragedy of all human life and, perhaps, to action. All this is accomplished through feelings of value; rational judgement and criticism arise only later, if at all. Thus, our conscious grasping of propositions and feelings of value, the 'intuitive knowing' that allows us to acquire knowledge without the exercise of the formal process of reasoning, is a more basic form of knowledge than what we call 'rational knowing'. To affirm the existence of 'intuitive knowing' is not to contradict, negate or deny 'rational knowing' but merely to confirm that rational knowing enables us to criticise intuitive knowing and action, thereby deepening and improving our knowledge (and to say this is, perhaps, to do no more than give 'common sense' its rightful place). So, Whitehead differentiates two distinct types of experience (conscious and unconscious) with regard to our feeling of and acting upon propositions, without the exercise of rational judgement.

But the integration of eternal objects with physical prehensions need not always result in propositional feelings. In the simplest case, as we have seen, the integration terminates the concrescence: a 'comparative feeling' is formed but not 'felt' as a proposition, since the concrescing occasion perishes immediately. In higher-grade occasions, the concrescence does not terminate immediately and the integration of conceptual and physical prehensions is felt as a new datum for the concrescence, which is 'prolonged'. Without consciousness, however, this amounts to no more than 'flashes of novelty' at the mental pole of occasions (Whitehead 1929: 184).

Therefore, Whitehead says 'a proposition is a new kind of entity ... a hybrid between pure potentialities and actualities' (Whitehead 1929: 185–86). Eternal objects, as we have noticed, do not in themselves possess any definite reference to any particular actual entities: ' ... an eternal object refers only to the purely general *any* among actual entities. In itself an eternal object evades any selection among actualities or epochs ... This doctrine is the ultimate ground of empiricism; namely, that eternal objects tell no tales as to their ingressions' (Whitehead 1929: 256). Actual entities, on the other hand, 'tell no tales' about what is possible; only what has been. However, propositions, being hybrid entities, bring a new possibility, a new form of datum for feeling: a possibility linked to a concrete circumstance in the real world. A proposition, says Whitehead, introduces 'the possibility of *that* predicate applying in *that* assigned way to *those* logical subjects' (Whitehead 1929: 258). It is an entity, but not an *actual* entity. However, provided the logical subjects of the proposition are found within the 'actual world' of the occasion, then *that* proposition will be present in *that* occasion to act as a 'lure' for *its* feeling.

Now, a proposition, unlike an eternal object, 'may be conformal or non-conformal to the actual world', says Whitehead. That is, whereas an eternal object simply *is*, a proposition, since it refers to determinate actual entities, may be either 'true or false' (Whitehead 1929: 186). However, considered merely as a proposition (that is, without reference to its logical subjects, the 'reasons' determining its truth or falsehood), a proposition, like an eternal object, is indeterminate; it 'tells no tales about itself' (Whitehead 1929: 257), proclaiming only its possibility. Metaphysically, what this means is that false propositions represent potential for creative advance: from a 'purely logical aspect, non-conformal propositions are merely wrong, and therefore worse than useless. But in their primary role, they pave the way along which the world advances into novelty. Error is the price we pay for such progress' (Whitehead 1929: 187).

In other words, whereas a true proposition may be regarded as a proposition that conforms to the 'actual world' of an occasion prehending it, a false proposition is one that does not:

When a conformal proposition is admitted into feeling, the reaction to the datum has simply resulted in the conformation of feeling to fact ... The prehension of the proposition has abruptly emphasised one form of definiteness illustrated in fact.

But:

> [w]hen a non-conformal proposition is admitted into feeling, the reaction
> to the datum has resulted in the synthesis of fact with the alternative
> potentiality of the complex predicate. A novelty has emerged into creation ...
> a new type of individual, and not merely a new intensity of individual
> feeling.
>
> (Whitehead 1929: 186–87)

The subjective form of a propositional prehension, like that of a conceptual
prehension, can be described as an 'emotional' reaction to the inherent
value of the proposition for the occasion's becoming. The concrescing occasion is either attracted or repelled by the possibility of actualizing it for
itself and a 'decision' is made. Propositional feelings, presenting the
contrast between what is (physical prehension) and what might be (propositional datum) encourage greater subjective intensity of feeling. This contrast,
felt in the concrescence, may 'lure' the occasion to 'decide' in favour of
actualising the non-conformal proposition and, if this happens, then it does
not merely repeat its inheritance from the past but introduces novelty into
the world.

We can now begin to compare Whitehead's analysis of intellectual feelings
and consciousness with this stage of propositional feelings. To summarise: (a)
a propositional feeling 'feels' the contrast between a possibility and a fact;
(b) the concrescing subject's reaction of the propositional feeling is an
unconscious evaluation of its worth to the concrescing subject; the concrescence may terminate with the formation of its 'unconscious purpose',
that is, the integration of the propositional feeling with the occasion's original
physical prehension.

However, the concrescence need not necessarily terminate here. This integration may itself become the datum for a further feeling, evoking consciousness as the dominant subjective form of feeling. This is an intellectual
feeling. That is, an intellectual feeling not only 'feels' the contrast
((a) above), but can distinguish possibility from fact. In other words, the
intellectual feeling not only apprehends the propositional feeling as possibility ('theory') and the physical prehension as fact but is also aware of the
contrast. This awareness is consciousness, the subjective form of the intellectual feeling. Thus, while a propositional feeling merely 'feels' the contrast
between fact and possibility, an intellectual feeling may be said to *know* the
contrast between fact and theory. That is:

> [i]n awareness actuality, as a process in fact, is integrated with the
> potentialities which illustrate either what is and might not be, or what is
> not and might be. In other words, there is no consciousness without

reference to definiteness, affirmation, and negation ... Consciousness is how we feel the affirmation-negation contrast.

(Whitehead 1929: 243)

Thus, in the case where a conformal proposition is consciously apprehended and evaluated, there is at the same time an awareness of the possibility that the character of the propositional feeling might be otherwise; that is, even while and although the conscious intellectual feeling compares the propositional feeling with the data of its physical prehensions and judges that it is not, in fact, otherwise. Similarly, in the case of the conscious apprehension and evaluation of a non-conformal proposition, where the intellectual feeling informs the concrescing subject that something is not but might yet be.

Moreover, without physical prehensions there cannot be consciousness: 'Wherever there is consciousness there is some element of recollection. It recalls earlier phases from the dim recesses of the unconscious ... [C]onsciousness enlightens experience which precedes it, and could be without it if considered as a mere datum' (Whitehead 1929: 242). The conscious intellectual feeling recalls the propositional feeling and the initial physical prehension (both of which are unconscious) to 'enlighten' the 'earlier' experience. Just so, 'this character of our experience suggests that consciousness is the crown of experience, only occasionally attained, not its necessary base' (Whitehead 1919: 267).

How do intellectual feelings function and why are they important? According to Whitehead's scheme, 'the primary function of conscious intellectual feelings is to shed light on the grounds for "decision" and so assist in the formation of an occasion's subjective aim. The importance of intellectual feelings rests in the fact that consciousness introduces critical ability into the concrescence of the occasion. It enables the occasion to form a judgment before it commits itself to the possibility contained in the propositional feeling' (Hosinski 1993: 113). In unconsciousness, 'decisions' involve valuation (the attraction to the possibility embodied in an eternal object or a proposition), but not criticism. 'The primitive form of physical experience', says Whitehead, 'is emotional – blind emotion'. That is, the occasion commits itself to actualising a possibility that it does not visualise. It is consciousness that allows the occasion to evaluate critically a proposition before it 'decides' to actualise it, and also to criticise its own unconscious valuations. Consciousness prepares the way for a formation of judgement:

> an intellectual feeling is aware of the difference between the mere possibility represented in the proposition and the actual facts represented in the physical prehensions. The intellectual feeling integrates these two, the merely possible and the actual fact. The subjective form of this integral feeling must include judgment of what is, what is not, and what might be in its datum.

(Hosinski 1993: 114)

Conscious perception is, Whitehead maintains, 'the most primitive form of judgment' (Whitehead 1929: 162). Consequently, the most primitive form of knowledge is conscious intellectual feelings, the form of knowledge that is shared by most animals. Judgement (not, that is, the rational judgement of higher animals but this primitive form of judgement) allows a concrescing occasion the opportunity to alter its decision regarding how it will form itself. Intellectual feelings allow the concrescing subject to criticise its pro- positional lures: '[a] judgment weakens or strengthens the decision whereby the judged proposition, as a constituent in the lure, is admitted as an efficient element in the concrescence, with the reinforcement of knowledge. A judg- ment is the critique of a lure for feeling' (Whitehead 1929: 193). Further, 'consciousness is like a spotlight', says Thomas Hosinski, 'focussing atten- tion on something that matters to the concrescing subject at that moment ... There is a vague awareness of [everything else], but an intense awareness of what matters most at the moment' (Hosinski 1993: 115–6).

In this sense, then, we can see that the judgement we are concerned with in conscious intellectual feelings relates entirely to the immediacy of the becoming of the judging subject:

> an actual occasion ... is the whole universe in process of attainment of a particular satisfaction ... The final actuality is the particular process with its particular attainment of satisfaction. The actuality of the uni- verse is merely derivative from its solidarity in each actual entity ... [J] udgment concerns the universe as objectified from the standpoint of the judging subject. It concerns the universe through that subject.
>
> (Hosinski 1993: 200)

Thus, it is not so much the truth or falsity of the proposition that is impor- tant in this respect but the question of the possibilities offered through the proposition given the physical data of the immediate situation. In other words, in relation to its particular attainment of satisfaction, the concrescing subject is concerned solely with the question of *this* possibility and *these* facts: the judgement made will determine *its* self-constitution in *this* moment.

How then, does Whitehead's theory of concrescence contribute to our understanding of the present problem? While this theory, as we have seen, is extremely complex, our everyday understanding of the world (and of legal reality) is characterised by the attempt to reduce complexity, to make things simpler and more manageable. Is it not a retrograde step, to recognise the achievement that is (for example) law and to then begin to reintroduce com- plexity? Is this not simply to make our understanding unmanageable again, rather than to aid or improve understanding? We need to recognise that reduction is only a limited achievement that helps us to communicate within boundaries and that, in fact, the greater achievement is to forever push at and expand those boundaries for, as the old saying goes, a horizon is nothing but the limit of our sight. The problem is that our ideas, our conscious awareness of things, are too simple, not that they are too complex. We *train* ourselves to ignore the complexity of the world and our participation in it. 'In this way', writes Hosinski, 'we are like swimmers on the surface of the ocean, aware of a very small area in our immediate vicinity, but unaware of the immense depths beneath us' (Hosinski 1993: 117).

How does this increase of complexity that Whitehead's theory represents contribute to our understanding? As we have seen, Whitehead's analysis confirms that it is in the later, responsive phases of concrescence in the higher organisms that sense perception occurs (i.e. in the integrative and reintegrative phases of physical, conceptual and propositional feelings). Furthermore, its occurrence here is dependent on the earlier, simpler, unconscious phases. Sense perception is understood, in Whitehead's terms, within the whole act of perception, which he calls 'symbolic reference' (Whitehead 1929: 61ff). Symbolic reference (which corresponds to an intellectual feeling) is the integration of 'perception in the mode of presentational immediacy' (which corresponds to the conscious apprehending of a propositional feeling) and 'perception in the mode of causal efficacy' (which corresponds to the initial physical prehensions). It functions by the referral of data given in one mode to that given in the other mode. That is, symbolic reference integrates the data in the propositional feeling with the data in the initial physical prehension. It is therefore utterly dependent upon these. Physical prehensions are, then, the more primitive form of ingredients of our experience; sense perception is utterly dependent on perception in the mode of causal efficacy.

Whitehead maintains that his theory, in showing how a moment of experience includes within itself several types of relations between a concrescing subject and the actual world, not only reveals but corrects a defect in modern epistemology. Ever since Hume and Kant, the difficulty of showing a relationship between a knowing subject and an object that is known has plagued epistemology. Both Hume and Kant assumed that the most primitive ingredients in experience are sense perceptions, abstract universals not referenced to any particular. This meant that it became impossible to identify and demonstrate any sort of fundamental, necessary relationship between knower and the known. While Hume concluded that it is doubtful whether we can ever really know anything at all, Kant affirmed that all knowledge is knowledge of things filtered through the structure of our minds (phenomena) and not of things in themselves (noumena). Nonetheless, knowledge as such multiplies! Whitehead's answer to this is his identification of the ontological ground for the possibility of knowledge; the revelation of those of a concrescing subject. It is these relations that make knowledge possible: 'all relatedness has its foundation in the relatedness of actualities' (Whitehead 1929: xiii). More:

'Actuality' is the decision amid 'potentiality'. It represents stubborn fact which cannot be evaded ... Bradley's doctrine – Wolf-eating-Lamb as a universal qualifying the absolute – is a travesty of the evidence. *That* wolf ate *that* lamb at *that* spot at *that* time: the wolf knew it; the lamb knew it; and the carrion birds knew it.

(Whitehead 1929: 43)

What the problem of concrescence illuminates is:

how the many components of the objective content are to be unified in one felt content with its complex subjective form ... [I]n its phase of satisfaction, the entity has attained its individual separation from other things; it has absorbed the datum, and it has not yet lost itself in the swing back to the 'decision' whereby its appetition becomes an element in the data of other entities superseding it. Time has stood still – if only it could.

(Whitehead 1929: 154)

There is one further consequence of Whitehead's thinking that we need to deal with before we can turn to consider properly its significance for law: the relation between rational knowing and ontological knowing. On the one hand, we have already pointed to the distinction between these two forms of knowing. We have seen that, for Whitehead, ontological knowing rests on a judgement concerning the immediate becoming of a concrescing subject. What is at stake is not propositional truth or falsehood but self-constitution; that is, how the concrescing subject will form itself in *this* moment given *those* propositional and physical feelings. Rational knowing, however, is the product of many moments' inferences, reflections, balancings of weight of evidence, rational judgement. What is at stake here is precisely propositional truth. Here, 'there is abstraction from the judging subject. The subjectivist principle has been transcended, and the judgment has shifted its emphasis ... to the truth-value of the proposition in question' (Whitehead 1929: 191–92). On the other hand, as Hosinski points out, we can see how 'this distinction also reveals the connection between ontological knowing and rational knowing'. Rational knowledge requires insight (the ability to distinguish between different possible understandings of a problem) and reflective judgement (a decision in respect of the correspondence of possible understandings with facts of experience), both of which are momentary events and a type of intellectual feeling that Whitehead terms 'intuitive judgments'. Thus, rational knowing 'is based in all of its key points in the more basic ontological knowing' and, further, 'the structure of rational knowing, though it involves many individual moments of experience, is parallel to the structure of a single moment of experience'. Indeed, '[i]t seems clear that the three phases of rational knowing [particular observation; imaginative generalization;

renewed observation] correspond to the three phases of concrescence [physical prehensions; conceptual prehensions; integration of prehensions in decision]'. Moreover, the 'correspondence becomes even closer when we consider the concrescence of an actual occasion of higher grade' and, '[i]n an occasion that is conscious, the same correspondence holds, except that in this case the subject is aware of what is mere theory and what is fact ... This ... introduces judgment prior to "decision" and thus is the most primitive form of knowing. Here, the structural correspondence to rational knowing is even closer' (Hosinski 1993: 122–23).

We have seen that, for Whitehead, rational knowing finds its basis in ontological knowing. What is the purpose of rational knowing? We need to remember that the possibility of knowledge is found in the relations between a knowing subject and the actual world. But every moment of experience is a reduction from complexity, an abstraction from fullness and a selection (which begins in the first phase of concrescence and continues throughout). Further, each decision in an occasion of experience is a decision determined by a concern in respect of its own becoming. This introduces the possibility of error. Rational knowing, stimulated by a concern for self-transcendent truth, for a harmony of truth beyond a simple concern with the self, can be a means of refining, enhancing and correcting an individual's connection with the world of the past and the future (at least to the extent that this might inform acting). Reflective inquiry allows us to examine critically the commitments, decisions, judgements and purposes that condition our aspirations. Nonetheless, without exception, our use of reason always tends towards greater abstraction, a further reduction of, and an increase in, complexity. We look, select and act, grasping truth only incompletely and pursuing our purposes with blissful ignorance; unable to apprehend what does not fall within our field of vision and unable to comprehend that we have not seen it. It is just at this point, then, that critical reason may help to illuminate our understanding of the greater concrete reality from which we habitually abstract:

> Apart from detail, and apart from system, a philosophic outlook is the very foundation of thought and of life. The sort of ideas we attend to, and the sort of ideas which we push into the negligible background, govern our hopes, our fears, our control of behaviour.
>
> (Whitehead 1929: 63)

Chapter 4

Lessons from organisation theory

In the field of organisation studies, some theorists have begun to utilise a process metaphysics to argue against what they describe as a tendency towards reification. By means of a deconstructive analysis of organisation they are beginning to challenge approaches to organisation theory and management that view organisations effectively as outcomes of forgetting (as constituted by conventional wisdom but pre-existing our experiential knowledge of them) and argue for a refocusing on the practices of organising rather than the features and effects by which we define organisations (boundaries, environments, goals, strategies). Here, we find evidence of an increasing processual awareness of organisations as 'loose and active assemblages of organizings' (Cooper 1998), as ever-moving groupings of dynamic acts rather than static structures. Such an understanding, it is claimed, can help to foster a more constructive consideration of organisations than has been possible on the basis of ideas derived from the mechanistic and rationalist assumptions of Newtonian thought.

On this view, the problem as inherited is threefold: in the first place, Newtonian assumptions have now become 'so firmly entrenched that they [have] led to the creation of a disciplinary self-image, whereby the field [has drawn] the boundaries around itself so narrowly as to exclude th[os]e ideas and practices ... which [are] not modern' (Tsoukas and Cummings 1997: 657); second, theoretical development is now underpinned by 'progression': there is an 'assumption that we are part of a continuous progress in supplying ever more adequate unifying conceptions' (Tsoukas and Cummings 1997: 663); third, 'conventional analytical approaches adopted by mathematics and the physical sciences [have proved] impotent in helping us fully understand ... [our] experience of change' (Chia 1998: 349). This is because 'commonly held notions of time and sequencing of events ... [together with a] reliance on scientific systems for objective analysis fail to recognise [that] our experience of temporality and change is one of indivisible movement' (Dibben and Pantelli 2000: 6). Of course it is true that, at one level, 'formal organizations [do] accomplish through an architecture of constraints, ... highly stable and discriminate types of behaviour' (Kallinikos 1998: 372) but, in organisation studies at least, it is also quite clear that Newtonian terminology is gradually being replaced by a new, and 'significantly less mechanistic than before' (Tsoukas and Cummings 1997: 656), Aristotelian or Heraclitian style of thinking more in tune with a processual understanding of the world. This newer way of thinking both encourages a consideration of how a subject may intervene upon the experience of the object and discourages a view of chaos as antithetical to organisation; instead, there is a growing awareness of the importance of unpredictability, multiplicity, novelty and surprise. In sum, such a view cultivates 'awareness of dynamic processes; it encourages a positive attitude toward unpredictability and novelty; and it invites us to rethink the character of human intervention in the social and natural world' (Tsoukas 1998a: 292–94).

Thus, we find a significant shift in organisation studies from thinking of organisations as entities to a 'more ontologically and epistemologically aware understanding' (Dibben and Pantelli 2000: 6) of the process of organising as:

> a complex and dynamic web of interlocking visual acts of arresting, punctuating, isolating and classifying of the essentially undivided flow of human experiences for the purpose of rendering more controllable and manipulable such phenomenal experiences of the world.
>
> (Chia 1998: 366)

and the act of organising, as 'an interminable ontological quest of carving out a version of reality from what would otherwise be an amorphous and indistinguishable mass' (Chia 1998: 365).

Chia maintains that those 'common organizational attributes' that positivists and realists allegedly discover are in reality only 'mirror images of their own deeply-entrenched thought structures'. Alternatively, commitment to a 'process-based *becoming* ontology' would open up possibilities for 'rethinking' organization in terms that better reflect its essential characteristics as a process of 'world-making' (Chia 1997: 685). This alternative approach 'draws its inspiration from a vastly different set of ontological and epistemological priorities and … is more epistemologically robust' (Chia 1997: 687). He identifies six enduring 'instincts', characteristic of positivistic thought:

> First, there is an emphasis placed on the idea of empirical verification or some variant such as 'falsification' … Second, positivists … believe that what we can see, feel, touch or sense directly provides the best foundation for all forms of knowledge. Third … When one event follows another in a regular predictable manner, a causal relationship is said to exist. Fourth, positivists see the task of science as enabling the prediction of events … Fifth … primary importance is placed on observable

reality … Finally, empirically untestable propositions … belong to the
realm of idle speculation …

(Chia 1997: 688–89)

These six instincts provide the 'epistemological justification for a positivist
view of scientific inquiry'. However, this positivistic epistemology clearly
derives from a set of '*ontological* commitments' that has it roots in a
Parmenidean cosmology:

> First, reality is made up of discrete, self-identical 'things' … which exist,
> independently of our perceptual apprehension. Second, these things or
> entities are primary to process … Being precedes and is primary to
> becoming … Third, the state of rest, stability and equilibrium is a nat-
> ural state. Movement only occurs when things are 'disturbed' … Fourth,
> an external force is required to initiate change, … Finally, the commit-
> ment to a being ontology precipitates a subject-predicate mode of
> thought … deemed to be more able to accurately 'capture' and represent
> reality as it is in itself.
>
> (Chia 1997: 690)

Chia maintains that contemporary organisational theorising tacitly presupposes
this notion of the necessary pre-existence of enduring presentational forms in
that it more or less assumes an entitative conception of reality, in which
'clear-cut, definite things … occupy clear-cut, definite places'; that is, a style
of thinking 'in which the "thingness" of things, social entities, and their
properties and attributes are taken to be more fundamentally real than …
interactions and relationships' (Chia 1997: 690). Nonetheless:

> this very act of 'foregrounding' organizations as clearly circumscribed,
> legitimate objects of analysis, whilst at the same time denying the status
> of the network of organizing from which this theoretical object has been
> abstracted, is itself an ontological act of organization … Only by a
> dogmatic and intellectually convenient process of 'forgetting' its 'other'
> can positivistic organization theory proceed in the way it has done.
>
> (Chia 1997: 691–92)

We can see how this 'forgetting' happens from an explanation that Steve
Woolgar (1998: 68) provides. He identifies a five-stage 'splitting and inversion model of discovery' in the scientific research process: (i) first, there is the
production of (often speculative) documents; (ii) this is followed by the pro-
jection of the existence of that object that will become the legitimate focus of
investigation; (iii) at the same time, perception of this 'object' grows until it
attains an existence of its own, independent of all notions of it; (iv) next, the
relationship becomes inverted, and the idea forms that it is in fact the object

itself that stimulates attention towards it; (v) and, finally, this inversion becomes so embedded in the research process that stages (i)–(iii) are either 'forgotten' or denied. Woolgar believes that this model is sufficiently robust as an explanatory device to be generally applicable and useful for understanding the practice of all forms of representational thinking. Chia maintains that any 'findings' obtained in this way will simply mirror the tendency to think unquestioningly in static, structured and discrete ways, thereby reinforcing a belief in the validity of those findings.

This is precisely the point that Michael Baxendall makes in relation to Kenneth Clark's account of Piero della Francesca's *Baptism of Christ*:

> [W]e are at once conscious of a geometric framework; and a few seconds' analysis shows us that it is divided into thirds horizontally, and into quarters vertically. The horizontal divisions come, of course, on the line of the Dove's wings and the line of the Angel's hands, Christ's loincloth and the Baptist's left hand; the vertical divisions are the pink angel's columnary drapery, the central line of the Christ and the back of St John. These divisions form a central square, which is again divided into thirds and quarters, and a triangle drawn within this square, having its apex at the Dove and its base at the lower horizontal, gives the central motive of the design.
>
> (Baxandall 1985: 5)

The point is that Clark's use of language represents not so much a description of the picture as a representation of his own thoughts about the picture and his attempt to provide an explanation of it. For Chia, if we really want to understand the complexity of the world, we need to acquire a more dynamic understanding of complexity that will improve our awareness of the indivisibility of movement and change, the interpenetration of past, present and future. He suggests embracing a qualitative awareness of duration as an indivisible flux and becoming, a fusion of heterogenous instants; a corresponding relinquishing of the dominant spatialised conception of time that conceives of movement as a set of rests along the line of a trajectory. To think complexly is, he claims, 'to avoid the seductive appeal of the metaphysics of presence, to resist the overwhelming tendency to think in terms of simple location, and to recognize the immanent, enfolded and implicate character of phenomena' (Chia 1998: 357).

Nonetheless, social life becomes possible only when it is seen as 'simple location', when entities are in fact posited as discrete isolated systems existing in space-time. Understood in this way, organisation becomes a simplifying ontological activity in which 'subjective phenomenal experiences are simply located, fixed, externalized, and objectified into isolatable elements ready for reconstitution by the intellect' (Chia 1998: 365). That is, we perceive the world as the outcome of an organising process: 'All our belief in objects, all our operations on the systems that science isolates, rest in fact on the idea that time does not bite into them' (Bergson 1911a: 9). However, the point is that we need to balance this realisation with a deeper one, thinking in a complex way that will overcome this self-imposed simplification.

In various contributions to organisation studies, a number of writers have adopted Henri Bergson's thinking to present a fresh challenge to the notion that punctuated equilibria can ever form an adequate basis for under-standing radical novelty or creative advance. Their arguments indicate that, whereas Bergson's thought on the importance of intuition as a form of knowing allows normative concerns for the production and use of knowledge to be reconceived in terms of essentially dynamic movements of enfolded meanings relating all things at all places and times, organisation theory has failed to take this into account. For example, Martin Wood (2002), proposes:

> an alternative *becoming* ontology, in which theory becomes part of practice at the same time as practice becomes part of theory. There is a practice-becoming of theory and a theory-becoming of practice, a double capture since 'what' each becomes changes no less than 'that which' becomes ... The production-use relationship is therefore not one of integration between extrinsically distinct entities, but one of *internal difference* with a focus on differentiation and division.
>
> (Wood 2002: 157)

This substitution of a Parmenidean-based theory of unchanging reality with a rediscovered Heraclitean-inspired world-view, in which everything is in flux and nothing at rest, is a realization that 'we are living in a world of change whose processes are imperceptible: there is change but there are no things that change'. Reality cannot be analysed purely in terms of 'spatialized and localized end-states ... [I]nformation and communication do not merely convey representational contents that bridge the various stages of an evolu-tionary process but also contribute to the fabrication of new *assemblages* of movement, flows, stimulation and connections that cannot be simply located' (Wood 2002: 159).

Wood adopts Deleuze and Guattari's (1988) idea of 'creative involution' to express this 'relaxation of natural, obvious and reified forms, and the crea-tion ... of heterogeneous combinations and novel alliances ... cut[ting] across and beneath ... assignable relations', and to emphasise 'modes of "transver-sal communication" ... that scramble simple, genealogical lineages and allow heterogeneous assemblages to develop and break out across closed thresh-olds and species'. In this way, he is able to represent these in Deleuzian terms as 'rhizomic web[s] of continual transversal communication ... involv[ing] "unnatural" combinations, mergers, incorporations and associations ... '

Here, 'points are not real positions [but] a non-localizable line of *becoming,* a middle, an in-between that recognizes the continual participation of points *within* each other, even though in reality one does not become the other, or achieve any necessary correspondence with it' (Wood 2002: 160). But why, Wood asks, is involution creative? Essentially, because it involves 'communications that cut across distinct lineages' and 'have a tendency to break out of fixed or stable determinations'. Therefore, 'its inventions do not exist in advance but involve rhizomic modes of becoming ... bound up with [what Bergson calls] the creation of forms ... [and] the continual elaboration of the absolutely new'. The contrary idea that knowledge can be produced and subsequently used involves 'abstractions from an idealized space foreign to real movement' (Wood 2002: 160), a notion which, as Chia points out, is a 'confusion', resulting 'from a total misunderstanding of *movement* and *trajectory*, conflating one with the other'; in other words, a confusion of 'lived time' with 'clock time' (Chia 1999: 212).

For Bergson, intellectual analysis customarily proceeds on the basis of a reduction of the object of interest to an *a priori*, already established, set of conceptual elements; that is, a translation into pre-defined symbols of representation and organising codes. But this type of analysis can only ever express an object as a function of something other than itself, alienating it from itself. It 'multiplies without end the number of its points of view in order to complete its always incomplete representation, ... ceaselessly var[ying] its symbols that it may perfect the always imperfect translation' (Bergson 1913: 7). Intuition, on the other hand, attempts to help make contact with the reality of change and movement. It is a method of thinking in duration; a temporal synthesis of passing images into one coherent whole. He illustrates this point with the example of an artist visiting Paris. The artist makes numerous sketches of the city, writing underneath each the word 'Paris'. Because he has actually been there, he will be able to place this multiplicity of created images within his original intuition and synthesise them within his original intuitive experience of Paris as a unique whole. But only because he has been there: it would be impossible to achieve this synthesis otherwise. So, for Bergson, intuition is not mysterious; rather, it is a discipline, something we can all develop to a greater or lesser degree (Bergson 1913: 18). Nonetheless, in our favouring of the intellect as the more useful faculty, we have thereby neglected the status of intuition:

> It is a lamp almost extinguished which only glimmers now and then for a few moments ... whenever a vital interest is at stake ... [I]t throws a light, feeble and vacillating, but which none the less, pierces the darkness of the night in which the Intellect leaves us.
>
> (Bergson 1911a: 282)

Chia suggests that we should see here, in this comparison of these two modes of thinking, the beginnings of a more complex and dynamic mode of inquiry. 'What are subliminal about Bergsonian intuition are its fleeting

characteristics', he says, and this is something that 'finds sympathetic resonance with what the art theorist Norman Bryson calls the *logic of the glance*'
(Chia 1998: 360). For Bryson, 'the dominant factor in shaping our current
forms of knowing is that of ocular vision and in particular the "method" of
the *Gaze*'. However, comparing Western and Chinese painting methods,
Bryson comments that whilst the former is predicated on the '*disavowal of
deictic reference*' the latter is predicated on the '*acknowledgement and indeed
the cultivation of deictic markers*'. What 'deictic' refers to is that characteristic where '[t]he work of production is constantly displayed in the wake of its
traces', where 'the body of labour is on constant display'. But this characteristic, Bryson insists, is almost impossible to retrieve in Western paintings, where 'the viewer cannot ascertain the degree to which other surfaces
lie concealed beneath the planar display'. There, in Picasso's paintings, for
example, the work of erasure stops only when the original image becomes
totally invisible, indistinguishable behind the view of the completed picture
(Bryson 1982: 92). So we can see then, says Chia, how '[i]n one case the process
of becoming is incorporated into the painting whilst in the other the process
has been eliminated' so that '[t]he painting is placed outside duration' (Chia
1998: 361). Chia notes how Bryson develops this distinction between these
two attitudes to reflect on two logics of presentation:

> Painting of the Gaze attempts to arrest and extract from the fleeting
> process. It is a vision disembodied ... [T]he painter: 'arrests the flux of
> the phenomena, contemplates the visual field from a vantage-point out-
> side the mobility of duration, in an eternal moment of disclosed pre-
> sence'. The Gaze is penetrating, piercing, fixing, objectifying. It is a
> violent act of forcibly and permanently 'present-ing' that which other-
> wise would be a fluxing, moving reality. Painting of the Glance, on the
> other hand, addresses 'vision in the durational temporality of the view-
> ing subject' it does not seek to bracket out the process of viewing, nor in
> its own techniques does it exclude the traces of the body of labour ...
> calligraphic work cannot be taken in all at once ... since it has itself
> unfolded within the durée of process.
>
> (Chia 1998: 361)

We can see, then, says Chia, how 'Bergson's attempt to deconstruct the
symbolic systems of representation in order to achieve an Intuition with
mobile reality is a form of thinking in duration not unlike that exemplified by
Bryson's logic of the Glance' and it is precisely this 'peripheral vision', a
'corner-of-the-eye form of knowing', that constitutes our everyday unconscious
perception of reality (Chia 1998: 362).

Clearly, it is the assumption in favour of the simple location of 'things'
and their causal mechanisms that makes possible a correspondence theory of
truth between linguistic terms and the external world of objects they are used

to represent. Yet, this representationalist epistemology clearly involves a transfer of focus away from the processes of change and towards the outcomes of change. Understood thus, change is really not much more than the temporary bridging of a series of various evolutionary stages. The basic ontological assumption here is that reality is essentially separate, substantial and stable. Without this assumption the correspondence theory of truth falls and, with it, potentially at least, the whole structure of causal and explanatory linkages and categories upon which it is built. This way of thinking, as we have seen, still dominates mainstream legal theory. MacCormick's institutional theory of law with its framework of legal concepts regulated by a tripartite structure of institutive, consequential and terminative rules, with its articulation of the requirement of formal justice in terms of the universalisability of reasons and a dependence on the idea of the possibility of wholesale rational resolution to rational dispute, owes much to this post-Enlightenment-inspired world-view.

Chia notes three dominant emphases that characterise the process-metaphysical approach of writers such as Bergson and Whitehead. These are: first, 'an unequivocal commitment to a process epistemology and to ... the heterogeneous *becoming* of things'; second, an adherence to 'the logic of otherness'; and, thirdly, a 'principle of immanence' (Chia 1999: 217–18). Deleuze is clearly in the process tradition of Bergson and Whitehead. His main interest is with the articulation of a theory of change and transformation that, with the aid of a new vocabulary free from 'identitarian pressures' (Boundas 1993: 5), will help develop an understanding of pure heterogeneous becoming. His choice of the idea of a 'rhizome' offers an alternative conceptualisation that, at first sight at least, appears resistant to the reductionist trends of modernist theorising. As a 'subterranean stem', the rhizome is 'absolutely different from roots and radicles', says Deleuze. It 'assumes very diverse forms, from ramified surface extension in all directions to concretion into bulbs and tubers. The rhizome includes the best and the worst' (Boundas 1993: 29).

This rhizomic model appears to incorporate a way of thinking that is consistent with Chia's three main features of process thought (heterogeneous becoming, otherness, immanence); indeed, rhizomes epitomise indeterminacy and heterogeneity. Whereas the growth of tree roots commonly exhibit a predictable pattern according to the principles of binary logic, rhizomes can connect at any point to any other and this random connecting of any point forms a bulb, or tubers. Here, change spreads by variation, is restless, opportunistic and sudden. This subtle, agglomerative, often subterranean and heterogeneous form of change (Boundas 1993: 28–36) shows how '[r]hizomic change is *anti-genealogical* in the sense that it resists the linear retracing of a definite locatable originary point of initiation'. Change is 'multiple, unending and unexpectedly other. There is no unitary point to serve as a natural pivot for constructing subject and object, for drawing boundaries that define inside and outside and that distinguish "macro" from "micro"' (Chia 1999: 222). Such terms, which both derive from and are the foundation of a logocentric analysis, give way to multiplicities that 'have only densities, determinations and lines of connections that ripple outwards' (Chia 1999: 223). The pattern is not linear, but a three-dimensional net-working of change representing the opportunities for the actualisation of possibilities for becoming (Boundas 1993: 31). Change, transformation, is not pre-determined by any prearranged pattern.

This probabilistic approach to the dynamic of change is, Chia observes, 'reminiscent of Prigogine's powerful explanation of irreversibility and inde-terminacy' (Chia 1999: 223). Prigogine expressed deep unease about the inconsistency between the idealized, stable predictable world described by modern physics and the unstable, unpredictable world of living organisms. The real world, he claimed, evolved its 'most delicate and complex structure' only through irreversible processes of nature: 'Life is possible only in a nonequilibrium universe' (Prigogine 1996: 27). Therefore, life, nature, the world must all be understood in terms of possibilities and not certainties. Change does not take place along a single trajectory, but in multiple trajectories of 'probability clusters' (Prigogine 1996: 37).

In the same way, ideas of causality require to be replaced with notions depicting the 'coupling of events loosely analogous to the coupling of sounds by resonance'. This means developing a new, non-Newtonian vocabulary wholly '*incompatible with a trajectory description*', which requires instead a 'probabilistic description' (Prigogine 1996: 42). Importantly, there is no determinism involved here. Outcomes can always be surprises, other than expected. As Hart (1958) observed, the nature and limits of thought and language can serve as the precursor of an element of the surprising: surprise, novelty, creativity are all in-built, of the very essence and meaning of change and transformation. Precisely because we insist on encoding our experiences of reality into explicitly articulated rules and symbols, shortcomings are thereby built into our working model of reality. However, this is not because our model is incomplete, and must continually be updated with an explicit rendering of what is already implicit within it; on the contrary, it is because our models tend to distort and misrepresent the changing nature of reality. True change has something of the unexpected, unpredictable, and therefore unanticipated nature of surprise about it; something of the character of 'otherness'.

According to Chia, the point is that 'chance and necessity are not polar opposites'; rather, they 'implicate and structure the possibilities for one another'. In other words, they 'are other to each other and express them-selves through the operation of change. In the language of process meta-physics, we can say that *chance leans towards* otherness, *necessity leans towards* immanence. Thus, the change in continuity (otherness) and the continuity in change (immanence)' (Chia 1999: 223).

From the standpoint of a process metaphysics change, surprise and novel adventure are all essential conditions of reality, in particular of living systems, without which existence would not be possible. Therefore, conventional dualistic notions ought to be rejected:

> [c]hange implies its other ... [N]ot a 'thing' or 'entity' with established patterns, *but the repetitive activity of ordering and patterning itself.* It is the active intervention into the flux and flow of the 'real' in order to abstract pattern and coherence out of an essentially undifferentiated and indifferent whole.
>
> (Chia 1999: 224)

This is what MacCormick's theory fails to accommodate, preferring instead to identify institutions as objects, albeit 'thought objects', but 'things' nonetheless, with predefined arrangements and patterns of relations. Yet for process thought, as Chia demonstrates, law is not only the outcome but also primarily the act of stabilising and simply locating, this ontological act of halting, holding and handling what is otherwise the indeterminate flux of lived experience. In this sense, law is inherently simplifying: the 'taxonomic complexity' (Chia 1998) of theories of law and legal reasoning is a contradiction of process, rendering it as substance by the application of pre-structured formulae and symbols of representation. Nonetheless, following Chia, we might say that as law acts to constrain, constrict and control these otherwise unpredictable forces, the tension between law as simplification and reality as complexity acts as a creative mainspring for novelty and progress.

So we can see how the social reality that we think of as existing independently is really a construct, comprised of artificial arresting and stabilising institutional acts and simple location. Each act 'simply locates' as it halts and holds outside of the durational experience a *re*-presented version of a moment of changing reality. As many such versions merge, creating denseness, we see the emergence of phenomena of familiarity and social habit:

> [a] socially constructed reality, *alienated* from our raw experiences, is achieved in which all those practical norms that govern the stance of human beings toward one another and towards their particular historical environment become more and more established ... Organization exists as islands of order in a sea of chaos and change.
>
> (Chia 1999: 224)

In this way, process thought understands law as a complexity-reducing and reality-constituting enterprise that constitutes and coordinates a world of its own making via an *un*-natural stabilising of these natural forces. Nonetheless, it is also an extremely successful one: it is only in and through this mechanism for command and control of reality that any *things* as such appear at all: '[t]he concept of the entity can be preserved only by an optic that casts around each entity a perceptual frame that makes a cut from the field and immobilises the cut within the static framework' (Bryson 1998: 97); weaken the frame and the object merges with its past and future in a changing field that defies rational alteration and refinement.

We can see this if we think, for example, of a flower. A flower is only a phase of evolution and transformation, 'a continuous exfoliation or perturbation of matter' (Bryson 1998: 97). It cannot occupy a single place, for it 'is always implicated in the field of transformation of which it forms a part' (Chia 1999: 225). It is always changing, from seed to flower to dust:

> [t]he present state of the object appearing as the flower is inhabited by its past as seed, and its future as dust, in a continuous moment of postponement, whose effect is that the flower is never presently *there*, any more than seed or dust are there.
>
> (Bryson 1982: 99)

Thus, we understand that change is immanent in every quantum moment of the process of an entity's becoming and perishing. Understood in this way, law is an ongoing activity of resisting change, maintaining and stabilising as 'real' a moment *snatched* from the continuing flow, preserving it sufficiently for persons to act and further their purposes against a barrage of competing external inducements. Simplification, complexity reduction and economy of effort in control of reality are the aims of law. In this way, as a result of their institutionalisation in law, all the multifarious aspects of our experience, including the self as person, obtain immediate self-identity and become malleable.

However, what this also suggests is the possibility that legal 'change' might be effected without orchestrated external intervention; indeed, merely relaxing the constraints and ingrained behaviours that contribute to the perception of legal institutions as substantial may be enough to encourage change of itself. It is this relaxation of entrenched generalisations that a process approach would advocate and can explain. Utilising a metaphor of 'creative involution', such as Wood employs, can help demonstrate such an alternative understanding of how legal change can and does occur.

From a process perspective, law as an attempt to halt, hold and handle what is essentially a ceaseless flow, is a reduction achievement. It is an important and necessary attempt to create a more secure, regular and predictable world from a fundamentally indiscriminate reality. In this sense law as institutionalisation is primarily about legitimating social worlds, only subsidiarily about coordinating activity. Counter-intuitively, perhaps, law is the exception, change is the rule. Change always implies surprise and otherness because of its essentially indeterminate character, a unique and never-to-be-repeated coalescence of a multiplicity of potentialities. Law, as essentially rhizomic in nature, is the outcome of this creative tension between institutionalisation and change.

Thus, assuming Chia's distinction between dynamic and taxonomic complexity, we can see how the latter more correctly describes the method of ordering of modern Western legal thinking. Conversely, dynamic complexity recognises that human experience can be much more complex and fluid than any descriptions based on static states can account for. Dynamic complexity is qualitatively different from the discrete and stable states preferred by the taxonomic urge. Here, 'complexity arises from the increasingly bewildering array of possible combinations, but from the immanent *in-one-anotherness* of moments of experience and hence their intrinsic non-locatable and inter-penetrative nature' (Chia 1998: 349). The past is inextricably bound up with the present. There is 'a real persistence of the past in the present, a duration which is, as it were a hyphen, a connecting link ... Continuity of change, preservation of the past in the present, real duration' (Bergson 1911a: 24). The difference between these two attitudes is analogous to that between qualitative and quantitative change. 'I must willy-nilly, wait', says Bergson, 'until the sugar melts'; which implies that my sense of time in conscious experience is not that of mathematical time but 'coincides with my impatience ... with a certain portion of my own duration, which I cannot protract or contract as I like. It is no longer something *thought*, it is something lived' (Bergson 1911a: 10). It is something indivisible and inseparable from my own sense of becoming.

So we habitually think of time much like we think of space, as a homogeneous medium, but only because of the 'trespassing of the idea of space upon the field of pure consciousness' (Bergson 1913: 98). Only by the importation and imposition of spatial metaphors do we construe mathematical time. Our conscious experience of time is otherwise: 'nothing but a succession of qualitative changes, which melt into and permeate one another, without precise outlines, without any tendency to externalize themselves in relation to one another, without any affiliation with number' (Bergson 1913: 104). Experience, thought about in spatial terms, is translated as homogeneous. But duration 'prolongs the past into the present, the present either containing within it in a distinct form the ceaselessly growing image of the past, or, more probably, showing by its continual change of quality the heavier load we drag behind us as we grow older' (Bergson 1913: 38). Absent this endurance of the past in the present, there could be only instantaneous instants.

We see much the same picture in relation to movement when motion is thought of in spatial terms as divisible into discrete moments that represent the area traversed. But, as Bergson says:

> the process by which [a body] passes from one position to the other ... eludes space. We have to do here not with an *object* but with a *progress*;

motion, in so far as it is a passage from one point to another, is a mental synthesis ... We are thus compelled to admit that we have here to do with a synthesis which is, so to speak, qualitative, a gradual organization of our successive sensations, a unity resembling that of a phrase in a melody.

(Bergson 1910: 111)

We need therefore to distinguish between travelling over the ground and the ground over which we travel: reduction to the latter is a denial of duration. This is precisely what lies at the root of the confusion in those childhood puzzles presented earlier. Analysis on the basis of static states may make it possible to focus and act but it is nonetheless a mistake to think of reality as essentially stable and with only intermittent periods of change.

Chapter 5

Towards a process reconstrual of 'the middle'

We need now to bring this processual understanding to bear on the approaches to legal reasoning represented earlier and the problems presented for analysis in *Re A*. As we have seen, a fundamental tenet of any process-philosophical approach is the idea that knowledge cannot be simply located as the successive quantitative movement from one homogenous, stable, or independent, state to the next; on the contrary, knowledge is a relational effect and fixed states are but specific cases in point. On this view, legal knowledge is not something that travels across the gap between one pole and another; instead, the institutionalisation of knowledge in law constitutes a particular context that emerges to mediate the tension between these two poles and within which individual terms (such as universal and particular, rule-determination and rule-application) assume subsequent and relative meanings. Thus, where knowledge is institutionalised in law, this should not be understood as the outcome of some pre-existent structuring or patterning of positions but as an establishing of 'internal resonance' (Wood 2003a: 226). It is this 'fixing of tensions' that creates the abstracted structure that is subsequently commanded and controlled according to the conceptual categories of legal thought and representation.

What this suggests is a sense in which what we have called the institutionalisation of law is properly understood in terms of the means by which participants make sense of their social interactions. In this sense, institutionalisation comprises *both* the forces and tendencies that promote order and stability *and* the mechanisms that tend towards change and de-structuring. It is the continual fluctuation between these that momentarily results in an appearance of order, some thing achieved through reduction, but the two are really inseparable. Law, as a *process* of institutionalising information, is always-already the *outcome* of a previous process of institutionalising.

Two views of legal knowledge and its production

Commonly, when we think of law we think of it as a coherent resource, as something to be applied. As we saw in *Re A*, there are three aspects to this:

first, practical problems are confronted, recognised and addressed in a context governed wholly by the interests of the legal institution, problematised entirely as legal issues; second, all of this, including language, context, concepts and interpretations, is commanded and controlled in an essentially homogeneous, largely hierarchical manner; third, this hierarchical legal institutional structure prevails over the communication of outcomes, disseminated through legal institutional channels. In these ways, by its use of either/or distinctions, its courtroom terms and procedures and its control of the flow of decisions (through the doctrines of *ratio decidendi, stare decisis* and legal precedent), the legal community defines and deploys the criteria and measurements of its own success.

It is against this background that we must understand Bańkowski's suggestion that law's external audience should become more involved in decision-making: as the site of legal decision-making becomes more important so it becomes necessary to seek a more collaborative approach. What we find here is much less a sense of the fixed separation of theoretical and practical and more the recognition of a managed flow back and forth between the two with a movement across disciplines and fields incorporating, within legal decision-making, ideas, methods and procedures otherwise considered as outside. In this way, knowledge sites become more dispersed and new knowledge producers begin to emerge.

According to this view, law requires a more flexible, relational, context-based approach realised through the coming together of heterogeneous assets and continually shifting institutional forms and structures. This is something to be arrived at through participation, negotiation and mediation, and where results are communicated in and through the contexts in which they are to be applied. In this sense, this way of thinking about law might be considered more in keeping with the complexities of situations that law seeks to address. Here, legal practice becomes the difficult task of maintaining the middle position that opens up between abstracted representations and exacting contextual requirements, refusing simply to go one way or the other but always maintaining both the separation and the link, the continual movement or conversation to and fro, between them.

However, from a process perspective, two problems emerge with regard to this. In the first place, those advocating a new understanding of the relation between universals and particulars tend to overestimate the extent to which the determination of legal knowledge, and not simply its confirmation, may originate from outside the limits of the legal institutional structure. Notwithstanding the increased recognition of extra-legal influences, it is still the highly structured, hierarchically ordered institutional framework that is the main site for generating, developing and refining legal knowledge. Changes in law take place by law and according to law's *legal* structure, governed by the procedures and mechanisms that limit, order and subjugate according to law's institutional practices and routines. That is why, in reality, very few of the advances predicted ever amount to anything very novel or surprising. Superficial changes in the institutional context of law make little impact on the basic assumptions underlying and characterising law. Besides, while a more socially distributed form of legal knowledge might well be expected to generate a more relevant and socially applicable type of law, the degree of difference in the legal power/knowledge rhetoric always works, as we saw in *Re A*, to prefigure what counts as knowledge. It is precisely this ideological aspect of law that we found to be its most disturbing feature. Very little of what appears succeeds in altering law's privileged and self-legitimating, autopoietic, standpoint.

The second problem concerns the assumption, introduced earlier, of a one-to-one relation of correspondence between living experience and legal representation. In common law decision-making, legal practitioners have to provide justification for their legal decisions, attempting to turn thought back upon action. In doing so, they appear to engage in a sort of action-reflection, a process of *re*-deliberation or justification of the situations in which they perform. However, as Detmold and Bańkowski show, with their depiction of the 'anxious judge', judges inevitably face a crisis of confidence and legitimacy closely related to the adequacy of their legal knowledge reservoir. This crisis of confidence highlights a disparity between traditional representations of knowledge and lived experience, and thus the impossible complexity and the incommensurability of legal decision-making. While assumed forms of technical rationality are based on the presupposition of a correspondence of means to ends, those same means and ends often appear confused and conflicting.

In this way, a gap opens up that must be closed. This is why, for Bańkowski, judges need to attend to the 'outside', to bridge the gap between their professional knowledge and the demands of the real world. But even here, a judge's reflection on action is still always directed towards verbal descriptions, deliberate constructions that must be tested. It is in relation to these that Bańkowski suggests that a judge, in deliberating, must remain open to the unfolding story; letting the story speak for itself, talk back. It is here, with selected information, that the judge works reflectively, always leaving things open to change. We find a similar notion underlying MacCormick's sense of determining what the ratio of a decision is; that is, it is only when the enacted environment responds and a future judge answers the first that any real decision can be made about what the fuller meaning of the ratio is, what information will be retained for future use.

This distinction between law and its external environment as a critical separation that must be closed is also one which Christodoulidis refers to. With him, too, we can discern a form of attending to the outside that underpins his idea of an enacted environment; however, here, it is more correct to say that any 'outside' is created by the decision to 'draw a distinction'. For Christodoulidis, following Luhmann, a system's environment is not so much something already external to be reacted to but it is created by the actor through the processing of information according to her focus on a particular task, by the process of selection. Selecting has to do with deciding what is relevant, what to deal with and what to leave alone. Something can only become the object of attention *after* this selection has occurred. This is how everything becomes noticeable and noticed, registering as occurring only after it has occurred. In decision-making something is always acknowledged retrospectively, related to the specific concerns and motivations of the individual. In this sense, he is quite obviously correct: 'justification is always justification *a posteriori*'.

Given the disparity brought about by the lack of correspondence between living experience and legal representation, even paying attention to the particularities of a situation cannot fully account for the mutual inter-relatedness of elements in the originary assemblage. To achieve this will necessitate greater sensitivity to the temporal dimension; in other words, it is crucially important that paying attention always occurs retrospectively.

Employing a method of creative involution

To think about creative involution is, as Wood suggests, thinking differently. It is to treat relations as the primary objects rather than as linkages between separate things. However, this does not involve moving 'from one actual term to another actual term along a single line, but from a virtual term to the heterogeneous terms that actualize it along lines of divergence' (Wood 2002: 161). This is what Bergson refers to as intuition. For him, the key to true knowledge and understanding lies much more in asking new questions than in providing answers to already existing questions. While the latter practice is closed and regulated, the former is open-ended, its movement and flow forever resisting representation and regulation.

Traditional understandings of legal knowledge as institutional continue to follow along the route of an ordered, linear progression characterised by the procedure of applying general rules to particular circumstances. Here, and within the hierarchical structure that emerges on top, each discrete part has its own place, function and methodology, and is organised in relation to all other parts. A flow of information is facilitated, enabling predictability. However, even within this tightly fitting structure, legal practitioners and legal consumers all experience legal knowledge as a complex web of opinion, supervision, guidance, claim and control. In reality, all experience law, at some times more obviously than at others, as 'a continuous and unfinished process whose intrinsic nature resists the regulative model. ... self-organizing, non-linear and multi-stranded' (Cooper 1998: 143). In this sense, contrary to received wisdom, law grows from the bottom up and not from the top down and there is really no settled structure or definitive order that we can identify absolutely as legal institutional knowledge; rather, legal institutional knowledge appears as continuous becoming naturally resistant to this attempt to identify rule and application, law and fact, universal and particular, or the relations between them. Law appears as a communication that cuts across our carefully guarded distinctions, expanding forever outwards.

In a hierarchical model of structuring legal knowledge, the main emphasis is on the relative positions of distinct phases, stages or states. In this way, the method of investigation proceeds by way of the splitting up of a whole complex experience of interdependent and interpenetrating aspects into separate, immobile and distinct objects and behaviours with the assumption of the possibility of transfer between them. Contrastingly, on the alternative understanding outlined above, any investigation does not rely on some assumption about a whole being the sum of its connectable parts but on something beyond this, a middle place that is not defined, as it is in Bańkowski's model, as between set points, but is rather a pre-existing in-between where there is nothing but tensions and fields of force, continuous movement. It is this incessant fluxing of the real that points to the intuitive, sympathetic understanding of which Bergson speaks. Instead of assuming *that* the distinctions we observe between 'things' are straightforwardly given, the real problem is to understand *how* this division has come about in the first place, on the basis of which we assume that the subsequently divided pieces can be combined and recombined. Why has reality been divided this way rather than that? Why have we given knowledge this shape and not that? In other words, the entrance of essential knowledge into our experience requires the introduction of our consciousness within the continuity of the world. Everything depends on the relative weight we assign to each quantum of reality arrested from the flow of direct experience.

If we understand the structuring of legal institutional knowledge in this way, theories, concepts, doctrines, principles, values, rules and the rest, all become less clearly circumscribed. Knowledge no longer occupies clear-cut, stable positions adequately described and defined by clear-cut, established terms; rather, a complexity of real inter-connections, cleavages and coincidences intersect above, through and below the relative locations and meanings of all terms. What this means is that there is no single controlling mind, no hidden hand, no quantitative linear progression. In its place, we find that the mediums of information created by the institutional and institutionalising structure of law give way to a real interchange of ideas, a continuous swapping and substitution of meanings in which the limits of ideas, concepts and expressions are relentlessly in process of being shaped and reshaped. In this sense, the concrescence of legal institutional knowledge is forever ongoing, essentially transitive. Its continual reproduction and use is inextricably linked with the interpolation of our consciousness into the continuous succession and flow of the real world. This is the essential point that 'institutional theories' of law often ignore, imparting to the creation and utilisation of legal knowledge a concreteness that is misplaced;

thus, legal 'institutional facts' appear to benefit from an independent existence and the relations between them are considered as connections (and, crucially, all of this is assumed prior to any discussion about their individuation).

In reality, legal institutional knowledge is always an amalgam. Its outwardly homogeneous appearance as something defined and distributed, developed and deployed is always the result of a blend, a composite: it is both the sum of its parts *and* the degrees of difference of its terms. As such, legal knowledge is always indeterminate. Here, we cannot talk about applying a rule to factual circumstances, or even really of universals to particulars, because this derives from and depends on notions of substance and immobility where we address ourselves towards 'the ends of the intervals and not ... the intervals themselves' (Bergson 1911a: 9). Legal institutional knowledge understood in terms of creative involution is law understood as an *open system*.

Exploring the temporal dimension

According to Bergson we can conceive of time in two ways: either as pure duration or in spatio-temporal terms. In the latter, time fragments into separate parts, so that what we experience are characteristically bounded and distinct but connectable elements. We obtain this awareness by withdrawing ourselves from our involvement in the flow of experience and, having stepped out of it, then directing our attention back towards it. In contrast, pure duration is the experience of time as a ceaseless movement of flowing and fluxing, '[a] succession of qualitative changes ... melt[ing] into and permeat[ing] one another ... without any tendency to externalize themselves in relation to one another' (Bergson 1910: 104).

When we reflect on the particularities of lived situations we do so by trying to comprehend action in terms of a simple, straightforward, uncomplicated state rather than by following the continuity of its real movement. It is really this spatio-temporal idea of time that theories such as Bańkowski's, and Detmold's, and MacCormick's too, mobilise in their decision-making models. This presupposes the practitioner withdrawing to a position outside of the experience before and in order that her attention can be directed back to it and she can enter within it. Paradoxically, however, in directing attention to already lived experience Bańkowski and Detmold, as well as MacCormick, appear only to reinforce this sense of a 'gap' between legal representation and actual lived experience, a view altogether at odds with Bergson's notion of pure duration or *durée*.

As soon as we begin to focus on relations as things in themselves, rather than as linkages between separate things, then it also becomes clear how we should understand what we call the present; that is, as a temporal distinction between two horizons. Each present moment of experience is a tension between actual and potential, past and future: the present does not exist except in these terms:

> [W]e believe that the past is no longer, that it has ceased to be. We have thus confused Being with being-present. Nevertheless, the present is not; rather it is pure becoming, always outside itself. It is not, but it acts. Its proper element is not being but the active or the useful. But it has not ceased to be. Useless and inactive, impassive it IS, in the full sense of the word: It is identical with being in itself. It should not be said that it 'was' since it is the in-itself of being, and the form under which being is preserved in itself.
>
> (Deleuze 1991: 55)

Because the present never actually *is*, all our assertions about reflecting on actions in the midst of acting become, in this sense, merely evidence of a dependence upon an intellectual practice that reduces experience from the totality of lived experience in order to make it manageable. In this sense, a judge's reflections in the midst of decision-making are really no more than her experience converted into words, a way of presenting thought and action as if these were ontologically discrete and independent or autonomous categories. On this basis, even Bańkowski's attempt to provide a thoroughly pragmatic solution with his integrating and synthesising 'inside-outside' approach must ultimately break down. The dialectical model can never complete its task because we cannot ultimately and irrevocably say that either inside or outside exists prior, alongside or subsequent to the other, or that or how one is similar or dissimilar to the other. For this to be the case, we would need to be able to identify a boundary between the two, an edge or border that specifies their difference. But they are not identifiably separate. Our reflections in this way can produce useful knowledge, but not knowledge that provides an exact copy of the real movement of living experience to which it refers. The point is that all such understandings of reality are inevitably based on a falsity. While it might be convenient to reflect upon an event as if the whole of the event occurred as an instantaneous revealing, so that we might look at a situation as a whole from its beginning to its end with all its separate parts laid out, as if somehow at some earlier point we could even suggest what it will contain in its later parts, in fact, reality unfolds only gradually, as a living experience. Hartshorne (1987) makes the point that we cannot say about anything that it was possible or impossible beforehand because there is then no 'it' to which any such label might be attached. The object of the discourse is simply not there to be referred to in either way. What we are dealing with here, Hartshorne claims, is the law of the excluded middle. The criteria of the actual cannot empirically discover possibility. Taking something that exists now and reading it back into the past as if to say that it was possible then will not tell us anything about the past that could have been discovered by us then. To put it another way, there is always something more in the actual than in the possible; otherwise, why bother to actualise anything?

Understood thus, reality is the continuous and qualitative accumulating of actuality. But this presents us with a further problem: on this basis, how does it make sense to talk in terms of reflecting on one's decisions? A judge looks back on her own act of making a decision, but all this continuous qualitative accumulating of actuality is surely too much to carry forward repetitively: we have too much abstraction, too much reduction. Nonetheless, just because we abstract does not mean that anything ceases to exist. If we remember deciding then we also remember the process of deciding. The way to make sense of this is to think of the present in terms of subjective immediacy. Here, we can usefully employ a process/product distinction. A product is something positively prehended as an abstraction from process, a reduction. But this means that something else is always left out, negatively prehended. Product, as a reduction from process, cannot be properly understood apart from this act of negative prehension. Without it or a similar notion any process/product distinction would be untenable. This is just another way of saying that being cannot be abstracted from becoming: the two are inseparable. In other words, we can deal with particulars only in terms of universals and not otherwise. This indivisible continuity is what Bergson refers to as real knowledge. It is the forever becoming of living experience. But to be known it must be grasped under the forms of what is concrete.

Counter-intuitively, what is concrete is not and cannot be real. It is a perspective on the movement of reality, its symbolic reconstruction; put simply, there is always more in reality than we can apprehend through the concrete. Every reconstruction by which we try to reveal the real movement of experience is inevitably incommensurable with the experience to which it refers. Where we often go wrong is in our assumption that there is as much or more in our concrete representations of reality than in reality unrepresented. However, no matter how sophisticated our reasoning, there will always be more in experience than our accounts of it can record. Our perennial problem is how to stop ourselves confusing the two.

We can get close to an answer to this question if we recall that what we have termed the real is inseparable from the movement from potentiality to actuality in which it is realised. That is, it is only as we struggle to understand the real that we can discover ourselves as standing within the real: it exists, is present, precisely in the manner in which it is actualised. Everything hinges on this irreducible interpenetrating relatedness, this mutual constitution of the temporal and the spatial. The way that we understand the whole of something as comprised by the sum of its parts is only a perspective taken on it. The simple fact that this division into separate parts is something that must then actually be performed implies a temporal relationship between these; that is, the whole and the parts do not exist together at the same time, except as potentiality. The division must be made or at least be capable of being made. Hartshorne puts it this way:

> [t]he belief in a wholly determinate future is not translatable into action, and neither is belief in a wholly indeterminate one ... Action can only consist, not in simple foreseeing, but in step by step deciding, of the future, with each step in its concreteness left open until the previous step has been taken, and even then not simply predicted but created, settled by *fiat* ... The future, for all life, is what the past implies *plus* step by step decisions, none of which is concretely given until it has actually been taken ...
>
> (Hartshorne 1970: 92–94)

Hence, '[m]odal distinctions are ultimately coincident with temporal ones. The actual is the past, the possible is the future' (Hartshorne 1970: 61). On this view, 'our ability to understand universality or possibility, as well as particularity or actuality, is the same as our ability to grasp temporal distinctions ... [I]f temporal distinctions are modal distinctions, and if temporal order is independent of our thought and language, then so are the modal aspects of reality. And these are in part universal, not exclusively particular, aspects' (Hartshorne 1970: 62). Moreover, 'the precise qualities of particulars are themselves particular and unrepeatable ... irreducibly relational and historical' (Hartshorne 1970: 63–64). Just so, we can distinguish between the two: particularity is determinateness, universality is determinability. That is, '[o]nly the past alone is fully determinate within the limits of causal possibility. These limits are just the determinateness of the past as capable of being superseded by some kinds of successors but not by other logically conceivable kinds'. Alluding to an example of Bergson's, he describes this as follows:

> Before one cuts an apple in two, although there is not a possibility as determinate as either half which later results from such a cut, there is clearly the possibility of 'somehow halving the apple'. Actualizing a possibility is providing a determinate for a less definite antecedent determinable. Actuality is thus truly more than antecedent possibility, given a proper understanding of the latter ... [P]ossibilities are determinables not determinates. The apple can be halved *somehow*, but to suppose that the determinate *how* that subsequently results is included in the somehow is just to deny the distinction, determinable-determinate ... Given a determinate how we can relate it to the somehow, but given only the somehow we cannot relate it to a determinate how ... The "this" of an actuality simply has no advance status, modal or otherwise. Creativity does not map the details of its future actions, even as possible.
>
> (Hartshorne 1970: 64–65)

What Bergson's illustration proves is that both elements must be experienced or be capable of being experienced and this is only possible in the middle; that is, in the midst of a singular unifying temporality. Insofar as this may be understood to coincide with the creative advance in and through which we experience our own duration, our own continuity as living selves, then we can be relatively confident of correctly distinguishing the virtual and the concrete. We simply have to enquire as to whether what we are addressing can be qualitatively experienced and to situate ourselves in its flow, its unfolding continuity. It is this wholly qualitative conscious awareness of our reintegration into the duration of the things that marks out the difference between this and any quantitative representational scheme.

We can see then how we need our abstractions; they are useful constructs, tools. The problem arises when we begin to think of them as real, when we forget that they are symbols pointing to and participating in a reality beyond them. But we have forgotten how to think beyond the 'things' arrested from experience. As Deleuze puts it: '[p]roceeding "by dissociation and division", by "dichotomy", is the essence of life' (Deleuze 1988: 94). So the real problem becomes how to uncover the different processes by way of which legal institutional knowledge becomes actualised, rather than how the terms of any dualism are associated or integrated.

What is the relation of the universal to the particular? How do we decide whether a general rule applies in a particular case? How do the two meet? It is precisely this way of thinking, which understands the relation of particulars and universals as a meeting of oppositional terms or a synthesis of opposites, which is at issue here, proceeding as it does by way of linear progression from one immobility to another. Whether we think that it is by universals or by attention to particulars that our decision is controlled, or by any combination of these, any way of thinking that understands inner qualities or processes as determinate is not so much a discovery of movement and change as a slowing down of it; in other words, as we *de*fine we *con*fine.

Bergson's real contribution here is his identification of two ways of thinking: the first assumes the possibility of reflecting on what is near, conceptualising reality and shaping it into credible and distinct objects; the second proposes that we allow ourselves to be placed within the flow of experience, to 'enter into' it and identify ourselves with it. It is this second way that Bergson calls intuition, which is similar to the way in which we might identify ourselves with a character in a novel. But the essential difference between our reading a novel and our reflecting on a decision in a court of law is that the former unlike the latter can actually be understood as present experience. Once this difference is grasped, Bergson's model of 'intuition' may be seen to open up a way for the reconstruction of legal institutional knowledge: first, legal theory and legal practice should be understood as imminent within each other; second, the differences between them are not external relations but should be understood in terms of internal resonance; third, our understanding of legal knowledge finds its basis in our awareness of durée (cf. Wood 2003a: 235). Perhaps the most important difference between representations of knowledge as real movement and relative movement concerns the latter's notion of movement as instrumental, quantitative and transitional as opposed to the former's idea of it as continuous, indivisible and transitive (Deleuze 1991). Of course, this does not mean that real movement is without composition or arrangement, only that it is a 'fuzzy aggregate' (Deleuze 1988: 380).

Conclusion

The dominant highly structured, hierarchical model of institutionalising knowledge as law assumes almost unhesitatingly the ontological and epistemological inheritance from the rationalist tradition. Based largely on immobile and instrumental notions, law as structured institution orders a world of distinct states, stages or phases and, to analyse these, attempts to reduce the real movement of knowledge to its relative positions and functions between these. Because the flow of knowledge is a complex movement of ever-changing, immanent relations, it seems less demanding to analyse its singular, unifying flow in terms of discrete, immobile and stationary objects. But the flow of knowledge is not discrete, neither does it exist apart from the system of social relations in which it occurs. So we need to constantly remind ourselves of the uninterrupted nature of this flow, its lines of becoming that allow for and reveal the continual participation of every point within every other. This alternative approach based on process theory is not restricted by the number of connectable points that describe or compose it; it has no origin or destination, only middle. However, this middle is not to be understood as a position relative to other points, and from which these can be observed and negotiated; rather, it is a field of interactive tensions and stresses where, entering into the flow, we can follow its movements and changes. In this sense a process reconstrual of law can be both useful and practical. But this shifting of emphasis is really no more than a rediscovery of hidden tradition, in the absence of which we have all too often allowed ourselves to assume uncritically, often unwittingly, the idea of knowledge as instrumental, always-already convenient and available. We need to rediscover this healthy alternative understanding.

However, even the more socially aware forms of understanding the legal decision-making process still rely to some extent on this idea of separate but connectable domains. Paying attention, as Bańkowski calls it, requires more than simply identifying prior positions and taking up a mediating position in between. It must also include an understanding of how this middle pre-exists as a field of interrelations and interpenetrating tensions, ontologically prior to any of the abstracted points that we then describe and attempt to connect. Engaging with and immersing ourselves within this complex flow of knowledge and experience will require a more sophisticated understanding than the idea of any transfer and exchange of knowledge between two separate but connectable poles allows. It will require thinking about the way we think about law, thinking from *within* the flow, not so much adopting the position of an ideal, impartial spectator as adopting the position of each and every ordinary, partial, involved participant, understanding a narrative's flow *from within*. And what this suggests is a thorough-going empiricism in which primacy is conferred on process, change, movement, complexity, transformation and flux: the becoming of things over being, process over substance, change over order and stability. This is what Bergson refers to as durée: the indeterminate region in which there is no longer any sense of connections but where the interrelations exist in their own right prior to any identification of abstracted points. It is this field of relations that must, if anything, be understood substantially. Law, understood simply in terms of the institutionalising of patterns of behaviour in terms of a system of rules, can never be anything more than this structure that is created and utilised retrospectively. In what follows I will demonstrate how process thought can provide an adequate alternative conception with a prospective orientation.

Chapter 6

Two ways of thinking; two types of knowledge

Traditional notions of law rely on familiar dichotomies: thought and action, meaning and application, rule and fact. One example of this is the dialectical relationship of correspondence between universals and particulars. When law is conceived in static terms, the legal task is understood in terms of negotiating the gap between these two essentially separate but connectable domains; that is, securing the flow of knowledge, the delivery of communications, between them. Informed by this substance-based immobility, an important challenge for legal theorists and practitioners is to maintain the integrity of legal knowledge involved in this 'transfer' between one domain and the other. We can see how Ward LJ attempts to do this with his concluding remarks in *Re A*, offering his description of the justifying relationship between reason and decision that helps to secure and seal the gaping hole that has opened up in the seamless web of law (though nearly undoing himself as he appears to set *Re A* in a category of its own but not quite: 'this is a very unique case').

As a result of this, much of any sense of urgency within the legal theoretical arena has naturally gravitated towards the need for a more sophisticated understanding of the relationship between these separate poles (rules and facts, universals and particulars). But the problem with such an understanding, sophisticated as it is, is, as we have seen, that the underlying notion of legal knowledge on which it is based is still one of correspondence between connectable positions. Legal knowledge is still understood as something to be passed on, expanded and developed to meet the practical requirements of everyday life, a form of knowledge directly applicable to action in practical situations. Such a view unashamedly confers ontological priority upon categories of order, stability and communicability, constructing and categorising a world of disparate entities to which legal knowledge can then be applied in a top-down hierarchic, causal mechanistic way. This type of approach to legal decision-making precludes us from seeing the extent to which rule-determination and rule-application, universals and particulars, legal categories and living experience, already permeate each other, benefiting from this interpenetrative difference.

However, taking our cue from Henri Bergson, I have argued that we should *not* say that law is a system of rules applied to facts or, indeed, any form of reflection on this. On the contrary, rule-determination and rule-application, legal universals and legally relevant particulars, the ways in which we understand certain particulars as instantiating certain universals, our system of laws and our processes of decision-making, are all snapshots of reality, images extracted from an otherwise continuously moving and changing flow, simply ways that we break into this, halting, holding and handling what we abstract, in order to try and make sense of its elusive, enigmatic, otherwise inexpressible qualities. We can understand this as we realise that even our attempts to ground the act of giving justifying reasons for a legal decision in the particulars of the lived situation to which that decision refers is already something beyond the decision itself. A decision cannot be 'caught' because once a decision is made, it is gone: it is momentous, and all that we observe of it is its trace, the multiplicity of points through which the movement has passed, rather than the unity of the action experienced. In this sense, law can never deliver the reasons to justify a decision. Some gap always remains, the distance represented by the question concerning the appropriateness of *that* universal continuing into *these* particulars. (In the same way, we cannot capture the living experience of conjoinment in the legal representation of it.) Rather, we always miss the target we aim at, the decision-making act always remaining a decision already presented. Clearly, there is a flow of knowledge, but, on Bergson's view, not in the sense of some derived relationship connecting discrete spatial positions. For that to be true we would have to be able to completely isolate the different elements that occupy those positions so that we could identify them conclusively as like or unlike each other, spatially distinct and bounded (and to be connected they must be separate, they must each have a boundary and there must be a space between them). In spite of this, we continue to adhere to precisely this sort of unrealistic approach when we think about law as a system of known rules applied to facts. In addition, I have suggested that utilising Deleuze and Guattari's concept of the rhizome can help us to see how the movement or spread of information in law is best described as a forever jumbling up of distinct phases, stages and patterns, a complex form of growth like that associated with the roots of certain plants.

Employing a metaphor of rhizomic communication

Christine Battersby (1998) highlights five features of Deleuzean 'rhizomatics' that may help to show the relevance of this way of thinking about legal knowledge. First, the rhizome involves the bringing together of diverse elements. Second, the rhizome brings together elements that are not usually thought of as belonging together: it is based on heterogeneity. Third, the rhizome is not reducible to a series of points or individual parts. Fourth, the rhizome is 'subject to ruptures, breaks, discontinuities anywhere within it' while retaining its self-organizing structure. Fifth, the rhizome cannot be traced back to a principal root or source; rather, it is a form of nomadic mapping that 'moves across the landscape without fencing in the land' (Battersby 1998: 192). Rhizomes appear without recognisable beginnings or ends but are always an in-between, a middle that allows for the continual participation of all points within each other even if in reality one point does not become the other or achieve correspondence with it. In this way, the apparent stabilities of universals and particulars might be exchanged for the awareness that although we live in a world of change the processes of change are imperceptible to us. In this sense, the relationships between universals and particulars, rule-determination and rule-application, operative and evidentiary facts, legislation, adjudication and enforcement are not simply connective; rather, they involve the becoming of law through a movement that is neither universalist nor particularist, neither containing nor instantiating but always somewhere in-between. In this way, the assumption of a boundary between the legal and the extra-legal, law and life must give way to an understanding based on interconnections between different patterns of relations.

As an institution, law relies on explicitly formulated rules for its functioning, but law's institutional context relies on much more than explicitly formulated or formulatable rules. Through socialisation, judges internalise law-specific distinctions and their legal expertise is learned within the context of their discursive practice. This forms an unarticulated background that undergirds a judge's representation of their decisions. In this sense, the application of a rule is really not an individual achievement at all but derives essentially from collectively shared meanings, within a tightly related network of communications in and through which these shared meanings are attained. In this chapter I suggest that attempts to manage judicial decision-making actually involve *rhizomic systems of communication* rather than a series of linear connections. My aim is to demonstrate that the kind of continual movement being alluded to here already permeates the practice of law, at all levels, thus helping to prepare the way for a novel understanding of the diffusion of legal institutional knowledge.

It is often said that law is the prime example of a hierarchical institution, where normative procedures structure, order and shape all of its aspects. A taxonomic and classificatory urge controls the admissibility of its constituent parts – its formal and substantive rules, its rules of evidence, its requirements of coherence and consistency, its customs and practices, principles and values – all neatly ordered from the top down. Accordingly, legal professionals can be seen to approach their work in a pseudo-scientific manner, with judges in particular concerned to find the best possible fit of rules to facts, bridging the gap under the watchful eye and guidance of their peers and counterparts, whose control is exercised through procedural techniques such as the doctrine of precedent, *ratio decidendi*, and so on; indeed, any appreciation of law as an institution depends on a proper understanding of this hierarchical ordering of decisions. Simply looking to an individual judge's decisions in isolation will tell us very little. In such an environment only those aspects of a decision that can properly be said to form part of the *ratio* of the decision are authoritative, everything else is *obiter dictum*. The more that a form of reasoning can be considered part of the *ratio* of a decision, the more chance it has of being taken up in future decision-making. The more impressive an individual judge's justification of their decisions, the greater the impact and the more authority their reputation acquires.

But there is a flip-side to all of this, too. As we see in *Re A*, decision-making takes place under pressure of time and a lack of resources (and there is the inevitable threat of one's decisions being scrutinised by one's peers on appeal). The peculiar nature of the rules of evidence, and burdens of proof, and their corresponding impact on the public acceptability of decisions all, from time to time, provide sources of frustration for the judicial decision-maker. Therefore, in the real world of judicial decision-making there is a true sense in which, in tailoring his decisions, a judge 'cut his suit according to his cloth'. So law is a system of rules, yes, but it is a *very peculiar* system of rules, with the hierarchical ordering of its doctrine of precedent and *ratio decidendi*, examples of this. Precisely because of this, frustrations appear over and again, and we find that from time to time a decision is 'justified' where the facts and the rules do not overlap but public opinion or social mores have moved on to a position where the reasons given are deemed *sufficient to persuade* that the decision is acceptable, or a decision is deemed right and proper and in line with modern understanding, but that *cannot* be justified purely on legal grounds.

In this way, much of a judge's work in judicial reasoning can often involve cutting across recognised boundaries, developing new lines of precedent. Sometimes it will seem appropriate to question whether this is a new line of thought or a development of a previous one. Here, there is always a tension between the universal and the particular and, in such an environment, where the direction of the task seems co-determined by the interaction of these, this can often lead judges and others to reflect, as we have seen, that definition and application, theory and practice, are perhaps not really quite as far apart as they are sometimes thought to be.

But it can be rather unsettling to consider theory and practice as something other than two distinct things, two poles apart. In the first place, this presents a challenge to the dominant, hierarchical theories of law as institution. In the second place, this may also suggest that the ideological reading of the 'communicational transparency' of law as a cumulative flow of information (cf. Lyotard 1984) between areas of production and exploitation is itself a false one; that is, law, its manufacture and use, has always operated rhizomically. We can begin to see how such a challenge to traditional understandings of law might be presented by looking at Edward Levi's (1948) study of legal decision-making.

According to Levi, the notion 'that the law is a system of known rules applied by a judge' is no more than pretence; rather, 'the kind of reasoning involved in the legal process is one in which the classification changes as the classification is made. The rules change as the rules are applied'. Moreover, 'the rules arise out of a process which, while comparing fact situations, creates the rules and then applies them' (Levi 1948: 503). In this sense, 'the basic pattern of legal reasoning is by example. It is reasoning from case to case' by means of a 'three-step process' whereby 'a proposition descriptive of the first case is made into a rule of law and then applied to a next similar situation' (Levi 1948: 501).

As Levi points out, this method of reasoning brings to view 'characteristics which under other circumstances might be considered imperfections', in particular, that 'change in the rules is the indispensable dynamic quality of law'. And yet, although 'it cannot be said that the legal process is the application of known rules to diverse facts', nonetheless 'it is a system of rules; the rules are discovered in the process of determining similarity or difference', and 'the existence of some facts in common brings into play the general rule' even though 'no such fixed prior rule exists'. Moreover, 'there is an additional requirement which compels the legal process to be this way ... The categories used in the legal process must be left ambiguous in order to permit the infusion of new ideas'. In this way, 'laws come to express the ideas of the community ... molded for the specific case' (Levi 1948: 502–3).

Levi maps out the development of *danger* as a legal category, and the flow of ideas and definitions in and out of the legal system. First, a distinction is drawn, observed (though not articulated), and then refined. Afterwards, in a later case, the distinction finally achieves code value within the system. As Sean Smith (1995) observes:

> [p]atent dangers are illegal: they give rise to liability. Latent dangers are legal: they give rise to no liability. The one distinction is superimposed on the other ... , the distinction between patent and latent re-enters the legal system. It now has orientation value [and] can be used to guide further operations of the system.
>
> (Smith 1995: 195)

But it is important to realise that this '[r]e-entry cannot "solve" the paradox [of observation]', writes Smith, 'it merely disguises it'. Although the concept 'is treated as fixed and unchanging ... the context or precise nature of the distinction is constantly shifting'. Indeed, by explicit reference, implicit reference and an 'additional distinction (!) between explicit and implicit case reference' we now learn 'how to reconstruct the history of these cases. The "authority" is *Dixon*. The "development" is *Winterbottom*. The *Longmeid* case, therefore, represents the re-entry of the distinction between patent and latent dangers in the legal system'. Finally, in the next phase, the distinction 'becomes condensed and confirmed … Not only are different cases treated as identical, but the same distinction gains in authority from its repeated application in … new contexts and acquires additional meaning'. Eventually, '[e]ven the confirmations … get condensed', the distinction is 'turned … into a contradiction', and there is 'a crossing of the code values themselves'. In other words, what was once the exception now becomes the rule (Smith 1995: 195–96).

Particular attention must be given to the process, says Levi. What is important is the mechanism of transformation. The law is both certain and uncertain, changing and unchanging. It is an example, we might say, albeit a sophisticated one, of an ancient abstraction, the *unchanging subject of change*: '[t]he law forum is the most explicit demonstration of the mechanism required for a moving classification system' based on 'the presentation of competing examples' (Levi 1948: 503–4). So, while it is true that, '[i]n case law, when a judge determines what the controlling similarity between the present and prior case is, the case is decided', nonetheless, it is with 'a set of … satellite concepts that reasoning by example must work'. And, crucially, 'no satellite concept, no matter how well developed, can prevent the court from shifting its course, not only by realigning cases, but by going beyond realignment back to the overall ambiguous category written into the document', a procedure which, 'in other words, permits the court to be inconsistent' (Levi 1948: 505–6).

Levi's account of the process is clear and precise: the 'movement of concepts into and out of the law' begins with the recognition of similarities and differences, and the emergence of a word which, when accepted, 'becomes a legal concept'. Even so, 'its meaning continues to change', since 'the comparison is not only between the instances which have been included under it and the actual case at hand, but also in terms of hypothetical instances which the word by itself suggests'. At this point, 'reasoning may … appear to be simply deductive', though '[i]n the long run a circular motion can be seen' where concepts are built up and fixed before finally breaking down again. During breakdown, 'there will be the [inevitable] attempt to escape to some overall rule which can be said to have always operated and which will make the reasoning look deductive'. But '[t]he statement of the rule' is mere 'window dressing', and 'it can be very misleading', for 'it will have to operate on a level where it has no meaning'. For instance, '[p]articularly when a concept has broken down and reasoning by example is about to build another, textbook writers, well aware of the unreal aspect of old rules, will announce new ones, equally ambiguous and meaningless, forgetting that the legal process does not work with the rule but on a much lower level' (Levi 1948: 506–7).

In seeking to expose the '"lower level" operations of the common law process', Levi, Smith observes, 'stresses the contingency of change', noting 'how the legal system fumbles its way in an environment which is in principle inaccessible to it and can only be reconstructed using its own categories, its own distinctions'. Through its use of 'distinctions, the legal system ... break[s] up the "seamless web" of decisions based on decisions, construct[s] lines of argument, trends and patterns of development ... observes every-thing, including itself' (Smith 1995: 192). Here, with the construction of trends and patterns, the system receives its pedigree, and we discover 'one way of neutralising the paradox of the legal system'. To put it another way, as cases are ruled in and out as authority, 'history has to be rewritten'. 'The key thing to note', says Smith, 'is that these are not separate operations but separate ways of looking at the same operation – they occur simulta-neously ... This is redundancy ... , the attempt to reduce the element of surprise in the system ... to convince that a particular decision is compelled by the history of the system' (Smith 1995: 197).

For Levi, therefore, the attempt to 'soar above the cases and find some great overall rule which can classify the cases as though the pattern were not really a changing one' (Levi 1948: 510) is 'mere window-dressing' (Levi 1948: 507). But, for Smith, Levi 'dramatically underplays the significance of legal reasoning' being always 'at pains to stress the contingency of the system'. For Smith, rather, 'the decisional structure of law requires a certain style of reasoning', and systems theory describes this 'particular account of reasoning as taking place within the context of the common law process, and of the common law process within the legal system as a whole' (Smith 1995: 200). It thus 'compels us to look at the role of law in society and therefore, here, the role of common law and legal reasoning in society ... [L]egal rea-soning is important not because it is caught up in resolving the internal paradoxes of the system, but because it ultimately provides the link between law and community, between system and lifeworld'; ... although 'there is good evidence that courts do resolve paradoxes, and ... this distinction between law and community ... is just another way of resolving the paradox. But ... the question for systems theory now becomes whether this is a good way of solving the paradox, and to ask whether there are not better ways' (Smith 1995: 201–2).

What Levi shows us, concludes Smith, is that '[l]egitimation does not come through legal reasoning but through the legal process. It is law as system ... that legitimizes itself'. What this means is that:

> there is no simple exchange of ideas between law and its environment. Any idea has to be read together with the past and the future decisions of the system which gives it is legal sense ... What is important is not so

much the substantive values of the ideas themselves, but the institution
of a procedure of revisability ... a procedure [that] provides the forum
for the making and the unmaking of ideas ...

(Smith 1995: 203)

Taking account of Levi in this way, we can affirm the notion that judges'
actual experience of decision-making better resembles a Deleuzean rhizomic
web than an hierarchically ordered structure of linear progression, its natural
tendency to resist systematisation, to spread out, integrate and incorporate
in all directions, a 'self-organizing, non-linear, and multi-stranded' organism,
growing, as it were, 'from the *bottom up* and not from the *top down*' (Cooper
1998: 143). In this way, the metaphor of the rhizome helps to promote this
sense of an assemblage of incongruent parts, the bringing together of elements not normally considered as belonging together. This might help us to
understand how it seems that so much of a judge's work in decision-making
actually involves developing lines of thought that cut across boundaries. Just
as the rhizome is not reducible to an ordered sequence of individual component parts but is 'a non-localisable relation sweeping up the two distant or
contiguous points, carrying one into the proximity of the other' (Deleuze
1988: 293), so, in the courtroom, the rule that is supposedly to be applied to
the facts is actually just as much in wait of its appearance on the basis of
these facts. In this way, the process of judicial decision-making as a whole is
perhaps more accurately described under the metaphor of the rhizome given
this inherent vulnerability to irruption, disruption or interruption, all without
fatally undermining its continuing capacity for self-organisation.

Furthermore, in the same way that a rhizome does not appear to have any
identifiable start point, so, as Levi claims, concepts, definitions and lines of
reasoning seem to move freely across the judicial landscape without identifiable start or end points. In constructing their opinions, judges can actually
be seen to use deliberate engagement strategies within their *obiter* remarks to
achieve this. For example, a point of view is expressed that does not contribute to the overall *ratio* of the case, and may even be part of the minority
view, but which is intended to set out an alternative strategy. While it might
not impact on the case at hand in any significant way it may nonetheless be
picked up later and used by another judge somewhere else in support of a
future decision. In this way, although it does not have the force of a *ratio* in
terms of the doctrine of precedent, it is accorded informally and assumed
unofficially to have some credible force simply by way of the reputation of
the judge, and, by extension, the status of the court in which it was delivered.
Like the analogue of the rhizome, it is simply not possible to reduce the
organisation of legal knowledge in common law reasoning to a single source;
instead, it cuts across established lines creating, combining and integrating.

While such a view may be considered a challenge to both dominant hierarchical and ideological theories of legal institutional decision-making there

is really nothing new in this. The simple fact is that legal knowledge has always operated as a rhizomic system of interconnections and intersections across and between professional groups. It is simply quite false to think that law consists in the simple application of known rules to legally relevant facts.

A second effect of viewing the organisation of legal knowledge as a continuous process of communication follows on from this. As we have seen, under a traditional common law model of legal reasoning, legal institutional knowledge is understood as a connecting of two or more separate points. Yet, as Bergson states, and as our look at Levi and *Re A* has confirmed, we cannot say that knowledge progresses in any uniform way along a pre-arranged pathway. Rather, instead of some rigid adherence to the dogmatic assertion that a rule is applied wherever the conditions of its application are met, where the emphasis is on the halts, 'universals' and 'particulars' as in some way ontologically prior to our understanding of the nature of the relationship between them, we should perhaps more correctly say that 'there is a becoming of law from universals to particulars'. In this way, our attention is drawn away from any suggestion of a transition between two definite points, or, indeed, of any notion of simple correspondence, and only towards that 'irreducible line that passes in and between the two … carrying them both away in a creative process whose inventions and forms do not exist in advance' (Wood 2003b: 63).

For legal decision-makers the continuity of becoming from rules to decision is realized through engagement with particular local fact situations. In this way, not only does the decision and its effects, both legal and personal/social, get communicated but a whole network of interrelations works together to make this happen. It is not just about communicating decisions, it is more about a type of personal, social and political engagement: reasons need to be accessible and meaningful for law's audience, its users. In Levi's study we can see this emerging. Legal decision-makers, at whatever level, mostly do try to relate their decisions to the concrete situations before them. In this sense, the development of law and legal change does not occur in abstraction, but in and through the real world where men and women live and work. In reality, rule-determination and rule-application, universal and particular, actually 'melt into and permeate one another, without precise outlines' (Bergson 1910: 104).

Conclusion

Perhaps we need to reassess our adherence to the logic of institutionalisation that segments legal knowledge into separate phases. There is a good case to be made for an account of law and legal decision-making that cuts across these quite arbitrary divisions and focuses more on their immanent relations. This is important because while it is true that we do act and think in law as though we possessed a storehouse of ready-made, clearly defined legal knowledge awaiting its application and implementation, nonetheless, as we have seen this idea is not as helpful as we sometimes think, for the delineation of legal knowledge is not quite as distinct as it appears. In our examination of both the macro and micro levels of decision-making, in *Re A* and in Levi's account of decision-making, we can begin to see how this comes about.

First, an obvious tension appears in law's prescriptive framework: from the beginning it is clear that there is an *uncomfortable coupling* of two very different versions of events running in parallel. There is a deep suspicion that this tension exists because these two versions or understandings of what is going on belong to *two quite different worlds*, and that the objective events or circumstances to which they refer and from which they derive their meaning are really quite different 'entities' in each. While decision-makers continue to profess adherence to the established institutional order to satisfy the burden of decision-making beneath the weight of an ever-changing social, political, cultural and religious climate that relentlessly requires results under pressures of time, etc., it is clear that, in making those decisions, judges actually articulate a wider, more complex, more openly receptive approach than is often suggested by the simple and straightforward application of rules to factual situations. There is more to decision-making than is accounted for in the 'official' version.

Second, as we saw in *Re A* and in Levi, the connections between legal concepts, doctrines and procedures described in legal judgements are not always as straightforward and obvious as they are assumed to be. Therefore, alongside of the official, hierarchical, institutional version of how law operates appears a more pragmatic account that better corresponds to what we actually find to be the case, an 'unofficial' version that helps to engender trust, legitimate and domesticate the official version. As well as being institutions, formal legal contexts are also 'practices', shared traditions in and out of which legal practitioners live and work, and in this latter sense, the structure of legal knowledge takes on a more narrative form.

Third, by utilising the notion of *becoming*, it is possible to cast a spotlight on some of the difficulties involved in the making of decisions in real-life situations. For example, there is a problem in deciding where exactly thinking, deliberating, reasoning *about* a case ends and acting *within* it begins, and a gap between rule-determination and rule-application that has important implications for decision-makers and addressees of decisions alike. We have seen how, in rule-based law, law's decisional imperative and the collapse of the supposed symmetry between addressor and addressee that alone could redeem the rule-based form, collapses and how, then, because of this, a continued adherence to rule-based law-giving performs a travesty that cannot be compensated for. Here, we see how law is violent, a double-edged sword, cutting into and out of the continuing flow and flux of life with its requirement for the rational resolution of rational conflict and its use of abstractions and representations to perform this; manipulating, controlling and transferring across fields, misrepresenting on the one hand and silencing on the other. But it is precisely because of this that judges must then begin to equip themselves bravely with abilities honed through experience and training to translate ideas across fields and disciplines, blurring boundaries, entering into the living narratives that are coldly set before them, frozen from time. Any judge will need to be 'a man for all seasons' if he is to sit straddling all the different social, political, cultural, religious and even legal boundaries that this entails.

In this sense, perhaps the most urgent task facing judicial decision-makers, law-makers and other legal professionals is to re-engage with legal institutional knowledge as it really is, and not just as it is sometimes supposed to be; that is, not in terms of an either/or preconception of reality as separated into prior domains that structure and prefigure reality determining what is experienced, but as a simultaneously 'not only/but also', interpenetrative, relational account of legal determination and legal application. But this is not as easy a prescription to follow as might at first appear. We are much more inclined towards order, stability and predictability than we are to opening ourselves up to experience and entertain elements of the novel and the surprising, its irruptions, disruptions and interruptions. Most of all, what this suggests is that we need to stop thinking about law under the terms of its decisional imperative and more in terms of a forum for encouraging free and unrestricted dialogue, an opportunity for distilling and discovering ideals that will lure us into future commitments. In the next chapter I consider one way in which we might develop this approach.

Chapter 7

Michael Polanyi's 'tacit knowledge'

What is 'tacit knowledge'? In his seminal volume, Michael Polanyi (1962) writes that:

> [t]he act of knowing includes an appraisal; and this personal coefficient, which shapes all factual knowledge, bridges in doing so the disjunction between subjectivity and objectivity.
>
> (Polanyi 1962: 17)

One of the strengths of Polanyi's thought is its strong rejection of dualistic tendencies; such as between theoretical and practical knowledge. For him, '[a]ll knowing is personal knowing – participation through indwelling' (Polanyi and Prosch 1975: 44). Therefore, the idea that there could be such a thing as objective knowledge is mistaken and destructive; rather, all knowledge involves the active participation of the knower. The act of knowing is skilful action.

For example, imagine that I wish to construct a model airplane. In order to achieve this from a boxful of plastic pieces of different shapes and sizes I might make use of a set of diagrams and instructions. Each diagram is an explicit representation of something other than itself, a model airplane. It is, in this way, similar to a system of rules, aimed at bringing about purposeful action. But in order to utilise the potential of those diagrams I will first need to be able to relate them to the physical world outside them: I must *read* the diagrams. In fact, I must do three things: identify the pieces that I have, choose what I want to make, and decide how to put them together. According to Polanyi, all such acts are acts of skilful judgement and they are both cognitive and sensual (Polanyi 1962: 10–20). The diagrams assist me in constructing the model, matching individual pieces to their diagrammatic representations, but this still requires some personal judgement on my part to match the two, a mental and physical effort, in short, a skilful action. Personal judgements such as this are involved whenever we try to bring together our experience of the world and our abstract representations of it. We often say that certain laws can predict certain outcomes, but what we really mean is that *we* can predict certain outcomes by *using* these laws as *tools*. The outcomes are not given; rather, they need to be calculated, checked and authenticated, comparing expectations with results, calculating margins for error and assessing and reassessing the reliability of our rules (Polanyi 1962: 19).

In arguing that our tools of perception, intuition and reasoning are not self-applying but require an action on our part in order to apply them, Polanyi, like Whitehead, emphasises the importance of the physical body in the act of knowing:

> the way the body participates in the act of perception can be generalized further to include the bodily roots of all knowledge and thought ... Parts of our body serve as tools for observing objects outside and for manipulating them.
>
> (Polanyi 1969: 147)

In this sense, Polanyi argues that all acts of knowing are skilful presentations by the human agent which involve a 'personal coefficient' (Polanyi 1962: 17). Moreover, each skilful performance 'is achieved by the observance of a set of rules which are not known as such to the person following them' (Polanyi 1962: 49). Consider the driver of a motor vehicle. Although not well acquainted with the scientific principles of internal combustion such a driver may nonetheless be quite capable of driving proficiently. She will move off, effortlessly, from a stationary position and continue driving along a busy road, maintaining the car in a forward direction with good speed and with minimum discomfort to her passengers, accelerating and decelerating, changing gears up and down as necessary. Of course, if she were able, she might formulate rules based on scientific principles to explain why it is that the car responds in particular ways to the different actions she performs but it is not at all obvious that knowing any of these scientific rules would necessarily make her a better driver; much less, that she would require to know anything about these rules simply to drive. As she learns to drive and becomes more proficient at driving, any such knowledge will usually be held 'at the back of her mind', not *focused on* but taken for granted, accepted and held unconsciously. Just so, we might say that skills such as driving are not normally held to be accountable fully in terms of their particulars; indeed, these are often unknown to the person exercizing the skill. Knowing *how* a car works will not of itself make someone a good driver (Polanyi 1962: 88–90).

According to Polanyi, every 'mental effort ... tends to incorporate any available elements of the situation which are helpful for its purpose', even without the actor knowing them in and of themselves. Thus, it has a heuristic effect:

we feel our way to success and may continue to improve on our success without specifiably knowing how we do it – for we never meet the causes of our success as identifiable things which can be described in terms of classes of which such things are members.

(Polanyi 1962: 62)

Here, two types of awareness are involved. Polanyi uses another example to explain. Suppose that I am engaged in hammering a nail into a piece of wood. While I am aware both of the hammer and the nail, my awareness of the hammer is different to my awareness of the nail. Driving the nail into the wood is the main object of my concentration and I watch and correct my action as the effects of my hitting the nail drive it further into the wood: I am focally aware of the nail. I am also aware of the hammer: I feel it clenched tightly in my hand. However, feeling the hammer in my hand is not the main focus of my concentration:

I know the feelings in the palm of my hand *by relying on them for attending to the hammer hitting the nail*. I may say that I have a *subsidiary* awareness of the feelings in my hand which is merged into my *focal awareness* of my driving the nail.

(Polanyi and Prosch 1975: 33)

In other words, in performing an action, I am aware of some things that are not the main focus of my attention. More precisely, 'in an act of tacit knowing we *attend from* something for attending *to* something else' (Polanyi 1966: 10), which is why we always 'know more than we can tell' (Polanyi 1966: 4).

We can compare this understanding of skilful engagement with the legal method of deductive syllogism. On the one hand, we should note that on this understanding tacit integration cannot be undone: it is certainly possible to shift one's attention away from the object of one's concentration while driving a motor car or hammering a nail, often with significant results, but this will not take one back to the point of not knowing how to drive a car or hammer a nail. On the other hand, in the deductive syllogism we find that we can proceed step by step in a logical way from premises to conclusions and back again always without loss. In other words, because all the logical connections hold then the direction is reversible. Now, if we think of a particular instance of judicial decision-making, it should be clear that the moment of the decision in which the judicial decision is made is essentially one of tacit integration, while the subsequent act of providing justifying reasons for that legal decision is essentially, as MacCormick argues, of the nature of explicit or deductive inference. Clearly, the two are not the same. While the latter may build upon the former and may even explain it for legal purposes, this, as Christodoulidis observes, comes too late to justify it, for there is no going back. What is purportedly a justifying reason may indeed provide a reason to explain why the decision, already made, may now be used as a relevant datum for new decisions, but that is a quite different thing to saying that it provides the *justifying* reason in and through which *that decision* was made.

Clearly, much of this also taps into the familiar realist debate concerning the 'judicial hunch' and, in that respect, precisely what part is being played here by 'discovery' and what by 'justification'. This distinction was first made by Hans Reichenbach (1955) in order to differentiate between the description of the origin of a proposition (the 'context of discovery') and the demonstration of it (the 'context of justification'); indeed, Reichenbach argued that:

> [t]he act of discovery escapes logical analysis; there are no logical rules that could be applied to the construction of a 'discovery machine' that would assume the creative function of genius. But it is not the logician's task to explain scientific discoveries; all the logician can do is analyse the relation between the facts as given and a theory that is presented to her or him that claims to explain this relation. In other words, logic is not concerned with the context of discovery.
>
> (Reichenbach 1955: 199)

All of which brings us back once again to the central problem highlighted by Christodoulidis.

The structure of tacit knowledge: similarities with Whitehead

As Polanyi describes it, the character of tacit knowing as 'vectorial' (Polanyi 1969: 182) appears to embody the same sense of creativity that we find in Whitehead's analysis of the three phases of concrescence in the becoming of an actual occasion of experience. Polanyi explains what he means by reference to the way that a blind person might feel their way by tapping with a stick, or the way that one might use a probe to explore a darkened cavern:

> Anyone using as probe for the first time will feel its impact against his fingers and palm. But as we learn to use a probe, or to use a stick for feeling our way, our awareness of its impact on our hand is transformed into a sense of its point touching the objects we are exploring ... [A]n interpretative effort transposes meaningless feelings into meaningful ones, and places these at some distance from the original feeling. We become aware of the feelings in our hand in terms of their meaning located at the tip of the probe or stick to which we are attending.
>
> (Polanyi 1966: 13)

Of course, we could illustrate this with numerous examples from everyday experience: tacit knowing permeates all of daily living from casual acts of observation to performing simple physical tasks. But the point is that, as we take on more specialised tasks, in order to accomplish these we find that we must first have internalised (Polanyi 1962: 101) new knowledge: 'when we learn to use language, or a probe, or a tool, and thus make ourselves aware of these things as we are our body, we *interiorize* these things and *make ourselves dwell in them*' (Polanyi 1969: 148).

In other words, by indwelling in the tools that we use, we are able to use them as extensions of ourselves to increase our own powers and press outwards to further extend the boundaries at which we make contact with the world around us. But for this to come about, for our use of such tools to become natural, this must be something in relation to which we necessarily offer uncritical acceptance: we do not and cannot question their usefulness. On the contrary, their usefulness is always presupposed and taken for granted, something which cannot be stated; otherwise, we could make no claims and assert nothing. As Polanyi puts it, 'assertion can be made only *within* a framework with which we have identified ourselves for the time being; as they are themselves our ultimate framework, they are essentially inarticulable' (Polanyi 1962: 60).

So, internalising a tool to use it instrumentally in pursuit of some aim or goal enables the user to obtain new experiences that facilitate greater efficiency in carrying out appropriate tasks. Consider the novice rider. She has been told how to hold the reins, how to maintain balance and posture in the saddle and stirrups, where, when and how to give pressure when she wishes the horse to move and change direction or movement in a certain way. She feels the reins in her hands, her feet in the stirrups, the body of the horse beneath; but she has not yet learned how to correlate the responsive movements of the horse with their own bodily actions. Again, by contrast at the other end of the scale, an experienced equestrian will appear so much more skilled in riding, moving gracefully with her horse as if they were one. This is because all those skills that appear to the novice as things to be remembered and attended to with concentration have become actions of which the experienced rider has become unconscious. They are skills that have been mastered and need no longer to be focused upon but are now used 'naturally' for the purpose of guiding and instructing the horse. Having thus developed an *un*awareness of certain actions the experienced rider is now able to concentrate more on what is going on around, to notice changing conditions underfoot and to observe the actions and positions of others, and generally to move on to perform and enjoy an ever-expanding horizon of equestrian experience. As Polanyi states:

> by the effort by which I concentrate on my chosen plane of operation I succeed in absorbing all the elements of the situation of which I might otherwise be aware in themselves, so that I become aware of them now in terms of the operational results achieved through their use.
>
> (Polanyi 1962: 61)

This, then, is how we get things done, becoming efficient and proficient through developing an *un*awareness. We can learn all there is to know about the working mechanisms of a motor car or the anatomy of a horse, and how to make proper use of these, but until we have actually succeeded in putting all of this into 'the back of our minds', we will not finally have acquired the skilful ability necessary to master and experience fully the art of driving or riding. As Polanyi says:

> [t]his lapse into unconsciousness is accompanied by a newly acquired consciousness of the experiences in question, on the operational plane. It is misleading, therefore, to describe this as the mere result of repetition; it is a structural change achieved by a repeated mental effort aiming at the instrumentalization of certain things and actions in the service of some purpose.
>
> (Polanyi 1962: 62)

This is not to suggest that Bańkowski is wrong to say that we must pay attention to the story; on the contrary, it is to affirm that in order to be free to pay attention to the story we have to develop an *un*-awareness of the methods and the tools that we employ. Focusing on the methods and tools of legal argument simply causes us to stare at a situation and to deal clumsily with it (cf. *Re A*). Instead, we need to develop the ability to glance rather than gaze and to recapture the dynamic of movement in each story by skilfully entering into it in this way. As our consciousness of some things in a certain context contracts, so our consciousness of other things expands and enlarges. In the same way that particulars such as 'releasing the clutch' and 'keeping your heels down' are known subsidiarily to those persons involved in the skills of driving and riding we must also learn and develop the skills to enable us to attend with confidence to the art of judicial decision-making.

In this sense, then, we can affirm all knowledge to be contextual and operational, related to action within that context: in the context of driving I know about releasing the clutch; in the context of riding I know to keep my heels down in the stirrups. Moreover, it is in these contexts that I have a subsidiary awareness of these. Of course, if I were also a bicycle designer, or a motor car engineer, or a riding instructor, the focus of my attention would be significantly different, and rightly so. But that is just another way of saying that in some situations, and depending on context, I have a subsidiary awareness of certain particulars; in other situations, and depending on context, they constitute the focus of my attention. In this sense, my knowledge may be described correctly as recursive (cf. Tsoukas 2003: 418). Depending on context, I must have the ability to absorb, internalise and use unconsciously certain things in pursuit of some other purpose or goal; changing context, I must be able to turn or *re*-turn back on my self and concentrate on these.

In mathematics, the recursive application of a function to its own values will generate an infinite sequence of values. So here, too (though there are institutional checks to limit its effects), if a judge also happens to be a mother and a driver then she will have acquired different bodies of knowledge in respect of each of these, and these, with their own relevant degrees of abstraction, come together to provide the judge with her depth of knowledge and understanding and expertise. But the extent to which an individual judge will draw upon each of these depends on the present context of decision-making. Each of her various bodies of knowledge and understanding exists independently and cannot be replaced by or reduced to any other. That is to say, her practical knowledge cannot be replaced by theoretical knowledge.

Although MacCormick agrees that legal reasoning is a form of practical reasoning his use of the metaphor of communication whereby ideas are understood as objects that can be extracted and packaged or communicated to other people by means of a structure or channel of communication, appears to reduce legal reasoning to a sort of technical knowledge. For him, the form of legal reasoning associated with his institutional theory of law is that of deductive reasoning. Clearly, judges do learn a technique for the presentation of the results of their decision-making in their formal legal training but they also learn and gradually assimilate more than technical knowledge, even if they don't realize this. They not only learn how to present and re-present their decisions in the accepted institutional forms but also begin to acquire rudimentary forms or basic skills for decision-making that will later be further developed and refined, skills in the art of decision-making that represent a knowledge that cannot be precisely formulated in propositions but which will, nonetheless, become manifest in their decision-making (which is one reason why judges tend to develop recognisable 'styles' in decision-making). To regard such practical knowledge as having content capable of being defined with precision so that it may be converted from a thought in the head of the judge to explicitly formulated propositional knowledge is to confuse the distinction between knowledge and articulation and to diminish the idea of practical knowledge.

Polanyi goes even further. For him, since a judge could not possibly know all the rules pertaining to the activity she is engaged in, then, although these rules may be useful, they cannot determine the practice; rather, 'they are maxims, which can serve as a guide ... only if they can be integrated into the practical knowledge ... They cannot replace th[at] knowledge' (Polanyi 1962: 50). In other words, it is because the knowledge necessary to the activity of decision-making is not able to be stated in any detailed way that it must be handed down from master to apprentice. That is why, for Polanyi:

> By watching the master and emulating his efforts in the presence of his example, the apprentice unconsciously picks up the rules of the art, including those which are not explicitly known to the master himself.

These hidden rules can be assimilated only by a person who surrenders himself to that extent uncritically to the imitation of another.

(Polanyi 1962: 53)

Thus, to the young law student, for example, everything is alien, because the relevant and requisite knowledge for how to do law has not yet been internalised. Nonetheless, over time the student does begin to assimilate that knowledge and becomes subsidiarily aware of what they are doing in answering legal problems. In this way, they can also begin to turn their attention to and become focally aware of what is really going on in the case at hand, instead of simply trying to 'answer' the question. Now, a different type of understanding develops and knowledge is used instrumentally: it is tacitly known and unquestioningly used.

Just so, it is clear that the activity of thinking about decision-making is different from decision-making, just as the activity of finding justifying reasons for decisions is qualitatively different from the moment of making of those decisions. In seeking to present justifying reasons for her legal decisions, a judge is no longer involved in precisely the same activity; namely, the making of the decision. Contra MacCormick, Polanyi argues that the particulars of any skill are '*logically unspecifiable*'; in fact, 'the specification of the particulars would logically contradict what is implied in the performance or context in question' (Polanyi 1962: 56).

However, we do still speak of a judge as afterwards reflecting on the decision she has made, discussing her decision-making with her colleagues and articulating it in written judgement as explicit legal knowledge. But this is surely mistaken. It is the same decision that is referred to, but the judge is no longer describing the decision-making event in its entirety, the moment of decision, only that technical part of it that can be articulated in the form of rules, principles and values, and embedded and embodied in propositional statements. Contrastingly, what is tacitly known cannot be put into words., Here, then, is the force of Polanyi's argument:

> Subsidiary or instrumental knowledge … is not known in itself but is known in terms of something focally known, to the quality of which it contributes, and to this extent it is unspecifiable. … The knowledge of such particulars is therefore ineffable, and the pondering of a judgement in terms of such particulars is an ineffable process of thought.
>
> (Polanyi 1962: 88)

In other words, tacit knowledge cannot be transferred or transformed into explicit knowledge. Contrary to MacCormick's argument in relation to the instance of Solomonic wisdom, stating Solomon's act of judging in propositional form does not capture in any detailed form the essence of Solomonic wisdom or, even, its moment of decision. Such skilful knowing has in it an ineffable element based on personal insight (intuition, call it what you will) and will not admit of articulation. But does this mean then that we cannot speak about decision-making as a practical activity and that such skills must inevitably remain mystical, outside the forum of reasoned debate? Of course not. What we actually do when we engage in reflection on our practical activities of judging is *re*-visit the distinctions underpinning them, highlight previously unnoticed or unconnected aspects, understand and relate to the situation we are in, in a new way.

What all this points to is that our engagement in the practical activities of decision-making takes place in and through our participation in social practices under the tutelage of those more experienced than us. This is how we come to know the 'hows', the 'whats', the 'wherefores' and the 'whys' of that practice: we acquire its knowledge and gain its understanding by having our attention directed, through a hidden persuasion. In this way, we keep getting re-told what we already know, taught again a language that we have already learned but cannot yet speak. Perhaps this is what Augustine meant when he complained that, although when he thought about time he knew what he meant, if someone were to ask him to give an account of time he could not (cf. Wittgenstein 1958: 89). Quite possibly this is why the practice of decision-making continues to fascinate us: we constantly practise it but we need forever to be reminded of it. Indeed, when we recursively interpose our understandings in the process of finding justifying reasons for legal decisions we do in fact bring light to bear on previously unseen or un-emphasised distinctions that our everyday use of language often easily passes over. In this way, the simple, familiar, but often unnoticed aspects of decision-making, the things that are there but always remain hidden, can be talked about; the 'ineffable' can be described and previously unnoticed or forgotten aspects viewed afresh in new connections.

We misunderstand tacit knowledge, which is at the heart of judicial decision-making, if we think of it as MacCormick does as knowledge awaiting articulation. Tacit knowledge is ineffable; it cannot be reduced to what is articulated or articulate-*able* but it exists in our subsidiary awareness of something when we are focally aware of something else. We cannot examine subsidiary particulars directly: it is like trying to catch a moment of time. If we do focus on particulars, it is in the sense that we are engaged in activities in which we have a subsidiary awareness of them. For example, while we are focused on the flight of an arrow in its unitary motion we are subsidiarily aware that it is forever occupying different positions but if we try to focus on any one of its positions independently our awareness of its flight disappears. In other words, in trying to focus on the particulars of a decision after that decision has been made we are not focusing on them as they are in the original moment of decision, for they derive their meaning from their association to that original focus of decision; rather, when we focus on the particulars of a decision we do so in a new context of decision under which lie a new set of subsidiary particulars. Thus, the notion that we can focus on a set of subsidiary particulars and transform them into explicit knowledge cannot be sustained. We can talk about the decisions we make and our reasons for making them but only in so far as we refrain from insisting that in so doing we are somehow transforming tacit knowledge into explicit knowledge; instead we must understand this whole process as an ongoing process of considering how we give consideration to certain things. That is, not so much in terms of a process of providing rational conclusions to rational arguments but as the continual uncovering and discovering of ideals that will lure us into further commitment.

In this way, written judgements help us understand how we relate to each other and the world in the web of legal settings that we have woven for ourselves. They help not only to remind us of how but also of why we do things in the ways that we do and they encourage us to develop our understanding of this in order that we might do these things differently, with more clarity and better: previously unnoticed distinctions emerge and we highlight their importance. So, what we need to promote in considering justification of judicial decisions is not the institutional explication of tacit knowledge, which is perhaps something of a contradiction in terms, but this process itself; that is, the opportunities it offers for new ways of doing dialogue and interaction, new ways of making distinctions, connecting and re-connecting: the end of the process is the process itself.

Tacit knowledge in the context of decision-making cannot be stated in a captured form; it cannot be transformed or transferred, only demonstrated in what we do. New knowledge comes about not when what was hitherto tacit is made explicit but when our judicial decision-making process is interrupted and shot through with new social forms of mutual and reciprocal action and influence. The important question, then, is how, if at all, this can be said to take place.

Part III

Exploring formal legal contexts

Chapter 8

Legal institutional knowledge

In this chapter I describe the different types of institutional knowledge that exist in law, how they interact with each other and how they may be seen to be founded on different features of the legal institutional context. Following Tsoukas (1996, 1998b, Tsoukas and Vladimirou 2001), I will argue that while it is true that the propositional structure of legal knowledge is fully realised within formal legal contexts this tells us only part of the story. As well as being institutions, formal legal contexts are also *practices*; that is, *shared traditions* in and out of which legal practitioners live and work. In this latter sense, legal knowledge has a narrative structure, maintained by story, anecdote and example. However, these two features of legal institutional knowledge sit uncomfortably alongside each other: there is an uneasy tension between the propositional form of legal knowledge fundamentally associated with law as an institution and the narrative form of legal knowledge associated with law as a shared tradition or practice. In order to survive as a practice, law requires its institutions to be strong but these same institutions, by their very nature, as they strengthen and become more autonomous, begin to act as a corrosive influence on the shared tradition; nonetheless, without its foundation in a shared tradition law as an institution is weak and unproductive and incapable of functioning. Thus, some equilibrium must be achieved, its tension negotiated and maintained.

Here are two examples of propositional statements in statute:

If a person–

(a) drives or attempts to drive a motor vehicle on a road or other public place, or
(b) is in charge of a motor vehicle on a road or other public place,

after consuming so much alcohol that the proportion of it in his breath, blood or urine exceeds the prescribed limit he is guilty of an offence.

(Road Traffic Act 1988, s.5(1))

Any person who, being a person to whom [Civic Government (Scotland) Act 1982, s. 57] applies –

(a) has or has recently had in his possession any tool or other object from the possession of which it May reasonably be inferred that he intended to commit theft or had committed theft; and
(b) is unable to demonstrate satisfactorily that his possession of such tool or other object is or was not for the purposes of committing theft, shall be guilty of an offence and liable, on summary conviction, to a fine not exceeding …

(Civic Government (Scotland) Act 1982, s.58(1))

At common law, the following statement by Lord Sutherland exhibits a similar structure and has been taken, for the purposes of decision-making in Scots Criminal Law, to provide a working definition of 'wicked recklessness':

If you act in such a way as to show that you don't really care whether the person you are attacking lives or dies, then you can constitute this degree of wicked recklessness which is required to constitute murder. It may, in the end of the day come as a considerable surprise to you, and indeed a matter of regret too that your victim dies, but that doesn't alter the fact that you have committed murder.

(Lord Sutherland in *H. M. Advocate v. Hartley* 1989 SLT 135 at 136)

In each of the above examples, the preceding conditional statements operate to identify as significant recurring events or behaviours that serve to provide a basis for the formulation of rules to guide future adjudication. Such recurring events are assumed to be patterned, ordered and non-random, made up of elements that are objectively available and which can be re-presented in an abbreviated form. That is, the elements are seen to be ordered according to a pattern that can be replaced with a rule to capture its information content, doing away with the need to list repeatedly the whole contents of that pattern. In this way, the mass of observed events and the statements made about them can be compressed into a small number of propositional statements with the same informational content, permitting economy of effort, transferability, and remote control.

However, for social reality to permit its abbreviated representation in this way, and for propositional knowledge to be possible, the world must first be capable of being understood in such regular, patterned and non-random terms. In what sense might we affirm this to be the case? According to Peter Berger and Thomas Luckmann (1996):

[a]ll human activity is subject to habitualization. Any action that is repeated frequently becomes cast into a pattern, which can then be

reproduced with an economy of effort and which, *ipso facto*, is apprehended by its performer as that pattern. Habitualization further implies
that the action in question may be performed again in the future in the
same manner and with the same economical effort.

(Berger and Luckmann 1996: 70)

For Berger and Luckmann, institutionalisation provides the context for linking
habitualisation and typification: it occurs 'whenever there is a reciprocal typification of habitualized action by types of actors'. Within such contexts, intentions and purposes are assigned to actors and, when certain actions recur,
these intentions and purposes are also held as recurrent. Reducible to role
and rule, behaviour becomes to a large extent routine and predictable and
'[t]he institution posits that actions of type x will be performed by actors of type
x' (Berger and Luckmann 1996: 72). In this way, the social world is seen as sub-
mitting to an ordering and regularity that makes it possible for us to arrest from
it patterns and routines and to represent these formally, in an abbreviated way.

Clearly, the more that human social life becomes institutionalised, the
more concentrations occur, then so the more accessible to regular pattern
and ordering it becomes and the easier it is to represent this in an abbreviated form as propositional statements. In this way, rules become a means
for the prescriptive ordering of human behaviour in specified circumstances.
As Twining and Miers put it, a rule 'prescribes that in circumstances X, behaviour of type Y ought not to be, or may be, indulged in by persons of class Z'
(Twining and Miers 1991: 131). Rules, as generalisations, connect types of
behaviour by types of actors to types of situations (Schauer 1991). To affirm
that a rule exists is to generalise, to institutionalise behaviour is to affirm the
existence of rules (MacCormick 2007). Between rules and propositional
statements there exists a sort of mutually dependent relation.

Legal rules and facts

What, then, is the relation between general categories and the particular
instances they seek to relate? Obviously, any particular object, action or
event is subsumable under a whole range of separate, though not mutually
exclusive, categories; for example, I am white, married, middle-aged, bespectacled, driver, ex-army officer, dog lover, keen gardener, and so on. However,
not all of these or my other attributes are always necessary in order to offer a
full and relevant description of me in every situation. Only a very limited set
of descriptors will often be all that is required and my choice of action in
any given situation will not depend so much on any of these generalisations
as on the type of situation I find myself in or the discursive context in
which I am described. Indeed, we might go even further and say that I am
not always the same person in all of my different situations in life: there
is not one over-aching community to which I belong and by which I am

adequately or completely described but I belong to a number of different communities and I am a different person in each one of them. Within these situations, I as I am in these situations make my choices, and my possibilities for future choosing are shaped by and depend on the possibilities that I choose to actualise, make concrete, in each present moment of choosing.

This is important. Through my ability in any given situation to generalise in one direction, to choose A and thus to actualise its possibilities, I not only accept the consequences for my future choosing that are given by my choosing A but also, by default, I choose not to actualise other possibilities. Therefore, in this sense, we can say that particular situations or discursive contexts make institutional action possible, for saying that I am a white married male is quite different from saying that I am a bespectacled driver, and the presence of these different particulars will assume greater or lesser significance depending on the context chosen. In some contexts, the fact that I share particular characteristics with other persons will have significant consequences; in a different context, and depending upon the context, they might assume greater, lesser or no significance at all.

Put differently, generalisations as category descriptors are necessarily selective: inclusive as well as exclusive, suppressing as well as revealing. But, what determines which generalisation will constitute a given rule's factual predicate is its purpose: the goal prescribed (or permitted) or the evil pro-scribed by it. What is significant about institutional rules is that while their consequents are forward-looking (meant to be applied to future instances) their factual predicates are backward-looking (in the sense of having been derived from regularities viewed retrospectively) or forward-looking in the limited sense of being based on current assumptions about future behaviour. But there is a difficulty here. While propositional knowledge can provide an explanation retrospectively as to why a social system functions as it does, it cannot prospectively inform actors as to how to apply any given set of rules or how to create new ones.

The reasons for this are famously stated by Hart and developed by others. First, there is the inherent instability of language and representations of meaning. Any illusion of stability is only temporary, and new definitions and new symbolic representations are forever emerging to overtake, overshadow or erode old established ones. Thus, while on the one hand a social system such as law tries to fix its definitions and representations with regard to its purposes, inevitably, at some point, definitional control passes over to the context in which it is set; if we affirm the inherent and ultimate instability of knowledge representations in institutional contexts then we must also acknowledge the same in respect of its functional rules. Second, if it is to be suggested that a rule must always be followed in the same way repeatedly in the future, then what determines this cannot itself be a rule (Taylor 1985: 57). Rules, as guides for social action in open social systems, are fundamen-tally imperfect tools: the definition of a rule cannot itself determine how, on every occasion, it is to be applied, and there is no point in pursuing the argument *ad infinitum* by formulating ever more new rules to determine the use of the first rule, so we can only conclude that the application of rules cannot itself be determined through a rule; that is, it must be rule-less.

To put this more concretely, suppose that law books containing codified rules were issued to all judges. The abstract representations of actual situations imagined behind these codified rules will be only weakly related to the actual situations that later confront the individual judges. The application of rules falls to take place in social contexts the details of which cannot possibly be known in advance and fully to the rule codifiers. Moreover, just because some generalisations are selected does not mean that those that have been suppressed are irrelevant. This will depend on the circumstances within the context. In certain combinations of circumstances they may become central, but the point is that there is no way of knowing beforehand what particular combination or type of combination of circumstances will make a certain feature salient. Only the decision-maker faced with making the decision in respect of the actual circumstances of the case before them will be able to make that decision and make judgement accordingly. So not only is what is going on in an institutional context not static, and indeterminate, but the rules governing situations are bound to be to some extent of limited utility: all sorts of things are going on at the same time that cannot be described in advance, and can only be known at the time from the particular perspective of the observer as an involved participant. There is no escaping the difficulties that arise with new circumstances and even the most informed and imaginative codified system will come up against this problem in the end.

MacCormick argues that if we can identify regularities of behavioural patterns then it should be possible to state these in the form of conditional, 'If, Then' propositional statements, which will be valid under certain stated conditions: 'Whenever *OF* [operative facts], then *NC* [normative consequence]' (MacCormick 2007: 24–25). This accords well with the idea that propositional knowledge is necessarily concerned with generalisations, connecting *types* of behaviour and circumstances and environments. However, the *actual* circumstances of any behaviour are always bound to be in some sense *un*-repeatable, so that the particular decision-making context within which adjudication is made in respect of any such behaviour is always bound to be, in some sense, unique. So how can a judge acquire the necessary knowledge of any particular set of circumstances to link these to rule-like generalisations in order to formulate a decision? Put differently, in judicial decision-making, how do the universal and the particular ever meet?

We might suggest that rule-like generalisations could be subjected to ever more refinement and, in this way, shaped to meet the specific requirements of a particular situation. But this does not solve the problem: even conditional generalisations are *universal within the scope of their applicability* (Schauer 1991: 24). In other words, universal statements, as generalisations – where time and space have effectively been removed – cannot connect with the local knowledge of conditions of time and space.

Thus, following the argument presented by Tsoukas and others in the context of management and organisation studies, I argue that in decision-making, judges do not simply use instrumentally already existing propositional knowledge in the form of explicitly articulated norms, or rules, but they also draw upon the reservoir of their own factual knowledge and upon a collective knowledge of which they may or may not be wholly aware, and create new knowledge. These sources of knowledge are used differently by different judges in different decision-making contexts, and the variety of ways in which such resources can be used to inform decisions can potentially create an almost limitless pool of new knowledge.

My claim here is significantly different from MacCormick's, who suggests that judges construct the rules upon which the justification of their decisions is based on the basis of principles and values underlying legal institutional normative order and are thus not really creating new knowledge or rules but only making explicit what was hitherto implicit in that order and system of rules. Such an attempt to classify institutional knowledge and to continually draw out its implications exemplifies a positivistic view of law, where we find legal analysis in decision-making concerned primarily with the construction and testing of ideas, the introduction of new ways of understanding the system and its environment. On that basis, knowledge is articulated explicitly or implicitly and more or less abstracted from practice. Thus, in MacCormick's model of legal reasoning, explicitly articulated (new) knowledge is created in precisely this sense, by extracting or revealing implicit knowledge through a process of drawing out and testing possibilities (universalisability and consequences) and converting this into concepts (rules) that are justified in terms of the institution's overriding mission or purpose (principle). Those concepts are then made more tangible (legal rule coherence) and disseminated (consistency, non-contradictoriness).

Such a model advances understanding of legal institutional knowledge, helping to demonstrate the interaction of various aspects of legal knowledge, but it also possesses some severe limitations that stem from a tendency to think in 'forms'. The taxonomic urge that produces systems of classification is based on the assumption that it is possible to identify similarities and differences between distinct, independent objects of study, and for this type of thinking to be possible conceptual categories are also assumed to be discrete, separate, and stable, yet they very rarely are (Chia 1998).

Beyond thinking in forms: relating tacit and explicit knowledge

Tacit knowledge and explicit knowledge are not two different types of knowledge but are mutually constituted (Tsoukas 1996: 15). However, while explicit knowledge is always grounded in tacit knowledge, tacit knowledge is not explicit knowledge 'internalised', something rather weakly and precariously held. On the contrary, the tacit dimension is a dimension of all knowledge. Just so, what we call the 'social' is not an aggregate of individuals' experiences but a set of background distinctions undergirding individual action.

Similarly, a judge's decisions are part of a complex practical activity involving both language and procedures. Looking at a judge's decisions over time we can observe how she follows certain rules and procedures and how these rules and procedures do not just lend shape to her decisions but function as normative constraints, criteria against which her decisions are assessed and guided. As a judge, she knows to follow these rules and, because she has been trained to follow them, she possesses certain skills that make it possible for her to engage in such norm-bound activity. This is just another way of saying that she engages in a particular 'discursive practice'. Such practices are what they are by virtue of the background distinctions embodied within them and whose meanings are established through their use in the discourse. Thus, in a courtroom, for example, much of the interaction between counsel and judge would likely be unintelligible and futile unless one had some idea of the meaning of the words, phrases and gestures used and how these have tended to be used within that discourse over time. So not only does a judge possess certain skills that make it possible for her to engage in norm-bound activity, but she also knows how, when and in what relation to use them because there is something in her mind that tells her how, when and in what relation to do so (cf. Jackson). In this sense, a judge is 'primarily a subject of representations ... about the world outside and depictions of ends desired or feared' (Taylor 1993: 49).

But if a thought lies in the mind of a judge telling her how to follow a rule, how is it possible that some rules have been misapplied, or misunderstood? It is unsatisfactory merely to say that a further rule is necessary to determine how the first rule should be applied; it is equally unsatisfactory to suggest that all possible interpretations and misinterpretations of a rule could be shown in advance, for that would mean every judge having an infinite number of thoughts in their head even to follow the simplest of instructions. Rather, the application of rules must be based on some 'unarticulated background of what is taken for granted' (Tsoukas 1996: 16; Taylor 1993: 46). In this way, a judge's understanding finds its roots in the practices in which that judge participates; misunderstandings arise from a lack of or inadequate engagement with a common background. Thus, knowing and understanding how to follow a rule and procedures is implicit in the activity in which a judge engages: it comes with familiarity. We might say that it is the social and professional activity of judging, not the individual thinking judge, which is where the ultimate ground of this understanding lies.

At this point, let us recall Polanyi's notion of how this unarticulated background is related to human understanding. When I have an awareness of something, I have a focal awareness of it; I know it as a whole. But I know something by integrating particulars that are known to me subsidiarily; that is, I tacitly integrate those particulars. In this way, tacit knowledge has a 'from-to' structure. The subsidiaries remain essentially unspecifiable: the moment I gaze at them I lose sight of their meaning.

In discussion of the industrial firm as a distributed knowledge system, Tsoukas (1996) identifies three themes that bear directly on our present argument and may be adapted in relation to judicial decision-making, as follows. First, following Polanyi, all articulated knowledge is based on an unarticulated background, a collection of subsidiary particulars resident in the forms of life or social practices that we participate in and which are tacitly integrated by us as participants in those forms of life or social practices; thus, a judge's decision, her opinion or declaration, is made possible because and only because of the tacitly accepted background that she inhabits. Second, a judge's capacity for rule-following is founded on her own unarticulated background; in other words, the rules that an observer would be able to identify or represent in a practice are different from the rules that actually operate to guide the judge as an agent in that practice. Third, our awareness of this unarticulated background through our having been socialised into a practice by others is 'not only cognitive but embodied' (Taylor 1993: 50); 'the process of learning is constitutive of what is learnt' (Tsoukas 1996: 17). In other words, through socialisation into a practice we internalise a set of background distinctions constitutive of that practice and, through dwelling in these, live both in our own memory and in all of those experiences through which that language has been acquired by us.

Viewed as a social practice, then, several features of legal decision-making are important. First, the normative expectations that are associated with being a judge and held by others above, below, and across legal systems. To enquire about these is to ask questions about how a judge has been socialised into her particular role, both formally and informally. Second, the patterns of recognition, discernment, and adjudication acquired by an individual judge and brought to bear on particular decision-making situations, which Tsoukas calls the 'dispositional' element (Tsoukas 1996: 17). Bourdieu (1990) refers to this as 'the *habitus*', which, as:

> a product of history, produces individual and collective practices – more history – in accordance with the schemes generated by history. It ensures the active presence of past experiences, which, deposited in each organism in the form of schemes of perception, thought and action, tend to guarantee the 'correctness' of practices and their constancy over time, more reliably than all formal rules and explicit norms.
>
> (Bourdieu 1990: 54)

For Bourdieu, the 'active presence of the whole past' ensures for social practices both continuity and 'a relative autonomy with respect to determinations of the immediate present' (Bourdieu 1990: 56). In simple terms, every contact leaves a trace: history leaves its mark on us and every time we act we do so through the habits of thinking acquired through past socialisation: our habits of thinking are formed 'through our participation into historically constituted practices' (Tsoukas 1996: 18). To find out why a judge decides in a certain way we really need also to ask about the past socialisations to which she was subjected to in and through her involvement in a number of social practices (family, school, religion, and so on); in other words, her *habitus*. Finally, to complete our investigation into how and why the judge decides as she does, we will also need to ask about the particular context within which the normative expectations and the *habitus* are triggered, the active unfolding of her concrete interactions with others within a specific socio-temporal context (Tsoukas 1996: 18).

Looking at a judge's behaviour in decision-making as a whole we will observe regularities: actions and patterns of actions in decision-making will be repeated. The normative expectations associated with being a judge, together with her past socialisations, will have developed ways of thinking and deciding that are triggered every time she engages in decision-making. In which case, we might be tempted to develop rules about her behaviour and to conclude that these rules completely describe, or represent, her practice. But these rules will be created from the point of view of a spectator and there is always something more to an actual practice than can be conveyed by any representation of it, a persistent asymmetry between 'rules-as-represented' and 'rules-as-guides-in-practice' (Taylor 1993: 55–57).

Of course, our spectator might well be able to infer the existence of certain rules and procedures (doctrines of *ratio decidendi*, *stare decisis*, precedent, and so on) that inform a judge's decision-making from studying that judge's decisions, but there will also be much else that a judge does that will not be adequately represented by these. Ostensibly, she is a member of an independent judiciary but she will, nonetheless, also be conscious of a wider, more complex network of human social and political relationships that will be just as important to her and bear directly on her ability to do her job efficiently and well. There is, indeed, something about a judge's role that cannot be captured simply with rules, however regular and patterned it might appear. To assume otherwise would presuppose that we had the ability to foresee all future occasions of decision-making and were endowed with a language through which to faithfully reflect it unequivocally. But we do not know all the answers to all the future questions, much less do we know beforehand what questions will later be asked.

So, in decision-making, judges make use of the explicit rules provided for them by the law as enacted, but the actual activity of decision-making takes place in a social context the actual details of which cannot be known beforehand. Consequently, in striving towards a decision, a judge needs to attend not only to those strict and rigid aspects of the law as laid down, or what Bańkowski calls its machine-like quality, but also to the human social and political context within which her decision-making is set, the wider effects of applying a particular rule here-and-now; for example, the impact of that law on the life of the accused. At the same time, she will be acutely aware of the need to create and maintain public trust in the law and the legal system and also of the need to maintain her own reputation in the community of judges. In any given situation any number of concerns might appear as relevant and important but there is no way that she can say in advance which or when.

We can see then, how, in spite of the normative expectations and social dispositions associated with being a judge, a mix of consistency and diversity will still be found across decision-making: different judges will negotiate the tensions between role expectations, dispositional attitudes or *habitus*, and the actual situations where these interface with each other, in different ways. Through explicit rules formally associated with being a member of the judiciary, together with training and socialisation, the law seeks to define the normative expectations of an individual judge's role and homogenise decision-making, but these normative expectations are rarely if ever identical to an individual judge's habitus, since each judge's dispositional attitudes or *habitus* is the result of past socialisations that are different for each judge. So, when normative expectations and dispositional attitudes are triggered, and interface with each other within actual decision-making situations, how this happens will always be unrepeatable, unique. A judge will always be confronted with specific choices under specific conditions and the way that those conditions are made relevant will always be distinctive to each specific context and situation. She will select out what she considers to be relevant in relation to her role-related expectations and relevant in relation to the local context or conditions and fuse the two together, which is precisely what she does when she attempts to identify the *ratio* of a previous decision and use it, or not, in the present case. In this way, every moment of her decision-making contains within it the essence of the past, the whole of its social structure, but how that structure is instantiated in the present unique moment of deciding is always a local matter. This is what Whitehead understood so well: the many become one and are increased by one.

In light of all of this, we might be tempted to conclude that decision-making must become an impossible task: concrete situations are infinitely concrete, particular situations are infinitely particular, relevant features are infinitely relevant, and there is no limit to the ways that a social practice can be described from an infinite number of viewpoints and perspectives. The reason that this does not paralyse us is precisely because the legal institutional context within which these are articulated acts as a halt on this, imposing limits on how each of these may be described. However, merely because some descriptions are selected and others are not does not mean that those others are not also present or that they may not be relevant in other sets of circumstances: I may choose to select as relevant in the present circumstances features that I will disregard in a future circumstance depending on my purpose in any given case; equally, I may choose to disregard now features that in another instance and under different conditions I will later consider to be relevant. The point is that I cannot know in advance what those relevant descriptions are going to be: both my characterisation and my reasons for decision are inseparable from the occasion of my deciding.

We can pull much of this together by considering, for example, the role of *ratio decidendi* in relation to the Common Law doctrine of precedent. Here, courts draw upon a shared pattern of decisions in relation to particular types of situations and the system of precedent is closely tied to the legal situation in which it is generated to enable judges to make sense of their particular environment. In other words, it arises because of the judges' need to communicate by word and act and because of the uncertainties of the institutional set-up in which that communication is to take place. Thus, a system of precedent is essentially a discourse developed over time within a particular judicial context, and consists of a set of background distinctions tied to a particular field of law. Those distinctions relate to a number of characterisations and issues that a judge must comprehend if she is to be able to deliver a justified decision and, through a process of socialisation, a judge internalises those law-specific distinctions. But judges are also presented with an almost infinite number of meanings unrelated to their legal-specific roles but which they must nonetheless familiarise themselves with if their roles are to be efficiently pursued. Internalising these distinctions is not simply a matter of learning by rote or of gaining knowledge from law books but is learned within the context of the discursive practice. Legal expertise in this sense is gleaned from and embedded within legal conversation, interaction and institutional procedures; that is, it forms an unarticulated background that underlies and undergirds a judge's representation of their decisions and operates to allow the justification of decisions, a form of tacit knowledge that permits a judge to construct within an otherwise *dis*-ordered array of conflicting or unrelated circumstances some sort of institutional ordering. It is the judge's *habitus*, the set of dispositions acquired over time which ensures within the present the active presence of past experience. But a system of precedent offers decision-makers more than just a language; it also provides structure, syntax. The core of a system of precedent is much more than can be represented by the sum of its parts. It concerns not just the accumulation of individual decisions but also the way that these cohere within a rational structure and, in this sense, such a system can never be wholly rigid; indeed, it must guide as much as direct in order to allow for a finely balanced shifting of emphases and meanings as necessary.

Precisely because of the unique character of every new decision-making situation every judge will inevitably have to improvise. Those uniquely different circumstances may prevent a judge deciding in the way that the system of precedent implies, and a case may have to be 'distinguished'. It is in this way that a judge is called upon to close the 'phronetic gap', to cross the 'particularity void': through a personal judgement about the relevance of a ratio to her present decision. This tension between the legal-specific *habitus* and the particular local circumstances of decision-making explains why a judge's decision is not always, or ever, either a simple replication of previous decisions or an altogether completely new invention by the judge. It is created by a judge out of the tensions experienced by *that* judge with *those* resources in *this* particular situation.

However, it is important to note that what is being suggested here is not that a judge's *habitus* is tied solely to the legal system but it also includes the whole of her entire history of past socialisations and the tensions that these may produce; for instance, the personal private experiences of a judge or the tensions between normative role expectations and dispositions acquired through extra-legal socialisations. An example would be Lord Atkin and his presentation of the 'neighbour' principle in *Donoghue v. Stevenson*. To understand this fully would also require some understanding of Lord Atkin's religious disposition, his historically formed *habitus*. The neighbour principle is the outcome of a correspondence of appropriatenesses (cf. Günther (1993)). It is a contingent outcome of decision-making in a specific situation with a particular set of circumstances.

Conclusion

In this chapter I have utilised the analysis employed by Tsoukas in the field of organisation studies to note how the different types of institutional knowledge that exist in law may be seen, similarly, to be founded on different features of the legal institutional context. While the propositional structure of legal knowledge is fully realised within formal legal contexts in terms of law as institutions, these formal legal contexts are also practices, shared traditions in and out of which legal practitioners live and work, and, in this latter sense, legal knowledge has a narrative structure that is maintained by story, anecdote and example. In this way it has been possible to extend that analysis to demonstrate: (a) the resources that a judge uses in decision-making are, to a large extent, constructed by that judge in the process of decision-making (Levi 1948). How they can be used depends on how they are viewed, which, in turn, is a function of the knowledge applied to them. In this sense, we can see how law functions as a system in which the bearer of legal institutional knowledge is law's customs, habits and practices. (b) As institutional actors, judges make use of a knowledge that is not and cannot be known completely and entirely by any single judge. (c) Legal institutional knowledge is itself inherently indeterminate: not only can the factual knowledge of particular circumstances of time and place not be envisaged as a whole, but no one can know in advance what legal institutional knowledge is or can be. In this sense, judges cannot know what they need to know. (d) Legal knowledge is dispersed in another sense, too, in that it is partly derived from the wider context in which a judge is set and is continually reconstituted (the classification changes as the classification is made) through its decisions. Therefore, it is not and cannot be self-sufficient. This is because of the nature and structure of social practices within law, which are made up of the following: role-related normative expectations, dispositions acquired by past socialisations, and the local circumstances in which a decision is made. While law has some control over normative expectations, with procedures constraining judicial discretion ensuring a degree of consistency across decision-making contexts, it has no control over the dispositions acquired through past socialisations in extra-legal settings. Moreover, these role-related normative expectations and dispositions of judges are instantiated within particular contexts the character of which may not be known in advance in any detached way but is fashioned only in and through a particular judge's encounter with them. In this sense, not possessed by any single judge, partly dependent on or originating within extra legal contexts and always incomplete, law's knowledge is forever continually evolving. (e) There is an inevitable tension between role-related normative expectations, dispositions acquired through past socialisations, and contexts of decision. This results in a persistence of shortfalls, deficits, or gaps between them: between universalist and particularist practices; between formal and substantive rationality; between the ideal and the actual; between 'rules-as-represented' and 'rules-as-guides-in-practice'; between 'the model of reality' and 'the reality of the model' (Bourdieu 1990: 39). Such aporias, gaps, or voids are closed only through judges exercising their discretion in judgement, selectively including and excluding different features of each of these three characteristic elements of social practices and attempting to link them together. It must also follow, therefore, that how these elements are linked together in decision-making is always contingent and evolving, vague and indeterminate: judges will inevitably differ. However, understood in this way, what requires explanation is not divergence of opinion in decision-making but the processes and procedures that ensure similarity or conformity and the progressive development of consistent and coherent judicial action; in other words, how the tensions are negotiated and brought under control by the system. (f) Understanding law as a dispersed knowledge system in this sense helps us to understand what legal institutions are and, consequently, what legal decision-making is about. Subject to constant change, law as an institution is inherently creative. Its institutional agents, the judges, adhere to a practice of rule-following that is contingent and context-related or situational. Thus, throughout, both rule-following and novel adventure, continuity and change, uniformity and creativity, are always present. In this way the practice of law becomes a never-ending process of harmonising purposeful decision-makers whose particular decisions stem from their own application of their (at least partly) distinctive interpretations to the situations confronting them. Those decisions can often presage unanticipated consequences and precipitate paradoxical interpretations that are further interpreted, and so on. In this way, given the dispersed nature of legal institutional knowledge, co-ordinated decision-making depends not on the accumulation of knowledge within the higher echelons of the legal institutional structure, but on ordinary decision-makers forever inventing new ways of tapping into and sharing each other's knowledge. To acknowledge this is to recognise the importance of maintaining law as a discursive practice, a common form of life in which individual judges as decision-makers share an unarticulated background of shared understandings.

Chapter 9

The judge as institutional actor and decision-maker

Stanley Fish argues that contemporary thinking about law, as with thinking across all disciplines, has fallen victim to what he calls 'theory–hope'. In the end, all 'the troubles and benefits of interpretive theory ... disappear in the solvent of an enriched notion of practice' (Fish 1989: ix). According to Fish, all that theory can ever hope to do is offer an after-the-fact explanation of already firmly held beliefs which function to allow and confirm within an 'interpretive community' those convictions which its rhetoric asserts. The reason that we are able to interpret a text is because we belong to an interpretive community which supplies us with a particular way of interpreting it. Moreover, because we can never escape our communities our readings of a text are always in this sense culturally constructed. So we can never know of each other whether we belong to the same interpretive community, for that would require that each act of communication itself be interpreted. Thus, what is important is how an utterance affects a hearer, not any question about locating the meaning that is assumed to reside within it. In this way, arguments appear intelligible and convincing.

Fish's response to Ronald Dworkin's rendering of the process of constitutional interpretation, the judicial use of precedent, demands mention here. According to Dworkin (1986), the interpretation of the constitution, and therefore the role of precedent in judicial decision-making, can be likened to the production of a serial or chain novel, in which judges take turns consecutively to add one chapter upon another. With the steady accumulation of chapters each subsequent writer's freedom and choice in interpretation becomes increasingly constrained: the author of the last chapter is more constrained in relation to that task than her fellow authors, since she has to contribute her chapter under the accumulated burden of their chapters; the first author is unconstrained.

For Fish, however, this understanding of what is going on is erroneous. A reader's approach to a text can never be completely subjective. On the contrary, an internalised understanding of language shared by native speakers generates normative constraints in respect of their experience with language. In this way, Fish's argument questions Dworkin's understanding of the role and function of a doctrine of precedent. Indeed, for Fish, since all our attempts to gain access to the meaning of a text stumble on the fact that our interpretation is based upon the interpretive community of which we are a part, then a system of precedent cannot truly constrain judges; rather, constraints in judicial decision-making must arise out of the process of judging itself. Moreover, since all judges appear equally constrained, we are left with the question of whether, at any point in this process, there is really any text as such that awaits interpretation.

According to Balter (2001: 384), 'Fish's theory of interpretive communities provides valuable insight into the norms of the legal community' and how the legal interpretive community 'legitimizes a way of thinking about the law that is inculcated into its practitioners at each level of participation from law school through judgeship. Central to this socialization is the judicial opinion ... studied by law students, read by lawyers, and written in respect to other opinions by judges'. In this manner, a judge 'begin[s] the discourse with a particular case' and 'past cases are read in relation to the present circumstances'. While the legal community 'expects that the present case will be understood in relation to the past, ... the present case also moulds the past'. That is to say, a writer is free to manipulate a text on which her opinion is based, provided this manipulation can be justified within the bounds of the expectations of her interpretive community:

> Interpreters are constrained by their tacit awareness of what is possible and not possible to do, what is and is not a reasonable thing to say, what will and will not be heard as evidence in a given enterprise; and it is within these same constraints that they see and bring others to see the shape of the documents to whose interpretation they are committed.
>
> (Fish 1989: 98)

Tacit knowledge and socialisation: understanding interpretation

As we have characterised it, modern accounts of legal decision-making proceed on the basis of an assumption that a judge will look at an ordered sequence of events, produce a context-based arrangement of these showing the relations between them and make a judgement as to their significance in respect of that context or theory. In this judgement process, what appears as straightforwardly presented to the senses is subjected to our craving to *re*-order, *re*-arrange and *re*-design, to create new perspectives on knowledge and new knowledge. However, this attempt to see things differently and to disclose hidden meanings always takes place from within a particular standpoint or tradition. We draw distinctions against shared backgrounds, 'forms of life', 'practices' or 'horizons of meaning', where certain evaluative criteria are found to control, and we do so by bringing to the fore the parts we are interested in and ascribing significance to them. Training and practice allow us to produce ever more delicately balanced and nuanced distinctions and judgements until, over time, we acquire an ability to make judgements on the basis of very finely tuned accents and emphases. Polanyi makes this point when he describes the training of a medical student:

> He watches in a darkened room shadowy traces on a fluorescent screen placed against a patient's chest, and hears the radiologist commenting to his assistants, in technical language, on the significant features of these shadows ... [H]e can see nothing that they are talking about. Then as he goes on listening for a few weeks, looking carefully at ever new pictures ... a tentative understanding ... dawn[s] on him ... [E]ventually, if he perseveres intelligently, a rich panorama of significant details will be revealed to him ... He still sees only a fraction of what the experts can see, but the pictures are definitely making sense now and so do most of the comments made on them.
>
> (Polanyi 1962: 101)

This understanding is the result both of personal exposure to the material and of the specialised terminology that the student is taught to apply to it. What appears initially to preconceptual experience as a mere shadow is gradually processed through successive stages of revision and refinement, as the student relates his knowledge to the picture and to the words of his instructor. In this way, he progressively *re*arranges, *re*orders and *re*designs his descriptions, and his descriptions of descriptions, recursively modifying and transforming every successive representation. Over time, newer distinctions are created and, as a result, so too is new knowledge.

We have found that a similar thing takes place in the legal context. For any judge to be able to discern a legally significant pattern of events from a collection of data, she must draw upon a collectively produced and sustained body of legal knowledge. This is because the significant categories implicated in her individual action as a judge derive their meanings from the ways in which they have been used within that particular form of life that we refer to as the legal community. For example, as a student of the law she learns how to recognise certain features of the law of contract because she is taught to use the category contract within a certain domain of action. Knowing how to act and judge according to law is assumed to be precisely this: learning how to make proficient use of the categories and distinctions that constitute the domain of law. In other words, judges, as students of the law, learn first of all, upon entering the legal sphere, to assimilate the distinctions appropriate to law; that is, they engage in a discursive practice and learn how to use its normative system to influence a course of events.

This capacity to exercise judgement derives from an understanding of context, and of having become knowledgeable in respect of the significance of certain acts within particular contexts, achieved as a result of having undergone a process of socialisation: we know how to recognise and do certain things because we have learned how to recognise and to do them. We have an awareness of the normative expectations relevant to them and an intuition of the consequences that follow from breaking these. We might say that our ability to exercise judgement comes in large part with our appreciation of theory, our ability to generalise a finding across contexts (cf. Bergson 1913). This application of a set of generalising principles across contexts involves judgement, and the capacity to do this is knowledge. So, when a judge applies a set of legal principles to a particular factual situation, she uses theory to generalise across contexts, which then becomes an additional basis for exercising judgement.

Judges apply rules in specific decision-making contexts. However, there is nothing within a rule itself that can fix its application in a particular case: 'there is no "fact of the matter" concerning the proper application of a rule, ... what a rule is actually taken to imply is a matter to be decided, by contingent social processes' (Barnes 1995: 202).

Similar to Levi, Barnes argues that to follow a rule is to extend an example:

> To understand rule-following or norm-guided behaviour in this way immediately highlights the normally open-ended character of norms, the fact that they cannot themselves fix and determine what actions are in true conformity with them, that there is no logical compulsion to follow them in a particular way. Every instance of a norm may be analogous to every other, but analogy is not identity: analogy exists between things that are similar yet different. And this means that, although it is always possible to assimilate the next instance to a norm by analogy with existing examples of the norm, it is equally always possible to resist such assimilation, to hold the analogy insufficiently strong, to stress the differences between the instance and existing examples. If norms apply by analogy then it is up to *us* to decide where they apply, where the analogy is sufficiently strong and where not.
>
> (Barnes 1995: 55)

In this way, the application of a rule derives essentially from and contributes to a collectively shared meaning. But for this to occur, members of an institution 'must be constituted as a collective able to sustain a shared sense of what rules imply and hence an agreement in their practice when they follow rules' (Barnes 1995: 204); in other words, the justification or purpose beneath a rule needs to be made clear and its meaning integrated within the institutional collective. Law exists as an institution as a tightly related network of communications in and through which shared understandings are attained.

On this view, it is institutional knowledge as the *collected and collective* wisdom or knowledge of the judges as a whole that enables each individual judge to put the sources of law to their respective uses and to develop and employ their own distinctive ways of thinking and acting.

This is, of course, very similar to Polanyi's idea of personal knowledge since, no matter how abstract the formalistic notions that judges use are, their effective use depends ultimately on social definitions. For Polanyi, all abstract systems involve an essential element of human experience, an encounter with the real world mediated through human judgement. In other words, if we affirm some degree of 'personal participation as the universal principle of knowing' (Polanyi 1962: 44) then all knowledge becomes, in one way or another, an art, a skilful achievement. Inasmuch as judicial decisions, like abstract mathematical formalisms, require formal justification by the comparison of predictions with measurements there will be gaps between theory and observation that require to be assessed by the personal judgement of the judge (cf. Polanyi and Prosch 1975: 30).

How should we understand this art or skill? As we have seen, to gain knowledge of something is, according to Polanyi, to integrate a set of particulars of which one is subsidiarily aware. So, to make sense of something, we depend on some aspects of it subsidiarily and concentrate on our main aim focally; that is, we tacitly integrate certain particulars in order to comprehend something focally as a whole. In this way, knowing has a 'from-to' structure: the particulars bear on the focus *to* which we attend *from* them. Nonetheless, subsidiary awareness and focal awareness are mutually exclusive, so that if we shift our focal attention towards the particulars that we had previously been aware of only subsidiarily then our acting becomes confused.

We may recall that there are three elements present here – subsidiary particulars, a focal target, and a linking agent (Polanyi and Prosch 1975: 36) – and, because 'the relation of a subsidiary to a focus is formed by the *act of a person who integrates one to another*' (Polanyi and Prosch 1975: 38), then practical knowledge is always 'personal knowledge', a knowledge that has to be applied as a tool (Polanyi 1962: 59). As we become more familiar with the use of such a tool so our awareness and understanding of how to use it instrumentally increases and we begin gradually to feel it as an extension of our own body. Through this process of assimilating the tool, 'indwelling', we begin to make sense of our experience and, as we become more *un*-aware of using our tools, so our awareness of the uses to which they may be put increases and we develop and refine our ability and skill to use them instrumentally. This refinement in the purposeful use of our skills and abilities provides a form of 'justification', which enables us to develop further our understanding of the situation before us. Thus, we can see how, in this way, a judge might properly develop the ability to 'read' a situation before her, 'pouring [herself] into the subsidiary awareness of particulars' (Polanyi 1962: 64).

We might say, then, that the particular type of knowledge that a judge possesses could be described as the capability to draw distinctions within a certain area of operations based on her grasp of context and theory. In decision-making we are concerned with three things: the concrete settings within which decision-making occurs (the facts); the normative background against which decision-making takes place (the rules); the historical continuity of the community of decision-makers (the judge(s)). Legal institutional knowledge is the capability that individual judges have developed as members collectively of the judiciary to draw distinctions in the process of decision-making in respect of particular concrete situations through the use of generalisations whose application is tied to shared understandings and experiences previously acquired and developed within and by the professional community of decision-makers to which they belong. As propositional statements and shared communal understandings are used, and experiences processed both individually and collectively in a reflexive manner, so they are pushed into subsidiary awareness. Individual judges, as members of this community, dwelling increasingly within these shared understandings are enabled to turn their attention towards new experiences that arise within their own particular area of expertise.

In particular, we can see how opinions expressed *obiter*, remarks and ideas shared in extralegal contexts, together with the provision of more formal justifying reasons for decisions all come together to create an environment in which communal professional judicial ties are strengthened, collective memory improved and individual knowledge augmented. Within this environment, individual judges draw upon the wealth of each other's accumulated experience and knowledge of decision-making, consulting with each other on professional judicial decision-making matters and also communicating less formally and naturally with one another, creating a culture and an environment of storytelling that reflects and reinforces communication. In this way, a shared background, individual learning and storytelling are all linked together in decision-making.

Judges draw upon a generally accepted body of law provided in the form of statutory texts, printed decisions, rules of evidence, court procedures, and so on, much of which is codified in one way or another, officially or unofficially. So if, for example, a defendant in criminal proceedings pleads guilty in relation to a particular offence she will often receive a standard sentence, which suggests that lesser crimes are capable of being handled lower down the judicial ladder (at these lower levels, often the most difficult question requiring the answer is how quickly this workload can be shifted). Here, justices and magistrates may be expected to draw on all the resources available to them, whether printed in official documents or taken from their own life's experience, to find the answers to nearly all of the questions likely to be posed. In diverse ways they are encouraged and expected to draw upon each other's experiences and upon their own knowledge of the judicial process and decision-making. Here, an environment of story telling strengthens the bonds between decision-makers and reinforces community ties and the collected and collective memory, thereby enriching and enhancing individual knowledge.

Nevertheless, not all of the questions or legal issues presented in cases before a court are straightforward and unambiguous. Where ambiguity occurs, judges need to be proficient at articulating the facts before them to clarify the precise nature of the legal questions being addressed and requiring answer. For example, is a skateboard a vehicle under the terms of a regulation prohibiting vehicles in the park? Most experienced judges would be aware of the reasons for the regulation and how these relate to its proper functioning in society and, through proper questioning, would be able to ascertain the extent of the uncertainty that required to be addressed. A judge's ability to discern the nub of the problem in this way, to determine the crux of the legal issue by making ever finer distinctions, is a skill that is acquired, developed and refined through training and experience in the practice of legal decision-making. In other words, through experience and through participation in a 'community of practice', a judge develops a 'sense' of what is going on, and of what is at stake, which is properly a legal skill that over time becomes instrumentalised. It is something that allows her to reflect on things as they are going on, a skilful intuition that she can develop and use as 'an extension' of her and which permits her to focus on the issue at hand.

Over time, judges develop a greater degree of sophistication in relation to these perceptual capabilities and the structure of authority and responsibility that we find in the judiciary develops. They learn how to recognise how certain concrete facts bring to light certain legal issues and how then to think in appropriate terms and categories. In this way, more experienced judges will often become admired for their ability to discern instrumentally nuances of difference, to draw ever more refined distinctions and decide on the basis of these: even their *obiter* remarks are referred to as if authoritative and quoted as such. Recognising nuances and being able to come to a decision quickly on the basis of these becomes an important part of a judge's skill. As part of the 'tacit' dimension of a judge's knowledge, it goes a long way to account for why a judge decides a certain issue in a particular way. It is, in a proper sense, 'intuitive', insightful'. It is, in fact, what accounts for the moment of decision in which a judge decides and is one reason why her decision must then be justified by way of providing justifying reasons for her decision. But, as part of the 'tacit dimension' of a judge's decision-making, it reflects a knowledge that cannot be told; hence, Lord Justice Ward's confession in his introductory remarks in *Re A* that he found it 'exceptionally difficult' and 'especially arduous', struggling to his description of the case as 'very unique'.

What we are dealing with here is knowledge that is difficult to put into words, let alone into the form of propositional statements. Of course, Lord Justice Ward does make use of a form of words and a recognised structure of argument, and he draws on the sources of law to justify his decision, but does so in a manner that makes it clear that it is his own personal professional judgement that is being exercised to identify the problem, however much that judgement has been moulded by the prevalent legal culture. All of this reflects the fact that in law we are just as much concerned with the act of decision-making as with the decision-maker and the decision itself; that is, it is *this* decision-maker who is *here* making *that* decision in respect of *these* persons, events and circumstances in *this* case that is of significance, not just the bald decision itself.

One important aspect of the doctrine of precedent that is of relevance here is the way in which the course of legal decision-making goes on regardless of the choice of decision. This is not simply because it flows on like a river forever coursing along the path of least resistance but because each new case presents a new and unrepeatable opportunity for decision-making with its own unique set of possibilities that might be actualised. Each decision is, to a degree, influenced or constrained by what has gone before and is now received as data, but there is freedom to choose not determinism; indeed, judges are drawing on a whole variety of different sources of data and information provided for them in written and oral form. Such data are offered as separate items of fact and information. What we see in decision-making is the transformation of these data and information into legal knowledge by the judges: its conversion and presentation into propositional 'If, then' statements.

To create 'If, then' statements, judges must take into account the particular context of the instant case and make a judgement under pressure of time as to what the proper outcome of the case must be. In doing this, they are not mindlessly applying general rules to particular facts but making an appropriate judgement as to how the body of rules must be adapted to include the circumstances at hand, however obvious that might sometimes appear to be. All of which is really just another way of saying that a norm requires a decision to claim its instances or that, to put it in Whitehead's terms, 'the many become one and are increased by one'. Thus, formal rules, as data in this encounter of experience, demand the exercise of human judgement to create new experience that is subsequently drawn upon and appealed to in later moments. If we accept Polanyi's claim here that all knowledge is personal, then, as far as institutional knowledge is concerned, there is *always* a question of appropriateness involved in the harnessing of knowledge for decision (cf. Günther 1993). This is precisely what distinguishes knowledge from information in legal decision-making: the former necessitates an active rearrangement of the latter on the basis of context or theory.

Consider this example: a judge hears a case knowing through experience that cases of a certain type with facts of a certain order present legal issues that fall to be determined in a particular way. But the same judge knows from her own experience of previous cases, and to some extent also from the collected and collective experience of the community of decision-makers to which she belongs, that there are difficulties that are often experienced by parties to such cases that are not apparent from a simple reading of the facts that fall for legal determination under the rules as prescribed. There may also be problems in relating the appropriate legal rules to those facts that could not have been envisaged by those responsible for making previous decisions, far less by those who constructed the relevant statutory authority. To decide in the obvious way would clearly be to create an injustice, and the judge knows this. But how does the judge know this? If we follow Christodoulidis' argument then we must acknowledge that 'the incalculability of justice is a result of the elision that every exercise of judgement enacts, of what finds no adequate register in judgement' (Christodoulidis 2004: 194). However, this 'knowledge' is not to be found in or derived from official written legal sources; on the contrary, it is knowledge derived from the judge's personal experience of encountering particular types of problems and, having worked those out, heeding their lessons. It is part of the development of her skill of understanding how to recognise and utilise appropriate responses in making decisions.

All of this implies that judges may have to improvise to meet the demands of decision-making under pressure of time and lack of resources and the expectations of their public and political audiences. In doing so, they may often have to use cases selectively to 'construct' the legal authority for the decisions they are making (cf. Levi 1948). In this sense, the 'sources of law' being appealed to as authority are not the formal, officially recognised sources of law but are more correctly described as informal, since in a very real sense law is being constructed 'on the hoof'. The type of knowledge involved here is a form of knowledge that is generated in the process of decision-making, fuelling decision-making and carrying it under its own momentum, rather than some pre-existent body of knowledge that forms a basis for decision-making and from which decision-making proceeds.

To press this point further, legal knowledge in this sense is not merely something that is to be found in the formal written sources of law but is rather something that continually evolves in the minds of individual judges and through the stories that they tell and share and which sustain their community of practice. Of course, such knowledge is often eventually given symbolic representation as institutional knowledge, cast in a relevant form through its structured use in decision-making, and presented as propositional knowledge. Nonetheless, while all of this happens, and quite properly so, it is equally clear that what this points towards is the fact that abstract generalisations, however necessary, are not and cannot in themselves be sufficient to capture the complexity of institutional knowledge in its entirety. In legal decision-making, *some creative element always accompanies every decision.*

What makes knowledge institutional is its codification in the form of propositional statements. However, institutional knowledge is always put into action in particular concrete situations and contexts. Therefore, the possibilities for individual judgement to be exercised and for novel adventure to emerge and be entertained are always open. That is to say, the world is not a closed system. It permits of new experiences and more advanced forms of learning and progression, and this gives knowledge its forever temporary and always provisional, ready-but-not-ready character. In this way, every application of general rules to particular facts, events or circumstances involves the instant case particularities in the constitution of its general principle in the sense of it being applicable to an instance that never before existed: the rule is supplemented, increased, by those instant case particularities and also in a very real sense determined by it. Levi understands this when he says that the classification changes as the classification is made; Gadamer makes the same point, maintaining that a general principle is 'always supplemented by the individual case, even productively determined by it' (Gadamer 1989: 38) so that each 'application is neither a subsequent nor merely an occasional part of the phenomenon of understanding, but codetermines it as a whole from the beginning' (Gadamer 1989: 324). This suggests that what is at stake is not really the application of general rules to particular facts, but that we understand generalisations only as and when we connect these generalisations to the particular concrete circumstances of the cases under consideration. We know and understand the general rule in and through the act of connecting it, relating it, to the present particulars. Thus, every act of applying a general rule to particular facts is a creative act, an act of creative interpretation in decision-making.

What is more, a condition for any judge to undertake decision-making is that she belongs as a bona fide member of the relevant legal institution. This professional organisation has its own intricate conceptual structure and theoretical framework of understanding, comprising generic categories and their interrelations, something that every judge must keep in mind when engaging in decision-making. But even this does not deny the fact that each act of decision-making is a personal, interpretive, expositional and creative act; indeed, it helps to underline it. In characterising or categorising a situation before her in a particular way, a judge already begins to explore the question of suitable responses: she decides to characterise it this way rather than that way because she 'feels' it to be of a certain *type*. Of course the situation may be a new one and in some sense it is always bound to be. However, it might strike her as new not just in the sense in which all situations are new but also in the significant sense that it does not quite exhibit those characteristic features that would suggest its 'fit' with previous instances of a similar type. Here, in starting to characterise the situation before her in a certain way she is already making a difference both to the category to which she refers and also, at the same time, to this new instant situation by the very fact of viewing it through, framing it with and imposing upon it, this template. Quite often (and quite likely) she may be wrong: her initial judgement is but a tentative 'shout', a well-educated guess. It is merely a hypothesis by which she attempts to extend an already formed analogy or theory to include this instance as an example. All she can do is test her hypothesis by considering the consequences. What results? She needs to consider these. Perhaps she must revise her hypothesis and test again, and so on. All of this abstract categorising and re-categorising, first this way and then that way, is a necessary part of her search for a decision and its formal legal 'justification'. In the end, her universalising may fail to find a 'match': the particularities of the present case may evade capture by her categories if only just because they are abstract categories. The question is: can she close the difference? Yes, of course, she will. This is what she is trained to do, personally skilled to do. It is *she* who *must* close the difference; indeed, it is *only* she, or another such as she who *can* close the difference.

Now what all of this points to, is the fact that we need to revise our understanding of what is going on here: somehow the idea of an unreflective institutional practice of applying general rules to particular cases must be transformed into a reflective one (cf. Günther 1993). The skill of legal decision-making needs to be augmented by an understanding of what judges are doing when they practise that skill. If legal judgement is, as surely it is, a form of practical judgement then this is entailed in affirming that. Legal decision-making must not be thought of as simply an unreflective practice, for it involves judges determining, often with great difficulty, how to observe the rules of their practice and the practice of their rules (the abstract rules of law and the historically formed, collected and collective, understandings of the community of which they are a part and to which they belong). Bańkowski alludes somewhat to this when he talks critically of the person who says 'I know nothing about art but I know what I like' (Bańkowski 2001: 165). If such a person was asked to explain what they meant by the statement that they knew what they liked, they would have to resort to, for example, indicating what it was about a particular painting that they liked. In doing this they would have to state it in terms appropriate to the art work, which would in fact show that they knew something about art after all. Their liking of a piece of art would show that they liked it but they could not know this unless they were able in some way to articulate it; that is; unless they knew something about art. So judges do not simply apply rules to facts, they also have to think about what they are thinking about and about how they are thinking about it. It is not enough just to make a decision, it must also be justified. It is just not acceptable for a judge to say 'I can't tell you why this is the right decision, but I know that it is'; equally, the idea that a judge could become a judge having mastered *unreflectively* the practice of judging. The practice of judging as involving the production of justifying reasons for decisions entails that the deciding should be able to be carried over, understood and employed by other judges: finding the *ratio*, articulating and elucidating the reasons for a decision, amounts to an engagement with and not blind observance of the rules and principles of law. All of this relates to what we have argued about communal understandings, practices, habitus, and so on, and it is primarily about turning an unreflective practice into a reflective one.

Today, technological advances and mass communication make possible ever more refined forms of abstraction that demand ever more sophisticated forms of codification of general rules for efficient and effective decision-making. In this ever-changing environment, our institutional abstractions must be able to help us navigate and negotiate the difficult pathways of life's experience. Yet this is only one side of legal decision-making. The other side, which I have been arguing for here, is that of the importance of *creative personal understanding*, a method of decision-making obtained and employed by judges using the exploration of possibilities rather than by following set rules: heuristic knowledge. MacCormick is forever pointing towards this but always stops short of openly acknowledging it; more so, Günther and Habermas; Detmold thinks of it as mystical; Bańkowski and, in a different way, Jackson, actively seek a way of articulating it; Christodoulidis argues that it belongs to the realm of ethics and denies its possibility in law. It is a sense in which judges depend on much more than a structure of general rules, principles and procedures of law, but engage their own personal experiences, skills, outlooks and understandings as well. It is precisely because of this that law as an institution in a sociological sense must endeavour to encourage, promote and sustain a sense of communal understanding, its collected and collective spirit, to harness the provisional and improvisational inventiveness, expertise and creative imaginations of individual judges within an overarching and undergirding sense of corporate, communal, membership and responsibility. Here, the effective development of legal institutional decision-making requires that the relation between personal creative knowledge and propositional knowledge be mutually supporting and sustaining: propositional knowledge is utilised by judges and instrumentalised in appropriate application within particular cases, thereby achieving representation as tacit; individually held and exercised creative knowledge must also be set forth in a way that can make it (institutionally) accessible to a wider audience. Therefore, developing legal institutional knowledge is not simply about the proper ways of handling or manipulating difficult 'pieces' of information, but also, and perhaps more importantly, about the nourishment and fortification of the social practices that make this possible.

Chapter 10

Legal contexts as practices

One widely accepted understanding of the institutional control of law is in terms of its capacity to stabilise and maintain relationships and expectations over time. In this sense, almost paradoxically, it is the dynamic nature of law as a social institution that is being highlighted. On the one hand, as a result of its application over time, and given the unpredictable nature of contingent social life, law is forever being confronted with new problems and new situations that it must constantly respond to. On the other hand, this dynamic nature of law as a responsible and responsive institution stems from the social values that undergird the legal system; thus, changing societal values will result in or be evidence of a restructuring and reorienting of law over a certain period of time.

Every individual judge is appointed to occupy a particular place within this legal institutional setup which, according to constitutional theory, is subject to regulation in two separate but related ways. First, the *legislature* as a political body sets the norms underlying legal institutional functioning and in this way the legal institution is made to adhere and correspond to the purposes and desires set for it by the body of elected representatives of the people. Second, the *executive* maintains the legal system to permit it to function within the circumference of the norms set by the legislature and to implement these. In this political conversation over the nature and performance of the *judiciary*, two different but interrelated sets of judgements are continuously being made: the first concerns the reality of the legal system, its proper purpose and function; the second is more instrumental and concerns its operation. In Parliament, this endless conversation concerning these two judgements takes place all the time under the shadow of an acceptance that the final say will always be with the former. In performing the duties of her office every individual judge, as a member of the judiciary, has in mind this endless political conversation and, to an extent, is constrained by it.

Now since the problems that legislatures deal with are always a problem *for someone*, then, in responding to a given situation, or the threat of one, we might reasonably assert that politicians, as elected representatives, will generally have in mind questions concerning how these actual or potential situations might be shaped in relation to their own particular purposes or goals. In this way, lawmaking by the legislature may be thought of as a socially grounded method of perception and action, founded in social practice but reflecting particular change-resistant self-understandings. So while, on the one hand, the subjective side of lawmaking may be seen to embrace the idea of creativity and change, on the other hand it exhibits a profound resistance to change due to its inherently self-referential nature. As a result of this contrast, the role of a judge must be understood not only to involve taking account of the reality judgements of lawmakers but also, in view of the endless political conversation referred to above, assisting in the redefining and introducing of new self-understandings through control of data and the way it is interpreted and presented.

Law, as Luhmann (2004) reminds us, is a social system, and social systems are constituted by self-understandings expressed through commonly held and articulated sets of background distinctions. According to Taylor, 'the language is constitutive of the reality, is essential to its being the kind of reality it is' (Taylor 1985: 34). In so far as our theoretical frameworks may be said to alter the background distinctions that make up the self-understandings of our social systems, they may also be said to modify the social systems themselves. In other words, there is an internal relationship between the categories of thought that we use to approach reality and the practices that we seek to address and manipulate. In an important sense, our theoretical frameworks, our models and categories of thought help to constitute the world that we then experience. Thus, a social practice, such as the way that fellow judges within a common legal system relate to each other and each other's decisions, is what it is in and through the main self-understandings that practice embodies; that is, these self-understandings are 'constitutive of the social matrix in which individuals find themselves and act' (Taylor 1985: 36). As the former change, so also do the latter. This means that the distinctiveness of a social system originates, at least partly, from the frameworks of understanding and categories of thought that have grown up in particular circumstances over time. But where do these self-understandings come from? How do they develop? What sustains them?

Alasdair MacIntyre's (1985) concept of a 'practice' helps point a way to an answer:

> By a 'practice' I am going to mean any coherent and complex form of socially established cooperative human activity through which goods internal to that form of activity are realized in the course of trying to achieve those standards of excellence which are appropriate to, and partially definitive of, that form of activity, with the result that human powers to achieve excellence, and human conceptions of the ends and goods involved, are systematically *extended*.
>
> (MacIntyre 1985: 187)

Thus, 'Tic-tac-toe' is not an example though 'the game of football is, and so is chess. Bricklaying is not a practice; architecture is. Planting turnips is not a practice; farming is' (MacIntyre 1985: 187).

In the context of our discussion here, two features of a practice emerge as significant. First, a practice is a complex, cooperative and coherent association of human beings bound together by rules and persistent across time. Second, every practice creates what MacIntyre calls 'internal goods'; that is, goods that cannot be known or acquired in any way other than by participation in that particular practice, which means that '[t]hose who lack the relevant experience are incompetent thereby as judges of internal goods' (MacIntyre 1985: 189). Obviously, internal goods are distinct from 'external goods', which are only randomly associated with practices and may be obtained in ways other than by participation in a particular practice; for example, wealth, rank, notoriety, and so on. In this way we can see how the key features of a practice originate from within; that is, the practice is self-referential. Those internal goods that make a practice that particular practice and not any other practices are grounded in the particular experiences that its participants gain from their involvement in the practice and, insofar as this is true, the values and cognitive categories that have evolved within a practice will specify and dictate the way in which its members relate, jointly and severally, to their external environment.

We might compare, at this point, MacIntyre's understanding of practices with Luhmann's account of social systems. For Luhmann, social systems interact with and relate to the environment that they perceive to exist externally. But while changes in its environment may trigger a response within a social system, this response is conditioned by the system's own significant structure. That is to say, social systems, through their own internal goods (to use MacIntyre's phrase), allocate significant patterns and pattern variations to their environment and react to these patterns and pattern variations. Knowledge emerges within a system as a result of this activity; not as a passive response to an objectively given environment but through a system's interaction with its environment. When faced with a change in its environment, a system will react in terms that reflect its own internal organisation: a change in one part of a system is coupled with changes in other parts. In this way, a system will always react to preserve itself, facilitating its own self-production by establishing continuous patterns of self-referential interaction. Thus, law as a social system in this sense will always react to its environment in relation to its own internal organisation. It will determine what it perceives and, likewise, what it perceives will thus determine the system. Therefore, wholesale change is difficult: a system will always react to preserve itself. Alternatively, significant change may take place generally across a system if the system continually receives information or generates information internally *about itself*.

To the extent that we might agree with this analysis, we may say that new practices and new ways of doing things are mutually constituted in a recursive manner; or, to put it another way, when new descriptions gain acceptance among actors then new ways of doing things arise; when new ways of doing things arise then new descriptions also emerge; and so on. Thus, new ways of thinking about a practice will give rise to new ways of articulating it and thus also, potentially, to new ways of acting. In this sense, there can be no permanent character to social practices; rather, since they consist of the articulation of a set of self-understandings, then, when the underlying way of articulating how those practices' functions changes, so will the self-understandings communicated in and through them. So, if we view what judges do as a social practice in these terms, then we can perhaps begin to understand in a new light the *obiter* comments that judges make in delivering their judgements. What we find is a set of internal goods developed over time, the main features of which are those associated with the work of judicial decision-making. To disturb the system, and thus activate it with a new set of self-understandings as to what judging is all about, would require the influence of one who straddles the threshold between inside and outside, and who might therefore be described as from the outside but with a recognised or legitimate authority and a far-reaching plan.

But how might this be brought about? In the UK, for example, we have seen how the use of tools such as statistics on clear-up rates, league tables and waiting list targets have shaken up not only the criminal justice system but also the education system and the National Health Service. This has taken place by forcing participants to respond to the messages expressed through these tools in ways that focus on these tools themselves. With attention directed more towards the tools than the essential workings of the systems, these rates, tables and targets gradually assume an importance independent of their initial projected use, and instead are thought of as important in and for themselves. As can be seen from the political fallout generated by these measures in the UK, they can have quite unanticipated effects, changing the systems quite radically in the long run.

In such cases those seeking to effect significant change commonly (a) have a particular goal and purpose in mind that they are able to articulate in a relevant way, and (b) are able to provide the system with information about its operation and about other systems. In this way they are able to create the conditions necessary for the implementation of the changes they wish to see taking effect. What is happening here is that a discourse is being founded to structure the debate that necessitates the use of their key categories. When that debate becomes so structured as to necessitate the use of their key categories, change becomes inevitable. From this point on, any attempt to object will fail to register since the very language in which any objection is composed and through which it is articulated will have to be consistent with those objects that the resistance strives in vain to oppose. In other words, when the way a participant talks and acts changes the practice changes too.

We can see then how institutions such as law may be seen as more than simply viewpoints onto the world; rather, they are collectively recognised methods of perception involving a set of cognitive categories, values and interests that originate in social practices, which are themselves founded on internal goods and self-understandings that have evolved historically and which are manifested as sets of background distinctions shared among members. Such practices are, of course, self-referential. Interaction is with members' *perception* of their environment rather than with any objectively identifiable environment, these perceptions emerging from the way that the practice is ordered and structured; that is, from the cognitive categories, standards and interests in terms of which it has evolved over time. In other words, to put it rather bluntly, in terms of the way that law functions as a practice, judges decide the way they do because they think the way they do, and they think the way they do because they decide the way they do. Law is a self-referential system, concerned with the persistence and survival of its own identity.

Therefore, to interrupt this cycle and to change practices, one would first have to recognise how it is that social practices are dependent on the language through which they are expressed, how it is that they may be said to be impressionable, for it is in this sense, if at all, that we might affirm it to be possible to introduce novelty; that is, through developing a coherent, credible and justifiable discourse equipped with those novel distinctions, definitions and self-understandings that will constitute the new institutional identity of the practice under modification. This battle over ideas, over the form and content of communication, must be engaged in with a vision of a new institutional identity, with a new conversation and a new purpose in terms of which those proposed changes could be conceived as possible.

In the second place, as we have already noted, regular information about the functioning of other systems or about the system itself might also offer the potential for challenging or changing this customary self-preserving behaviour of a social system. How? Not through any coercive behaviour but by means of persuasion. Such information, regularly received, might harbour the possibilities for institutional change through its potential for encouraging a system to be introspective to the extent of precipitating new descriptions of itself to engender new possibilities and patterns of acting. This reflexive aspect of institutions may resonate within that institution and lead to transformation, or at least prepare the way for future transformation. In this sense, institutional change, at least in terms of law as an institution, may be seen then to be as much about changing understandings as about changing procedure: it must involve the embracing and the articulation of a vision and a definition of a new institutional reality and the ability and the expertise to control information imaginatively.

Chapter 11

Chaos and complexity

Some years ago, towards the end of the Balkan conflict, I was stationed in Sarajevo with the NATO peace implementation force. As a result of the hostilities, much of the city's infrastructure supporting its public services was totally destroyed and daily life had either ground to a halt or become utterly chaotic. In particular, driving along the city's main highway and neighbouring streets was like manoeuvring around a giant-sized fairground dodgems track. With no electricity supply, there were no traffic lights: a large number of vehicles travelled at dangerously high speeds, their drivers negotiating not only junctions but also pot-holes, other vehicles, pedestrians, and many other obstacles. Nonetheless, seldom was there ever a serious accident or collision. Left to itself, the traffic had become a self-regulating system. So much so that when the traffic lights were eventually made to work the drivers had become so used to this self-regulating system that they appeared to have forgotten what to do. Sometimes, nearly all of the drivers ignored the lights completely: as they changed from red to green and back again they made little impact on the continuous flow of traffic. At other times, the flow of traffic simply petered to a halt, everyone unsure whether or not anyone else was observing the changes. In fact, it seemed that when everything was chaotic the traffic flowed well, but when the lights operated everything became *dis*-organised: its settled state was a form of *organised chaos.*

Perhaps we might more correctly describe it as *undesirably* organised. The problem was not that one system represented order and the other disorder, but that one kind of order appeared undesirable but worked and the other kind of order although desirable clearly did not. Left to their own devices, patterns emerged among the drivers that satisfied everyone's criteria, and the resulting (dis)order appeared fair and efficient. It may not have equated to what we commonly expect in terms of a properly ordered traffic flow but it was ordered, nonetheless. The point is that our natural instinct in social life is always towards establishing some sort of pattern, or order.

MacCormick's (2007) discussion of the social practice of 'queuing' and its subsequent institutionalisation deals with precisely this issue. However, the main point that I want to highlight here is not *that* this happens but *how* and *why* it happens, and *for what purposes*. MacCormick illustrates well our common impulse to recognise, impose and institutionalise patterns but results in a way of thinking that regards order and disorder as opposites. The upshot of this is that what becomes institutionalised is what appears to be classifiable and generalisable according to institutional categories, expected and predictable by a controlling agent. Behaviour at variance with this becomes thought of as incomprehensible, unpredictable or chaotic. However, on the view being argued for here, institutionalisation and surprise are not polar opposites. Because something could not have been predicted does not necessarily imply a lack of order any more than its predictability would imply order. Which is simply another way of affirming that pattern does not exclude novelty. Indeed, far from being polar opposites, order and disorder, like universals and particulars, appear to implicate each other.

To many legal theorists, law appears to fall naturally on one side of this pairing. But if the argument being presented here holds then the dualism is a false one and law might well be less deterministic than it appears to be. In this sense, far from reinforcing the Newtonian, mechanistic world-view underlying modernist legal theory, this argument would suggest that a revision of that understanding is urgently required. The suggestion being presented here is not that our idea of reality as a unity needs to be abandoned, but that the version of that idea of unity as derived from and expressed in a predominantly Newtonian mechanistic vocabulary needs to be discarded in law as it appears to have begun to be in some other disciplines. As Tsoukas observes, diversity, change and adaptability, rather than hierarchy, rigidity and standardisation are coming much more to the fore within contemporary scholarship (Tsoukas 1998a: 293). Gradually, a new language with a new attitude towards and an appreciation of ideas such as non-linearity, disorder and noise, fragmentation, unpredictability and marginalisation is emerging. We find a change in attitude that appears much more receptive to a sense of the chaotic and an awareness of dynamic process, an outlook more in sympathy with notions of the unpredictable and the novel and much less ready to impose a division of order and disorder. But with this new outlook we need to radically rethink our ideas concerning the use of law as a tool for intervening in the world.

Much has been said here about the Newtonian approach, but this now needs to be augmented with a fuller description of what that approach entails. In the first place, it is characterised by the search for the universal, general, timeless 'decontextualised ideal' (Toulmin 1990: 30–36). The ontological description is that of discrete, objective units linked through norm-like associations discoverable through abstract conceptual representation that can aid predictability and help to minimise elements of surprise. In this way, the subject under consideration becomes controllable. As Tsoukas argues, such a view 'assumes an objectivist ontology, works with a mechanistic epistemology, and enacts an instrumental praxeology' (Tsoukas 1998a: 294;

Tsoukas and Cummings 1997: 656). Such a view makes use of idealised models, created through abstraction, to estimate the complex behaviour of real entities. This assumes both that the behaviour of real entities will permit such an assessment of their various contingent factors and that by abstracting from the time-dependent historical pathways of their causal relations fairly accurate prediction is nonetheless possible. And all of this rests on that rather sweeping generalisation that we considered at length earlier; namely, that within institutionalised forms every activity of a certain type *can* be treated in the same way *and* that it is legitimate to do this.

To take an example, consider Mrs Donoghue in *Donoghue v. Stevenson* ([1932] SC (HL) 31). In MacCormick's account of the reasoning in *Donoghue* we find an argument being constructed in reverse to account for the judges' reasoning. We are directed to understand how it is Mrs Donoghue as ultimate consumer, not Mrs Donoghue as a vulnerable old Scottish lady or any other combination of actual real-time background qualities and descriptions that is significant. But Mrs Donoghue, the ultimate consumer, does not exist in a social vacuum in the way that this abstract conceptual reconstruction of her would seem to suggest. She, Mrs Donoghue, is not this a-contextual and a-historical representation that is given of her; indeed, one is almost tempted to interject: '*Will the real Mrs Donoghue please stand up!*' In a similar way, we might argue that in respect of the conceptual reconstruction of the manufacturer of the bottle of ginger beer containing the offending snail.

What is clear from MacCormick's account of the reasoning in that case, is that it is the purpose for which the institution of law is intended that determines the ways in which the various purposes of the characters involved are related; that is, their relative positions within the legal institutional structure. But what this implies is that the legal institutional answer does not arise as a solution to the social problem from which it derives; rather, the institution *re*constructs the problem according to its own aims and purposes and defines and modifies the limits of its relations, thus making it more malleable. However, none of this can be discovered from a simple viewing of these objects in their institutional incarnations. Such an analysis would reveal only the 'fact' that the system or institutional answer was created by and given in response to the environmental conditions; it would not reveal the underlying process by which one is modified or adapted by the other.

So we need to ask what demands the institutional perspective is making of the real life scenario. Why does it abstract from concrete reality sometimes this way, sometimes that, and what are the implications of this? On the basis of the analysis engaged in earlier in terms of the importance of practices, what other factors, both within and without the story, influence the decision? How is this particular set of real-life concrete relations related to the broader issues of legal structures and doctrines and social cohesiveness in which this particular scenario is set? If we choose to focus solely on the decontextualised abstract model we will not even begin to find a way to address any of these questions.

Clearly, some degree of generalisation is unavoidable. Here we notice again the movement from what we might describe as *simple data* (the multitude of descriptions and items of information that could be given in respect of a particular situation) to *legally relevant facts* (facts that can register in the legal decision-making context) to *legally significant facts* (those facts that are important to the actual decision or its future authority and use; that is, as part of the *ratio*). In MacCormick's view such generalisation is not only inevitable, it is essential and the very idea of legal institutions presupposes this. But the problem is that in order to see with any degree of clarity *how* and *by what means* that real-life concrete situation that is before the court *can* be represented in these a-temporal non-specific terms much of what makes that real-life event exactly what it is, its uniqueness, has to be dropped from view. The open-ended life narrative that gives rise to a particular episode has to be transformed into a scenario that is presentable before the court. In this process, the episode loses some of its particular features and characteristics and gains others, at least in the sense that the narrative structure imposed upon it by its institutional re-presentation embellishes it with a beginning, middle and an end. Within this structure, individual facts are relevant and important in relation to and in terms of the aims and purposes for which the court is constituted. Thus, it is not difficult to see how, in this context, generalisation and abstraction, this consequent reduction to role and rule, might be seen as an obstacle to a fuller understanding of the complexities of real-life situations, rather than an aid. Thinking about a situation in a legal context provides the thinker with a way of thinking that structures how that situation is thought about. The narrative structure imposed by law corresponds with the a-contextual, a-historical mode presupposed by law but not with the time-bound, context-specific situation experienced by those involved. In this way, the mode of thinking allows the thinker to construct certain expectations but it limits them to a certain type: those that can be expressed as universalistic expectations. Such a privileging of the a-temporal, a-historical, and generalisable comes at a price; namely, the loss from view of the temporal, the contextual and the historical. Accordingly, theorising about law that finds its roots in a post-Enlightenment-inspired mechanistic model of the universe generally assumes that the actual situations which are represented by legal institutions as institutional phenomena operate in a social vacuum. The narrative structure that they are assumed to have is in fact a narrative structure imposed by law, and this is the only narrative structure they are permitted to have; without this, as we have seen in relation to *Re A*, they cannot be heard in law.

Legal decision-making illustrates very clearly how this rational translation of multi-faceted, open-ended, real-life phenomena into the data appropriate to legal speech and then into legal decisions and thereafter into legal justifications that validate, corroborate and legitimate the institutional mechanism and structure, takes place. But we are only beginning to understand how such decision-making is decidedly self-referential and why this is a problem. Judges must justify or ground their decisions in law. But, as we have seen, at some point the infinite regression brought about by thinking of law as a system of known rules that can be straightforwardly applied to factual circumstances, persons or events must be called to a halt; which is partly why we are then able to see how judges' decisions must be rooted in their forms of life, within a historically developed body of collective knowledge that cannot be fully represented. It cannot be otherwise, for, as Derrida, observes, ultimately 'incalculable justice *requires* us to calculate' (Derrida 1992: 28).

Chaos theory

The world that is depicted in much of contemporary philosophy is a very different one from that represented by the Newtonian mode of thought. We can illustrate this by referring to some of the distinctions that map the difference between Newtonian ideas and Chaos Theory. Chaos Theory is a mathematical theory with widespread application. It has been described as *'the qualitative study of unstable aperiodic behaviour in deterministic non-linear dynamical systems'* (Kellert 1993: 2, quoted in Tsoukas 1998a: 297). According to Chaos Theory, each complex system is *unique*, with multiple interactions and feedback loops between elements. They are *dynamic*, which means that they exist in changing environments and therefore need to be adaptable. They evolve and, as they do, become more complex. Here, each element responds to *local* information and not to broader system information, and interactions are *non-linear*; that is, they contain multiple components that are rarely explainable in simple cause and effect relations. Moreover, because complex systems constantly change in unpredictable ways as a result of non-linearity, it is impossible to make accurate predictions; instead, they contain *attractors* which operate like magnets for chaos, attracting and causing turbulence like rocks in a stream. Therefore, we study them and how they emerge as a means for understanding; that is, we study *how order emerges from chaos in the form of self-organisation*: as patterns, habitual activity, and so on.

More exactly, a system is termed dynamic when the state of the system, changes with time. Normally, '[t]he rules specifying how the system changes ... are ... written in the form of differential equations which represent the rate of change of its variables ... [which] allow[s] one to calculate the state of the system at other times, given its state at one specific point in time. The rate of change of each variable is expressed in either linear or non-linear terms'. In this respect, while linearity dictates that 'a unit change in variable X will always cause a specific change in variable Y ... , non-linearity means that the change in variable Y brought about by a unit change in variable X will depend on the magnitude of variable X'. In other words, 'non-linearity means that a small change in a system variable can have a disproportionate effect on another variable' (Tsoukas 1998a: 297).

The character and utility of linear equations may be regarded as corresponding to that of syllogistic or propositional statements in law; propositional statements can also be reduced to a general formula from which, provided the initial condition and temporal duration of the period being studied are known, the future state may be calculated. Contrastingly, non-linear equations are not subject to any general formula from which solutions for successive temporal points may be obtained; therefore, rather than being concerned with the prediction of future states from present ones, mathematical formulae for non-linear systems are focused more towards the various accounts of their broad patterns of continuing behaviour.

To say that a system behaves in an unstable and aperiodic manner is to say that 'it never repeats and it continues to manifest the effects of any small perturbation. Such behaviour makes exact predictions impossible and produces a series of measurements that appear random' (Kellert 1993: 4, quoted in Tsoukas 1998a: 298). In this way, the question of how such an unstable system will evolve depends on these 'small perturbations', and small changes in original conditions can produce unpredictable results.

When the variables indicating a chaotic system are represented as Cartesian coordinates with a single point describing the whole system, then as the system changes the point traces out a trajectory. Now, the state towards which a system tends is called an '*attractor*' and, for a chaotic system, the attractor has 'an irregular shape'; thus, a *strange attractor*. Moreover, '[t]he existence of strange attractors shows that chaotic systems combine pattern with unpredictability, determinism with chaos, order with disorder ... [C]haos theory has made it possible, as well as legitimate, to overcome hitherto accepted conceptual dichotomies'. Finally, '[t]he pattern of a strange attractor is produced by the systematic operation of *feedback* ... the iterative operation of a function upon itself', which results in the emergence of properties that could not have been predicted beforehand. That is to say, 'chaos theory shows mathematically that with simple non-linear deterministic equations ... small changes in initial conditions can generate unpredictable outcomes' (Tsoukas 1998a: 298–99).

The important point for our purposes here that we might draw from this introduction to the basic elements of chaos theory is that prediction in relation to non-linear systems is impossible, since this would require an element of accuracy in relation to initial conditions that simply cannot be given, and this has clear implications for legal reasoning (cf. Jackson 1992). What this means is that institutional actors do not enjoy the efficient capacity for decision-making that institutional theories of law have often credited them with. The institutional capacity for reasoned judgement is founded on the *un*-reasoned corpus of shared understanding that the context-dependent social institution of law has developed over time. A judge's reservoir of knowledge evolves from a set of initial conditions that, however capricious, nevertheless provide the foundation for all her understanding. It is thus that concrete communal tradition, not its a-contextual and a-historical abstraction, which is the *conditio sine qua non* for judicial comprehension, decision and action.

What this suggests is that the boundary between law and politics is actually much more blurred than is usually supposed. It is precisely because our knowledge is incomplete that politics is possible. If we could gain an objective standpoint, some Archimedean point from which to survey all that happens in the world, then perhaps there would be no need for collective deliberation or communal action. Much of what we recognise as political activity would, along with the courts of law in which we seek agreement despite dispute and dissatisfaction, likely disappear. Therefore, in this sense at least, we can see how courts of law are inherently political entities, how judicial decisions are always political compromises; that is, they are always imposed as matters of opinion, not of knowledge as such.

Actually, it is only because we do in fact affirm the impossibility of any kind of accurate prediction that we are able to acknowledge any sense of human freedom: freedom is meaningless if we affirm determinism; determinism makes no sense if we affirm freedom. Rather, freedom is what helps us to make sense of the world and our place within it. That we are free to act really implies a non-deterministic world, but one in which acts, however unpredictable, are nonetheless intelligible. We do things and we make things happen. We make intelligent decisions and we make sense of them afterwards. That is why legal reasoning is a form of practical reasoning. Not because we are able to represent our decisions according to some symbolic code but because in and through them we are able to progress, to navigate and negotiate our passage through this world of which we are a part. As Aristotle was acutely aware, understanding, imagination and practical judgement skilfully supersede the ability to predict.

Why do we find this so terribly difficult to come to terms with? One reason is that we have erected a barrier of propositional statements, deductive syllogism, 'If X, then Y, in circumstances Z', that stands in the way. We cannot operate this system without dividing the world up into separate pieces, transforming what is essentially an undivided flow and flux into objects, re-presenting process as manipulable substance. Without such modes of abstraction, the instrumental application of propositional statements would not be possible. In this sense, law makes freedom, choice and creativity epistemologically redundant and dispensable, since all that such decision-making involves is instrumental application. Between these two worlds, the world as experienced and the world as explained an unbridgeable chasm exists.

Karl Popper has described the temporal characteristic of Newtonian determinism as being like in a movie, where 'the future co-exists with the past; and the future is fixed, in exactly the same way as the past' (Popper 1988: 5). But our experience of the world is different: we do actually experience the world as change, as emergence and recession, as the embracing of real choice and real possibilities, as actualised potential, as a contingent becoming. Moreover, this affirmation of complexity permits a much more accurate and coherent understanding of temporality, one that corresponds with our experience of lived time. In short, the irreversibility of the arrow of time need not signify lack of order or of *dis*-order, but can in fact also be understood as a source of order (Prigogine 1997: 26).

Associated with the temporal dimension, the historical dimension precipitates a similar problematic. A spectator joining friends at a soccer match some time after the start will usually ask, 'What's the score?' or 'What's happened already?' Likewise, a dinner guest arriving late at the table could not expect to understand the point of a story being told if joined half-way through, at least not without also having some knowledge of the patterns of conversation that led up to it, from which it arose, and of which the present story is but the latest chapter. Likewise, no judge can ever hope to understand the full significance of a particular case without having some background knowledge and understanding of, or at least familiarity with, the historically developed patterns of behaviour and interactions that form the backdrop to its current *re*-production. As Whitehead argues conclusively, our present experiences are brought about by our previous actions, and the choices that we now have are dependent on the choice path that precedes them; that is, the form and direction of our present choices depends on the sequence of events that precede them.

In this sense, we might also say that not only do our legal problems require legal answers, but our legal answers are searching for the questions that will host them. That is, the institutional structures and interrelations that we set up in law, and the way we set them up, may be seen to reflect not simply our need and desire for a deterministic universe, but the central cultural self-understandings of our society as they have evolved over time. As Robert Cooper puts it:

> Representation ... shows that the inside is always a doubling of the outside ... [I]t displaces the outside of the dispersed and macroscopic into the inside of the compact and manageable. Representation displaces the outside inside. In contrast, bounded rationality, as a singularity, must always be an inner resource which acts on an outer problem; it is allied to intentions and goals which are also presumed to be integral to the organizational decision-making apparatus directed from the 'inside' of the individual. For representation, however, intentions and goals are themselves displacements in the topological folds of organizational space.
>
> (Cooper 1992: 270)

In this way, law in the sociological sense, as a social institution, may be seen to reproduce in law in its philosophical sense, in its institutional legal practices and doctrines, the practices and beliefs of the social environment that surrounds it and of which it forms a part. Thus, we can see how it might make more sense to emphasise *patterns* and *relationships* rather than values. We can see how this might be worked out if we consider, as an example, recent calls for more engagement with narrative understandings of legal cases, institutional practices and doctrines. Qualitative descriptions are much better suited than their quantitative cohorts to reveal the unfolding nature of historical narrative, how and why the relationships, choices, actions and interactions combined to produce the complex unity of each particular case. Reducing the complex unity of the qualitative whole to a quantitative assessment of its individual parts is a vain attempt to discover and apply governing norms, for it cannot do justice to this historicity or evolution: the whole is more than the sum of its separate parts. There is something other, ineffably present in all social phenomena that cannot be captured in this way. In answer to the question, what then is the point of the process that we are beginning to describe as law, the answer must be that the end or point of the process, like its beginning, is the process itself. It is the discovery of meaning in concretisation, in the actualisation of potentialities; that is, law must be understood not simply in terms of rational conclusions to rational problems but in more aspirational terms as the continual uncovering of ideals which will operate to lure us into further commitment. In this way, law actually becomes understood as part of the ongoing process of life: not just as a tool for helping us to live, or even to live well, but to live better.

In what sense, then, if at all, is law as an institution a chaotic system? At first sight, law is typically non-chaotic. What is being argued here, however, is that law is not one way or the other. In other words, neither those who have argued for metaphors of complexity and chaos in legal theory nor those who have argued against such conceptions have grasped the essential point. Metaphors describe, they do not represent. *Law* is not one way or the other, but we describe the world from within those historically conditioned social, cultural and linguistic environments in which our use of language makes sense. We cannot escape that: there is no Archimedean point in respect of our use of language. For example, Bańkowski argues that we must let the story speak to us. But the story doesn't speak: only we do. The story, once we allow ourselves to read it in a different way, even to get inside it, may cause us to entertain different viewpoints, and to want to suggest things that we would not otherwise have suggested, but it can only speak through us if we first have a language to speak about or for it in. So really we can *never* be sure that the language through which we attempt to capture the nature of an event, an act, a person, and so on, and by which we represent it in legal decision-making, will actually capture its essential qualities. Language is a tool that provides us with indirect access to reality: analogical truth is a construct that stretches only as far as the analogy holds; metaphors do not disclose prior meaning, they shift our focus from the stared at to the glanced over features so that they may become clothed with meaning as and when they reverberate with the echo of another's experience.

So why then should we use metaphors of chaos and complexity to describe law? Simply and principally because they help to draw out aspects of and about law and legal decision-making that have for too long been overlooked or overshadowed. Terms such as non-linearity, sensitivity to initial conditions, iteration, feedback loops, novelty, unpredictability, process, emergence, help to equip us with a new vocabulary, necessary if we are to begin to describe and re-describe law and legal institutions according to the manner proposed here. Understanding law through these lenses may not endow us with 20/20 vision but it will provide us with a storehouse of alternative imagery that may help to make different things appear interesting and interesting things appear different. Understanding law's aporia, the particularity void, the phronetic gap, in terms of chaos may help us to see how it is that the unbridgeable gap is crossed, without doing violence either to law or to reality. Order and chaos are not so much polar opposites as two sides of the same coin – flip it and see! If we need, as we do, to find a way of understanding law and legal decision-making that accommodates the contextual, historical, temporal, processual, meaningful, political, evolving, contingent, reflexive, novel, complex and changing aspects of reality, this alternative imagery provides us with a wealth of resources that help point to a workable way forward.

Chapter 12

Closing the gap
Narrative and the law

How can we uncover the assumptions and presuppositions of 'institutional' law so as to understand better its underlying reality? This question addresses and forces us to acknowledge something that is easily and often forgotten when we start to think about and analyse law and legal reasoning; namely, that there is a difference between *thinking* of law as a structured institution and our *thinking about thinking* of law as a structured institution. So it may well be that although the propositional form of statements is characteristic of our thinking about law as a structured institution, precisely as MacCormick suggests, a narrative form might still be the more appropriate way to consider law in relation to practices. Indeed, if this is the case, then it may well be that the logic of the Institutional Theory of Law (ITL) is not incompatible with a narrative methodology. This chapter aims to explore these possibilities and to examine the usefulness of narrative as a means for understanding law.

Similarities between legal reasoning and literary studies are frequently noted by legal scholars. However, just as interesting as the question of the similarities between the two is the extent to which narrative theory may actually be applied to the study of law and legal reasoning. In this respect, what is being suggested is an extension of the argument presented above; that is, that the significant features with which we are concerned are not those which we entertain on account of their propensity to predict a certain future but which will act as signposts, pointing out a way forward by disclosing hitherto hidden associations and suggesting novel relations and connections. Rather than understanding the structural functioning of law as something which aims at a reduction of complexity by means of an underlying system of unifying doctrines and complementary principles, we are more concerned to look for ways of pushing at law's boundaries, expanding its horizons of possible thought and action and generating new insights through the operation of a narrative view-point and a metaphorical use of the idea of complexity.

According to MacCormick:

> It is of course the snake bite, not the theory that snake bites can be fatal because of the property of snake venom, that causes Cleopatra's death.

But what enables us so to conceptualize the death of Cleopatra is that the particular fact of the biting snake belongs as minor premise in an argument of which the major premise is a hypothesis culled from the snake-venom theory and the conclusion is the death.

(MacCormick 2005: 97)

But does this explanation really capture the essential difference between the two modes of thought operating here? In the logical proposition, 'If X, then Y', the word 'then' operates differently than it would in, for example, 'the snake bit, and then the queen died'. While the first precipitates a search for universal truth conditions, the second looks for probable connections between the two. In the first there is an assumption of conjoinment; in the second, connection; that is, the first emphasises separation while the second emphasises continuity. How can we understand these two modes of thinking and how are they related?

A senior army officer was sometimes heard to say to his junior officers when asked for their assessment of a situation and possible courses of action: 'Great idea, bad plan!' In other words, there is a difference between saying that something sounds good and that it argues well. Good stories do not always make sound arguments (but, arguably, sound arguments are always good examples of a particular kind of story)! Murray Gell-Mann defines complexity as 'the length of the shortest message that will describe a system, at a given level of coarse graining, to someone at a distance, employing language, knowledge and understanding that both parties share (and know they share) beforehand' (Gell-Mann 1994: 34). Thus, in the first place, complexity relates to the ease or difficulty with which information that conveys a sufficient and correct account of an experience of some phenomenon can be transmitted; it is linked directly to the subject experiencing the phenomenon, dependent on their ability to represent it. In this sense, complexity is 'necessarily context dependent, even subjective … In actuality, then, we are discussing one or more definitions of complexity that depend on a description of one system by another, presumably a complex adaptive system, which could be a human observer' (Gell-Mann 1994: 33). In the second place, complexity relates to the compressibility of information, so that information that can be condensed into short, sharp phrases will be less complex. Complexity, on this account at least, has more to do with the experiencing of complex phenomena and the amount of work involved in communicating this experience than with independent and objective complex states of affairs. It has to do with the compression and transformation, the reduction for simplification of complex sense experience into commonly recognised and accepted forms of speech.

Tsoukas (1998a) calls this 'algorithmic compressibility', and uses this to help convey the basic difference between 'propositional knowledge' and 'narrative knowledge' as that between conditional 'If, then' statements derived from empirical observation and knowledge expressed through stories, anecdotes and examples. He argues that while the former can be represented via an abbreviated formula the latter cannot, since no abbreviated formula exists by which it may be properly represented. In this way, what we experience may be considered simple or complex depending on how readily our experiences submit themselves to 'algorithmic compressibility'; that is, how easily they can be described and analysed. Notice then, that propositional knowledge, which is algorithmically compressible, is inherently reductionistic and therefore ill-suited to accommodating non-propositional forms of understanding, or complex experiences, at their own level of communication and how this then results in a deficiency, or deficit, that propositional knowledge cannot overcome.

Much of the recent trend in legal theory towards emphasising reflexivity, paradox, ambiguity and contradiction may, in this way, be seen as an attempt to overcome this difficulty by further complicating the language of law, as an attempt to render it more complex. But, against this, consider for example, Christoudolidis' objection to MacCormick's updating of the Solomonic tale with a number of contemporary maternity disputes. How, he asks, would a judge in this situation 'know' that she was faced with a new problem? 'How, *given universalizability*, would she know that "she has two choices?"' Christodoulidis explains:

> This is an argument directed at the potential of surprise and at how law might harbour this potential … On the one hand … every case is unique in its particularity … On the other hand … the recognition of a maternity dispute … already occurs in terms of classifications available in the law, so that *any 'first impression' is over-determined* by classifications … already in place.
>
> (Christodoulidis 2006: 106)

In other words, how can the complexity deficit resulting from law's inherent tendency to reduce complexity ever be overcome? By resort to what vocabulary could any legal practitioner even begin to make sense of it? What mode of thought could she utilise to accommodate it? This is a question that strikes right to the heart of any attempt *within law* to increase the complexity of our understanding so as to mirror the complexity of the situation before us. However, it also a question that while presupposing law's institutional and propositional structure appears to ignore the significance of its existence *as law* in terms of the narrative structure associated with law as practice. Might judges be able to increase the complexity of their *legal* understanding so as to mirror the complexity of the situation they are contemplating through equivocality; that is, through the formulation and accumulation of multiple inequivalent descriptions? We have returned to a familiar question: how, if at all, *in law and as law*, might it be possible, in

Bańkowski's terms, through 'paying attention to the story' to get inside it, to 'lift the veil'?

The difficulty with the argument being presented here is that features such as non-linearity, recursiveness, sensitivity to initial conditions, emergence, and so on, can be understood and articulated only from a position of second-order complexity; that is, by moving from a position where every focus is on the system's reductionistic tendency to one where we can entertain descriptions of the system as complex. For Christodoulidis, this is not possible: law's 'structural inertia' operates to cut off this possibility. However, for the moment let us simply note how, by moving from propositional statements to interpretative or narrative statements, we move from talking about properties of the system to understanding our statements in respect of the system as a part of a vocabulary that describes the system and, in this sense, they cannot, as Taylor argues, be separated from our beliefs and goals (Taylor 1985: 23). In the propositional mode, this is not obvious; in the narrative mode, the dependence is openly acknowledged.

How might a property of the system become accepted as a descriptor? In the first place, this must involve bringing the teller of the story actively into the focus of the story itself. Take, for example, the case of Lord Justice Ward's rendering of *Re A* as 'very unique'. It is precisely because we expect linearity here that the lack of proportionality between what we would normally identify as cause and effect secures our interest. So, we interpret the non-linearity of complex systems as surprising. However, the surprise itself is not part of the system but is down to our expectations not being met or fulfilled and depends on our perspective; similarly, it is our concepts that are indeterminate, not the system they describe. To alter our perspective on something, to try and define where an event or occurrence begins and where it ends, or to suggest that a certain coincidence of features mark it as systemic, each of these is an interpretative move. it does not identify system properties. Moreover, if we reveal complexity by using these methods, it is precisely because of our involvement that this is introduced. How, then, in law, can we gain access to second-order complexity, and how might a narrative approach help to do this? Here we will try to answer these questions by looking again at a Newtonian style of thinking and how it has influenced directions in legal theory.

As we have already noted, the Newtonian approach involves the adoption of a particular attitude towards the world. First, there is an emphasis on what is quantifiable and measurable. Second, in line with this, it operates by constructing ideal models, providing a method of analysis that is both a-contextual and a-historical so that the construct is released from the stimulation of temporal and situational influences. In this way, the phenomenon under investigation may be thought of as complete in itself, a self-sufficient bounded entity, at the point in time when the investigation takes place.

Examples of this style abound throughout the legal theoretical literature. However, for our purposes here, we will confine our interest to noting the relation of ITL to this mode of thinking. As we have seen, MacCormick moves effortlessly from talking about law as an institution to the institutions of law and their underlying structuring principles. If we ask how we discover these principles, the answer is that we discover them from the accumulation of identifiable, self-contained life-situations. In other words, abstracted from context and from diverse contingent influences we can proceed to discover the relevant universal, or generally applicable, principles. But notice how, in effecting this transition, we move effectively from the experience of events in their uniqueness to a theoretical construction of them that swaps contingency for necessity.

The methodological procedure adopted by MacCormick in ITL is that of seeking out regularities within situations marked by set limits and conditions. Under this procedure, rules can be constructed and codified, and their validity established, that can then be followed by legal subjects and legal practitioners alike. MacCormick's account of ITL may be seen to conform to what Jerome Bruner has described as logico-scientific thought. Bruner presents a comparison of 'two modes of cognitive functioning', the logico-scientific mode and the narrative mode (Bruner 1986: 11–43). According to Bruner, while each provides 'distinctive ways of ordering experience' and 'constructing reality', they are nonetheless 'irreducible to one another', so that '[e]fforts to reduce one mode to the other or to ignore one at the expense of the other inevitably fail to capture the rich diversity of thought'. Conversely, those tendencies within ITL which may be thought of as discouraging, or at least constraining, are those that find representation within Bruner's narrative mode.

For MacCormick, as we have already noted, legal institutional knowledge is organised around a propositional form of statements that relates a factual predicate to a consequent. These conditional statements are used to explain the recurrence of certain institutional phenomena and they also provide the basis for the framing of legal norms to guide subsequent behaviour. Here knowledge operates recursively inasmuch as it is used for both explanation and prediction of behaviour and for the guidance of legal practitioners; that is, events that occurred in the past form the basis for the factual predicate that will guide questions relating to future action. Thus, when the legal system is disturbed by encountering a 'new' situation, that new situation is reduced to and described by reference to those constituent parts that can be accounted for in the familiarity of past situations so that the behaviour in question may be examined by legal norms (rules). Therefore, in this sense at least, time is made redundant: the future is reducible to the past, in whose terms it is understood.

Of course, as MacCormick is quick to point out, regulating life by subjecting human behaviour to the governance of rules has its advantages, for once a particular interpretation has been assigned in a particular case they become applicable across a range of contexts. Nonetheless, as we have seen, with generalisations it is difficult to properly account for particular circumstances or experiences. Propositional statements have reference to purposes and motives that cannot be articulated propositionally. Moreover, because the propositional form makes time redundant this often results in paradoxes. In these ways, the propositional structure and form on which ITL is made to depend may be considered to be limited.

Just so, it is in order to address these limitations that the complementary capabilities of a narrative approach ought to be considered. The main point is to ask in what ways, if at all, a narrative approach may be thought to act in tandem with the sort of approach suggested by ITL so as to address the complexity deficit highlighted above; that is, in what ways may a narrative mode be considered to complement rather than to conflict with the mode of thinking engaged in ITL? MacCormick describes his model of legal reasoning as utilising the following method: universalisability; consequences; coherence and consistency. Here, the aim is to demonstrate the usefulness of the narrative approach as a necessary supplement, or corrective, to counter the perceived shortcomings of ITL. In other words, to ask how we may ally to those methodological features of MacCormick's approach, the following features characteristic of a narrative mode that MacCormick's approach seems to preclude: contextuality and reflexivity; the articulation of purpose and motive; sensitivity to the temporal aspect.

To say that a rule exists is necessarily to generalise: rules connect types of behaviour by types of actors to types of situations. Thus, to speak about human action as institutionalised is, MacCormick argues, necessarily to imply the existence of rules. But rules find application within particular local situations and in contexts where the configuration of events found to exist may not be seen to replicate those specified in the rule's factual predicate. In this practical sense, at least, law is indeterminate, because one can never escape the 'tyranny of the particular'. In this sense, too, the only persons capable of undertaking effective action in any situational moment are those with knowledge of its particular circumstances.

However, rules are not self-applying and neither are they simply applied in a mechanistic way through reference to other rules. Therefore, judges, in applying rules, can be seen to be dependent upon a historically derived knowledge concerning the previous application of these and other rules. Even so, all of this collected and collective historically derived knowledge cannot encompass the problem of the particularity of each new situation. Each new situation has its own history of how it came to be there, and no amount of institutional understanding can account for or encapsulate this: a judge cannot understand a situation at a certain point in time without some knowledge of how it got to be there. Consequently, every judge must appreciate and take of account two divergent historical 'tracks', and the one, the institutional, cannot render the other, the experienced, intelligible and articulate. To do so must involve the utilisation of the narrative mode and its understanding of contextual sensitivity, which, as MacIntyre, Bruner and others remind us, requires a 'story' with a 'plot'. So the problem that we are faced with is one of how, if at all, this narrative mode of thinking may be utilised within the legal institutional context, without contradicting, negating, or denying it.

Fundamental to the success of rule application is the bringing about of a pre-arranged state of affairs, which Schauer calls 'justification' (Schauer 1991: 26). This is the reason why law is composed not just of rules but also includes rule-like exceptions to those rules. In the criminal law, for example it is a defence to the charge of unlawful homicide that the accused acted in self-defence. The accused might have committed the *actus reus* of unlawful homicide but her use of fatal force becomes justified and her act of killing is permitted if it is used to counter unjustified and life-threatening aggression from her assailant. The justification for this rule and the consequent rendering of a notional infringement of the criminal law as lawful is the desire not to hold a person placed in such a situation, without other means of defence or escape, criminally liable. In this way we can see how the justification is related to the sort of society that we want to be, or to become, and the rule's factual predicate (the definition of the reasonable application of the defence) causally related to its justification; in other words, we believe that our preferred social order is brought about or hastened by adherence to the rule. Therefore, justifications lie hidden behind the rules: they are the reasons why we have such rules and they exist in the rules only by implication, not by explicit formulation. To try to include such a requirement within the propositional structure of legal norms would lead to unmanageable paradoxes.

To this extent, we might say that a rule's justification exists in a rule like Polanyi's tacit knowledge; that is, it is 'essentially unspecifiable'. We cannot focus on it and expose its meaning because to try to render it articulate in propositional form would introduce a never-ending dependence of explicit rule on implicit justification similar to that which we noted earlier. In this sense, it is completely wrong to think that a rule and its justification exist as two opposite ends of a continuum that can somehow be joined or connected. They relate more as east does to west than as north does to south: by reference to each other. One is the shadow side of the other, as it were. Thus, *why* we follow a legal norm cannot be expressed in legal propositional form: the rule is the instrument of the purpose, not the purpose itself. To engage with such assessment, with *thinking about thinking about* … , takes us beyond law as we know it, which is perhaps why Christodoulidis insists that is takes us into the realm of ethics.

So, we have seen how law in its institutional context operates through governing by a set of rules. We have also seen how this leads unavoidably to paradoxes that cannot be contained within law's logical structure, and how this is due, in part at least, to the exclusion of the temporal aspect from that logical structure; moreover, the circularity associated with causal statements cannot be conveyed in logical propositions without generating paradoxes. How, then, if at all, might a narrative mode of thought be legitimately utilised to provide support for the temporal dimension of experience, and so prevent the reduction of causality to logic? How might the narrative mode be engaged with to provide an alternative to the propositional mode that both complements and supplements it (cf. Tsoukas and Hatch 2001)?

There is a difference between something talked about and what is said about it. Thus we can rightly mark a distinction between, on the one hand, the meaning of what is said, the story, and, on the other hand, the particular situation in which it is interpreted, both by the teller and also by the hearer (cf. Jackson). When both the story and the story-teller are taken into account, the whole background of the story-teller, those purposes and dispositions alluded to earlier, must be brought into view. What do we mean when we talk about the story? In the context of judicial decision-making this might be taken to refer to the written legal judgement containing a judge's reasons for the decision; or it might refer to the actual events and relationships, the facts; or it might even refer to the actual moment of decision in which the judge by reference to those facts comes to a decision which will later be reported upon in the written judgement. Obviously, when we take into account both the written judgement and the relevant events and relationships to which the judgement refers, there is a gap that appears that concerns issues of application, interpretation and context.

According to Ricoeur (1984), 'narrative [is] exactly what Aristotle calls muthos, the organization of events' (Ricoeur 1984: 36) by which a story is 'pulled forward' by the 'successive actions, thoughts, and feelings in the story inasmuch as they present a particular "directedness"' (Ricoeur 1984: 150). Thus, the constituent parts of a narrative are organised sequentially according to a 'plot', and we understand one in terms of our understanding of the other: they are recursively ordered, mutually constituted, not reducible to each other or to anything else. But what Ricoeur then takes up with his notion of 'emplotment' and what Bruner takes up with his idea of the narrative mode is not simply the identification of similarities between narratives and plots or plots and their structural elements; rather, it is the deeper question of how, in constructing plots, we create and employ narrative thinking. Ricoeur notes how 'the definition of muthos as the organization of events first emphasizes concordance ... characterized by three features: completeness, wholeness and appropriate magnitude'. Here, the notion of a 'whole' is pivotal:

> Now a thing is a whole if it has a beginning, a middle, and an end ...
> But it is only in virtue of poetic composition that something counts as a
> beginning, middle, or end. What defines the beginning is not the absence

of some antecedent but the absence of necessity in the succession. As for
the end, it is indeed what comes after something else, but ... [o]nly the
middle seems to be defined just by succession ... If succession can
be subordinated in this way to some logical connection, it is because the
ideas of beginning, middle, and end are not taken from experience. They
are not features of some real action but the effects of the ordering of the
poem.

(Ricoeur 1984: 38–39)

On the one hand, thinking in the narrative mode can be seen as a way of
connecting and imputing meaning to what would otherwise appear as separate and detached events. Plots give meaning through connecting, sequencing
and relating, events within a context; that is, situating events. On the other
hand, thinking in the propositional mode, what Bruner calls logico-scientific
thought, connects not particular events but universal categories: *types* of
actions to *types* of actors to *types* of situations. However, once the plot is
assigned, those events and actions are no longer simply instantiations of
categories, but they are real: they have real, local, situational effects and
consequences. We might think of the narrative mode as breathing life into
these 'emplotted' elements. Nuances of relationships, reciprocity and purpose, all of those features denied expression by processes of abstraction,
categorisation and correlation are able to register within this more concrete,
historical and specific portrayal. Recall Whitehead's phrase, '*that* wolf ate
that lamb at *that* spot at *that* time: the wolf knew it; the lamb knew it;
and the carrion birds knew it' (Whitehead 1929: 43). In this respect, narrative thinking bestows and communicates context, in terms of situation and
circumstance, instead of contingency. Indeed, without such an understanding
of context it is difficult to see how the narratives that take place or are contextualised in institutional settings can be properly understood. A narrative
mode of thinking encourages or even demands an awareness of the concrete,
local, particular and situational aspects denied by propositional thinking.
And since narratives not only *refer* to contexts but also *have* a context – that
of the narrator and the act of narrating that goes towards interpretation of
the narration – then we can see how, in fact, a recursively symmetrical con-
textualising is built up with each new act of interpretation: it is impossible to
escape from context, no matter how many times the interpretive act is
engaged in.

Likewise, every decision presupposes a decision-maker. Each decision
presented in judgement is constructed by a human judge; it is not a product
of logical necessity but contingent. A judge is not simply some passive
computational device, a machine designed to compute decisions already
decided, but an active, perceptive and reflective agent who forms, and performs, the decision, and, in forming that decision, creates something new in
the present out of the materials received from the past. In this way, narrative

thinking may be seen to provide a semblance of reality considered lacking in propositional thought, since it provides a resonance with experience; that is, between the persons and events addressed by the decision and their appearance within the address in which the decision is given by the decision-maker. There is thus coherence between the decision as delivered, the decision-maker and the decisional moment.

Previously, we noted how a proper understanding of the significance of complexity requires us to be aware of the importance of the notion of thinking about how we think about complexity. For law, then, we might say that every judge not only engages with the practice of legal decision-making but must also deal with the matter of her own complexity. In other words, every judge is a part of the decisions that she makes and subject therefore to narrative analysis. Here we might allude, as Bańkowski does, to the distinction between coming to a decision from a perspective of being inside, of 'paying attention' to the story, and that of being outside it, and also of whether or not the decision-maker counts themselves in this sense as a part of the story that is told and whether that will be represented in the decision, the story that is told (which of course brings us back yet again to that sense of the recursively symmetrical layering of context). Narrative thinking discloses a legal decision delivered by a legal decision-maker in a particular legal position, interpreted by others, some of whom are legal practitioners in the same sense, who are also occupied collectively in the narrative act. Sequences of events, relationships, persons, etc., are contextualised by legal decision-makers whose positions as legal decision-makers offer the context by means of the insight that operates within the context of the legal decision-making process. To the extent then that a legal decision-maker's thinking is part of the situation to which the decision relates, a decision-maker who is aware of this interaction and dependence between their thoughts and decisions will be able to generate more descriptions of that situation.

In narrative, it is not simply a question of what comes next, but why: a plot implies more than mere sequence. 'The snake bit and then the queen died' narrates a sequential order through time. But 'the snake bit and then the queen died of poisoned venom' narrates a plot. While, according to the propositional mode characteristic of ITL, a particular event is accounted for by demonstrating that it instantiates a universal rule, in the narrative mode an event is accounted for by connecting it to purpose. This is possible because, as we have seen, although the propositional form excludes time, a narrative form accommodates time.

We can observe how the difference between propositional and narrative modes in relation to purpose operates by considering Alan Norrie's (1991) analysis of how motive and intention are handled in criminal law. The starting point for Norrie's critique is the Enlightenment ideal of the abstract juridical individual. This ideological form places the individual at the centre of moral and legal discourse, and is replicated in criminal law doctrine through principles of individual responsibility and rules respecting individual freedom. But, Norrie claims, as the product of a particular historical period it has distinct and severe limitations. Made possible only by the abstraction of the individual from her concrete reality, this ideological form ignores the social nature of criminality and so we find that, as a result, law must continually be searching for new ways to exclude this nature from its view. Moreover, at the same time, this individualism is political (Norrie 2001: 28–31): while the individual is presented as a rational, intentional, voluntary actor uninhibited by random political interference, this freedom is guaranteed only as long as, for example, the rational, deductive system that controls the state can constrain the judges within their politically neutral and value-free role. Judges, however, appear to form a value-laden socio-political class of their own, operating openly contradictory standards and moving, almost unreflectively, from rules that assert a more rigorous requirement of individual responsibility to rules that appear less scrupulous and exacting; moreover, their judgements can often appear unconstrained or ambivalent towards the requirements of logic (Norrie 2001: 26–28). So, Norrie concludes, it is a mistake to suppose that law can be understood as a politically neutral system of rules: having evolved out of the struggle for power between conflicting social classes, criminal law functions as a mechanism of social control mediated through an ideology of psychological and political individualism. Thus, it operates both to condemn and to protect individuals. Crucially, however, this contradictory, paradoxical state of affairs is maintainable only through the systematic operation of conflicting inclusions and exclusions of acts and contexts, individual and socio-political concerns. This becomes especially clear when we consider the relationship between motive and intention in the criminal law (Norrie 2001: 35–38). During criminal proceedings, an appeal is often made for the motive of the accused to be taken into account in relation to the crime committed; however, this is met every time with a stubborn refusal. Motives, it is said, lead to the formation of intentions and, as such, are psychological, not socially formed. No surprise, here, perhaps, for were the law to recognise the social context within which an individual's actions take place, and thus to understand motives as arising out of the locations of individual acts, it would then be extremely difficult to attach blame and to convict.

A similar result may be observed if we consider the defences of duress and necessity (Norrie 2001: 153–73) where a claim is made that the accused is not responsible for her motive, which results from circumstances beyond her control. What causes a person to form motives to commit crimes? Is it duress or necessity, threats of violence or their situation? Clearly, any attempt to reconcile the idea that 'she was forced to do it' with the free will notions of intention and rationality ('she intended it and her reason was unimpaired') is fraught with difficulties. And if a loaded revolver pointed at her head could excuse her action, why would 'an evil system' not do so?

Law's contradictory location may have 'its provenance in the enlightenment representation of a world of free individuals coming together in civil society', Norrie says, but 'crime is a social problem generated in ways that can be statistically correlated'. This 'social context is refocused through law into a matter of individual responsibility, justice and deterrence' as:

> [e]ach act of crime is relocated from the social sphere, where crime is produced, to the individual criminal agent ... It is the consequences of this translation, which is also a repression, a refusal to see the individual as always-already social, that lie behind the dilemmas of legal justice and criminal law. What is suppressed always returns ... [s]urfac[ing] and resurface[ing] across the terrain of criminal law's 'general part'.
>
> (Norrie 1996: 551)

Motives, as the interpretation of reasons for acting, permeate a narrative mode of thought being structured by and finding expression in the discourses in which they are set. However, they resist expression in the propositional mode since they cannot be fixed in propositional form but depend instead on viewpoint and perspective, where any number of different interpretations may be considered equally valid. Law, as a discourse in the propositional mode, provides the vocabulary for all human agents to justify their actions and decisions in ways that the institutional discourse dictates or allows. Just so, as the discourse changes so will the justifications; by the same token, as our use of language evolves and develops, so must the terms in which we express our motives. Nonetheless, while law can accommodate the first type of change, it is unable to accommodate the second type: it can accommodate change from one relatively fixed and stable position to another relatively fixed and stable position but not change rooted in interpretation, whose meaning is dependent upon context. Attempting to understand motive in relation to legal discourse would be an impossible complication of our understanding of law in the propositional mode: it quite simply could not be undertaken because this standpoint is not equipped to handle such levels of complexity. And yet, as we have already noted, a narrative mode of thinking is not only equipped for but best suited to handling these levels of second-order complexity. Indeed, to talk of law as narrative *is* precisely what it *means* to understand and to talk in terms of motive. Narrative thinking not only provides the vocabulary for conveying this but it also structures the discourse in precisely the ways that would accommodate it. Thus, narrative thinking can convey motive, and structure it, even though propositional thinking cannot. While propositional thinking aims at reducing complexity but in doing so forever increases its own complexity, creating an unbearable paradoxical burden, narrative thinking allows us to think recursively, providing for us a way of entertaining and encouraging complexity.

In light of this, we can understand Whitehead's point, referred to earlier, that it is much more important that something be interesting than that it is true, for the narrative style is much more concerned with the power of a story to evoke a response by the way it is put together than with analytic questions and debates over the veracity of claims. And here, in a sense, we pick up again Ricoeur's notion of 'emplotment', for inasmuch as a narrative style emphasises the sequential ordering of component parts then in that sense it may be said to be much more concerned with time than with truth *per se*. It is at this level, in the idea of emplotment, that we discover the means by which judges are able to perform the link between what they find in the rules on the one hand and the events, persons and relationships they must address on the other. Ricoeur claims that time is essential to narrative. He refers to Augustine:

> Suppose that I am going to recite a psalm that I know. Before I begin my faculty of expectation is engaged by the whole of it. But once I have begun, as much of the psalm as I have removed from the province of expectation and relegated to the past now engages my memory, and the scope of the action which I am performing is divided between the two faculties of memory and expectation, the one looking back to the part which I have already recited, the other looking forward to the part which I have still to recite. But my faculty of attention is present all the while, and through it passes what was the future in the process of becoming the past. As the process continues, the province of memory is extended in proportion as that of expectation is reduced, until the whole of my expectation is absorbed. This happens when I have finished my recitation and it has all passed into the province of memory.
>
> (Ricoeur 1984: 20)

In other words, the past that is memory and the future that is expectation interact to produce the present, and this coming together of the past and the future in the present means that memory and expectation can potentially reach across time to bring to consciousness in the present those things that belong to both memory and expectation. Thus, our *experience of time* is created out of a galvanizing of memory, expectation and attention.

In this sense, since the present is what exists between the horizons of past and future, and can be evoked by us in its various modes, then our experience of time is something that is created by us, and which, in narrative thinking, we can create and utilise by attending to the present as that which we hand on from expectation to memory and so consign to the past. In that sense, creating and employing an experience of the passing of time, narrative thinking allows us to do what Bańkowski asserts we must do and 'pay attention to the story'; in the terms of our earlier discussion, narrative thinking permits us to increase complexity by expanding our sense and understanding of the present.

We can see how all of this is relevant to our discussion of law as institutional. As we saw from Levi, making connections across time, situations and decisions, enables decisions, definitions and meanings from the past to be brought forward into the present, their importance re-presented in such new ways as allow for even wider implications and meanings. Thus meanings are stretched and widened across ever longer stretches of time and connections established in this way impart greater scope and flexibility to decisions. But the point is that this evolution of the collective mind, the collected and woven pattern of judicial decision-making, is really possible only on the back of a narrative mode of thought. As we have already noted, the propositional mode is unable to accommodate such levels of complexity.

But how is this judicial savvy managed? How do judges enrich and make more complex the collective mind of the law? Not by any way associated with the propositional mode, clearly, but by the harnessing and developing of their individual skills associated with thinking in the narrative mode. In this way institutional knowledge can become ever more complex, transposing and interweaving of past, present and future, make multiple connections across multiple time frames. In this way legal knowledge *can* be brought to bear on particular situations in a legitimately legal way. But the point is that it is not propositional thinking that provides the connection; rather, it is thinking in the narrative mode. Such connections are only possible on the basis of features that the propositional, generalising mode of thinking denies absolutely. There is something *qualitatively* different, and *dynamic*, about this moment, right now, immediately after I have pressed the space-bar on my computer that cannot be accounted for in any other moment(s), just as there is in the moment that followed immediately the snake's biting of Queen Cleopatra. Narrative thinking, narrative time, allows us to experience such complexity in a way that propositional thinking never can. In fact, it is in the narratives that we construct about the situations that we confront in and with law, and in the narratives that we construct about law itself, that our understanding of law is rooted. From this law derives its meaning.

So, also, in another sense, it really does matter when, where and how we ascribe initial conditions when we look at situations in an institutional context. When, where and how we do this can have radically different effects in terms of how we then see and characterise the system's development, and this introduces an element of surprise. The more that this happens, the more complex a system is and the more situations, events, actions and interactions that we have to accommodate the more intricate are the patterns of behaviour that develop. With this increase in complexity comes a theorising that we can understand as thinking in the narrative mode, as thinking about our thinking about complexity.

When does a line of people become a queue? asks MacCormick. He suggests that what we perceive, at the simplest level, is in fact only a grouping of persons, and that when we think of that grouping of persons as a queue we are in fact following a somewhat complex chain of inference from which we draw a conclusion. The way that this happens is that we recall the experiences and the training of past situations and we compare this to the present where, in order to satisfy a formed intention to travel, we conclude that this present grouping of persons is in fact a queue, and we move forward to join the queue in order to satisfy our intention to travel:

> To the extent that people 'take their turn', there is an orderly movement through ... From nearly everybody's point of view a kind of fairness and efficiency prevails ... Clearly, there can be a successful practice ... without perfect conformity to the practice. But there must be some minimum threshold of compliance below which the practice would be unsustainable.
>
> (MacCormick 1998: 304)

'Turn-taking or queuing is then normative', concludes MacCormick, so that 'where there is a queue for something you want, you ought to take your turn in it', which of course requires a decision that it is in one's best interest to queue. Of course, '[t]his does not mean that there is a single quite specific or explicit norm that everybody cites when queuing', and '[q]uite likely, my articulation of the queuing norm will differ from what you might offer in an attempt to make explicit what is implicit in a common way of acting'. Nonetheless, 'queuing is an intrinsically personal activity aimed at a common point ... at attaining a service or opportunity that others seek at the same time, and at facilitating its attainment in mutual civility rather than through open conflict' (MacCormick 1998: 305). Yet, when does a queue begin? How do people get to this position? What happens prior to this? How does what has gone before relate to identifying the 'start' of the queue, and how will identifying a particular point as the start impact in determining the significance of what follows? How do we perform the separation of this newly formed 'queue' from all that happens before, and what determines this? In one sense, if we really think about it, a queue has no identifiable 'beginning' as such. Queuing is an abstraction from process. Granted, we habitually and necessarily abstract in precisely this way in order to negotiate our passage through the multifarious day to day tasks of modern living. But we make a mistake if, after abstracting, we begin to treat our abstraction as if it were ultimately real instead of continually referring it back to the real and changing concrete situations from which it is abstracted. Why does this matter? Well, in the first place, as we have already implied, there is *history trailing behind* 'the queue', a history that is now in danger of being obscured, forgotten or overlooked. MacCormick seems to acknowledge this, in the sense that it is from *almost* everybody's point of view that a kind of fairness and efficiency prevails. But what about those other points of view not included there? How are their voices to register? To identify the character of the activity that constitutes the queuing process is one thing, to go on and treat the abstraction that we then term a 'queue' as if it were a precisely bounded independent entity without continually referring it back to the continuous process from which it is abstracted would seem mistaken. So we need to find ways to think about and question the abstractions that we make from reality and to refine them, in order to gain a better understanding of what is happening, how and why.

In this respect, imagine that I am a photographer, or an artist, or a writer. I may or may not have a formed intention to travel. But, instead of going over to the queue, I stop, take out my camera, sketch-pad or notebook and proceed to try and capture an image of the situation before me. What is happening here? As a photographer, artist or writer I am using my acquired ability and trained eye to contemplate the relative positions of persons standing in front of me. It takes effort of the imagination and not a little developed skill to resist the lure of that complex chain of inference that would lead me to the conclusion that what I see before me is a queue. This, perhaps, is what Bańkowski is arguing towards when he cites Gillian Rose's notion of 'suspending the ethical' and says that '[t]he action taken when I suspend the ethical is not one of self-assertion but of self-renunciation ... There is no final judgement; I can always be wrong'. In other words, '[w]e have to work from where we are ... engage and take responsibility' (Bańkowski 2000: 43–44). In this sense, 'our decisions whether to apply the law or not [will] always ... be arbitrary ... [W]e will never know for sure whether we are right ... ' However, '[w]e must realise that our life is never clear-cut and clean and is always something of a mess. But we must get hold of it as it is ... and we must use that anxiety creatively' (Bańkowski 2000: 38). In this sense, contra Christodoulidis' caution in terms of the absolute force of law's exclusionary rules, we can affirm a way of understanding Bańkowski's suggestion that '[r]easoning can be thought of as operating in a sphere which is barred by a thick almost opaque curtain ... You lift the curtain to look but the curtain is extremely heavy ... You have to drop it and remain on the side you were or move to the new side' (Bańkowski 2001: 174).

In this way, despite law's inherent tendency towards exclusivity in terms of its propositional mode of its thinking, reinforced through a strict understanding of the exclusionary force of second-order reasons, thinking in the narrative mode can encourage and develop that very approach to law that the propositional mode denies. In complementing and supplementing law's preferred mode of thinking in this way narrative thinking can extend law's reach into and find a foothold within the concrete, local particularities which it seeks to address. Moreover, not only is thinking in the narrative mode possible alongside of thinking in the propositional mode, but law as an institution (its sociological sense) supporting institutions of law (its philosophical sense) actually presupposes this. While law's propositional mode achieves reduction of complexity, this results in an increase in internal complexity that law's preferred mode is not equipped to handle. So it is narrative thinking, about law and in law, which provides a bridging of the gap here.

Part IV

Integrating law and process

Chapter 13

Law's institutional becoming

Creativity, novelty, change

> In order to think change and to see it, there is a whole veil of prejudices to brush aside, some of them artificial, created by philosophical speculation, the others natural to common sense.
>
> (Bergson 1946: 131)

Clearly, in terms of the philosophical approach that we have been pursuing here, traditional thinking about law, even more contemporary theories of law such as MacCormick's 'institutional theory of law', approach the idea of law and legal institutional change from the point of view of stability rather than continuing change. It seems important, then, to ask why and how it might benefit such views if institutional change, both as an object of investigation and as an everyday legal reality were approached from the point of view of continuous change rather than stability; in other words, if the ontological priorities were reversed and change was seen as the normal state and not just a special case or deviation from the stable and routine.

The argument being pursued here is that, first of all, it would provide legal theorists and other legal researchers with a more comprehensive view of the micro-processes of change that may be operating. What makes institutions change? How are new templates and models discovered and legitimated? Who does it? What this suggests is an enquiry into whether there is any alternative to the linear model of change characteristic of traditional legal theory. How might we account for the possibility of non-linear processes, of surprise? What connotations and consequences might this suggest for our ideas of law? Second, although change in law is often understood as the change from one stable condition or state to another, expressed in terms of often quite detailed descriptions of *what* these states and the differences between them are, there is little in the legal literature on *how and why* what happens, comes about. Even if we can say that a decision must be justified by the giving of justifying reasons for that decision (a movement from state A to state B), such reasons, as we have seen, do more to *explain* the decision rather than *justify* the decision-making. This 'justification' explains and describes the effect of the decision on the legal system and on the parties involved; however, it does not admit us into the experience of how and the why and by what means the decision was actually achieved: for example, how those legal rules were translated into, *became*, that decision, and how, in the process of being translated thus, they underwent change, modifying and being modified, adapting and being adapted. Justification for legal decision-making is always viewed retrospectively, more as a *fait accompli*, when understood in terms of the giving of justifying reasons for a decision that has already been made. In this sense, something important is lost: its vibrancy, its revelatory, evolving qualities are not only lost from view, obscured or denied, but perhaps also contradicted and even negated. When we view change in law as something exceptional to the stable state, we lose sight of the fact that change is happening all the time. On the micro level change is all pervasive; what we find is continuous change. In this sense, far from being repeatable and repeated patterns remaining essentially unchanged from instance to instance, institutions of law are actually perpetually moving waves or currents of ideas that act and interact and change in acting. Therefore, in so far as habitual patterns of behaviour are human actions then they too contain potential for change, since change is there all the time, unrecognised and unseen.

Perhaps the main stumbling blocks to any attempt at a re-conceptualisation of law and legal change are the ontological and epistemological assumptions under-girding our thinking about law. Nonetheless, there are inklings of a push towards a new way of thinking, or at least a restless dissatisfaction with the old way. Levi, for example, stresses how a legal concept changes asdecision-makers respond to previous decisions in the context of new decision-making situations. He notes how ideas develop, appear and re-appear in different guises, and how the classification changes as the classification is made. In this sense, every decision in law is a change in law. Others, like Bańkowski, Jackson and Detmold, note how in law the decisions that are made cannot be separated from the decision-makers who are making them. Generally, legal institutional change remains part of an ongoing process of legal decision-making, grounded in the decisions taken by legal actors, and arising out of their encounters with contingent everyday situations. Indeed, as long as human judges act in decision-making, the potential for continual change and institutional creativity always remains. Moreover, the development of an emphasis on the authority of the decision-maker rather than that of the decision itself is a further part of this same trend.

Here, the purpose is to show that and how it might be possible to build upon and develop these trends by proposing and explicating the philosophical basis that would sustain them. Our starting point is the recognition that to understand legal institutional change we need first of all to cease ascribing ontological precedence to the outcomes of institutionalisation, a view that understands change as something exceptional, a temporary aberration, deviation or unbalancing, that is produced by certain persons under certain conditions. Rather, change must be seen as the standard, base-line condition, permeating reality through and through, the inseparable, undividable, continuous character of reality and thus also of legal institutions. But this effort to push further at the boundaries of our present understanding cannot and will not follow without a reversal in the ontological precedence of institutional stability over change. Institutionalisation must be seen as a function of change; change as ontologically prior to institutionalisation, the condition of its possibility.

What, then, must institutions of law and law as an institution be like if change is constitutive of reality? Here, I will show that change is the result of the reflexive, recursive, inter-weaving of an institutional actor's intricate web of thoughts, values and routine behaviours as a consequence of new experiences obtained through interaction in concrete situations. Inasmuch as this is a continuing process, that is, in so far as it is an institutional actor's attempt to understand, comprehend and act coherently, change is intrinsic to human acting. Law is an attempt to try to make sense of this continuous tide of human activity, its to-ing and fro-ing, and to channel it, and shape it, through generalising and institutionalising meanings and rules. Yet, at the same time, law and legal institutions are patterns arising out of change. So, law is an accomplishment, an achievement, in two ways: first, it is a set of norms utilised in order to attempt to stabilise expectations over time of an always altering reality; second, it is a product, a pattern arising out of the reflexive application of these same norms in concrete situations, over time. Law aims at controlling change; it is also the product of change.

In law, thinking about change usually centres around the idea of change as a resultant state, whose significant features, causes and consequences require explanation and elucidation. This is the view underlying MacCormick's account of institutional concepts: change is approached from the standpoint of external observation. His institutional model therefore takes on a '3-stage' form with transition taking place between these stages over a period of time. In this way, 'frozen' pictures of key aspects along a temporal sequence are accompanied by explanations of the route traced. Nonetheless, however crucial such knowledge is to enabling our understanding, it has certain limitations; not least, because it is an overview, a series of frozen pictures. In this sense, it can never capture the inherent unpredictability and variability that we have been highlighting, the extent to which the continuity of connected micro-processes underlying the routes traced are characterised by indefiniteness and essential un-dividedness. But why is it that stage models, such as that of MacCormick's institutive, consequential and terminative rules, cannot encapsulate the significant characteristics of change?

The beginning of an answer is to be found in the age-old paradoxes of Zeno. Take, for example, the story of Achilles and the tortoise. The problem, as Zeno presents it, is that Achilles cannot ever catch up with and overtake the tortoise because every time that he reaches the tortoise's starting point the tortoise has already moved forward from it. But the real problem with this is not that Achilles cannot ever catch up with the tortoise; rather, it is that Zeno's paradoxes arise on the back of a misplaced assumption that space and time are infinitely divisible. MacCormick has the same problem in respect of the story about the poisonous snake's venom and Cleopatra's tragic demise. Why do we assume that space and time are infinitely divisible? The answer is found in our impulse to intellectualise everything. We try to make sense of what we experience by imposing on our perception a conceptual framework, a template through which to understand. We conceptualise perception in order to make sense of experience but, in so doing, freeze what is an otherwise essentially continuous, moving, ever-mutating phenomenon. It is, of course, our use of concepts that necessarily demands we impose such an arbitrary 'halting' on the continuous flow. Nonetheless, the result of this imposition of a series of static states or positions on what is otherwise an essentially fluid and ever-changing reality is our attempt to understand movement in terms of immobility.

Bergson, on the other hand, claims that to understand movement in terms of a series of successive points in space and time fails to capture what is distinctive about movement. Here, movement from A to B is understood in terms of the positions that something occupies in getting from A to B, in spite of the fact that none of these static positions contains any elements of mobility at all. Conversely, William James argues that the 'stages into which you analyze a change are *states*, the change itself goes on between them. It lies along their intervals, inhabits what your definition fails to gather up, and thus eludes conceptual explanation altogether' (James 1996: 236).

This is exactly the problem that we encounter in MacCormick's theory with his attempt to understand legal change by breaking it down into a series of stages understood in terms of the transition from institutive to consequential to terminative rules. There, too, we perform a reduction of change by converting it into a linear sequence of relatively static positions. But the point being argued here is that, in so doing, we actually lose its essential character and important quality. Instead of capturing what is significant about change, change itself eludes us and remains unexplained and unrecorded. The paradox is this: the conceptual apparatus by which we try to make sense of change fails to get to grips with change. We are unable to understand change *qua change*; that is, change in changeful terms. This is because we attempt to understand it using the language and terms of what it is not; in other words, we attempt to understand change through the use of a conceptual apparatus that denies change. In this sense, to understand change in terms of law is not a question of categories of universal and particular and how to communicate between them, but what both fail to grasp; that is, change, continuous process. To assert that what we need to do, since the universal cannot ever capture the particular, is to focus on the particular, itself misses the point, because that is still the same attempt to understand movement, change and process, in terms of immobility, stability and state. Put differently, we might try to represent change by a series of boxes, marked A, B, C, and so on, and explain that change is the process by which we move from A to B to C and so on. But the problem is that change understood in this way sees the boxes, not what happens between them (change); or, at best, it sees the boxes first, which amounts to the same thing.

If our customary methods of employing our conceptual apparatus in order to understand change continually issues in paradoxes that only serve to deny change, is there another way? Can we understand change in a way that does not contradict, negate or deny change? Bergson suggests that we must re-enter the flow, approaching reality with our senses and connecting through our intuition. For him, we must get to know reality from within. In this sense, only an *un*mediated perception of reality can glimpse its essential features – constant change, undivided continuity, the continual reiterative action and interaction of sameness with difference over time. But how do we get to know something 'from within'? For Bergson, this happens when we experience it directly. Through placing ourselves at the centre of something we can experience something directly and know it from within. We identify with something through intuitive sympathetic understanding; for example, drawing on the resources of our own experience to understand the complexity of someone else. Bergson cites the example of a man with photographs of Paris, arguing that he could 'feel' it from the photographs because he already knew it from being in it, but without that intuitive sympathetic understanding he could not. Similarly, when we listen to music, we do not hear simply a succession of static, individual notes but the continuing movement of the melody. We move with its flow, listening to it from within. Intuition, direct unmediated experience, insight, paying attention from within, sensual perception rather than intellectual conception, really are all pointing to the same thing: holding both continuity and difference, the homogeneous and the heterogeneous, together. But we are still left with the question: how?

Conceptualising change: the problem with universals and particulars

On the one hand, generalisations, or abstract universals, deny differences and seek to hide them; on the other hand, perception recognises difference and is responsive both to difference and to modification. Just so, when everything is the same, even very familiar, its essential character goes unnoticed. Thus, the visitor to a beautifully scenic place will often gasp in awe at the beauty to be experienced all around, while the local inhabitant hardly notices it or takes it for granted. For the one, difference heightens awareness; for the other, sameness dulls perception through the senses. In recent years, we have witnessed increasingly how the ability to produce a work, or technique, of art that shocks at the very least ensures that its author gets noticed. For Bergson

(1946: 135–36) we might say that this is the sign of a good painter, one who has the ability to bring to the forefront of our attention something that had hitherto gone unnoticed. But how does this happen?

One way in which this might happen is through encouraging a sense of detachment; that is, by resisting the obligation to look straight ahead and, instead, to engage what Chia calls our 'peripheral vision' (Chia 1998: 362), to notice fully what is on the fringes of our everyday life and experience in order to really see and understand. But we are too used to looking at things instrumentally, as means rather than as ends in themselves, as examples or instances of general categories, instantiated universals. By contrast, the artistic spirit naturally engages with reality in a different way: 'when they look at a thing they see it for itself, and not for themselves … It is because the artist is less intent on utilizing his perception that he perceives a greater number of things' (Bergson 1946: 138).

So we can gain greater awareness and appreciation of the dynamic complexity of reality by glancing at things rather than gazing, seeing them in and for their ever changing selves rather than in terms of their utility. But of course our minds and senses are not equipped like electron microscopes, to scan almost everything at once. There is a limit to our awareness and our abilities to perceive and to recognise difference and continuous change. We can only perceive to a certain degree of nearness and distance. How and at what point we perceive and come to recognise the effects of global warming on the polar ice cap, the rising of sea levels and the changes of climate that take place over tens and hundreds of years is certainly not comparable to the manner or the degree of perception involved in our experience of the difference between a heavy rainfall or a single day of scorching sun. For the former we cannot but utilise our conceptual apparatus. Therefore, our conceptual apparatus and our direct perception of reality must work together, one supplementing the other.

Looked at from the point of institutions, reality appears deceptively stable. Indeed, from a certain point of analysis stability appears to be correct: I am the same legal person I was yesterday, last month, last year. But I do not have exactly the same body throughout my life, it changes entirely, and from that point of view I am a totally different person. The apparent stability of institutions of law at a certain level of analysis, that of repeated patterns, is a function of the underlying and continuously changing character of all things. In this sense, stability, the static, divided nature of reality, presupposes change, process, un-dividedness. Thus also, in the same way, in relation to the distinction and relation between 'universals' and 'particulars', we can see clearly how it is that what we call the universal is an abstraction from the particular, and we can also see that what we call the particular is itself also an abstraction, from process, or continuous change; therefore, far from denying change, presupposes it. In this way, as Scott Veitch suggests:

[i]t may well be that while there are undoubtedly universal forms, universal and particular in practical reasoning (including legal reasoning) are no more than relative forms of abstraction or of generalization – more or less useful tools, stakes in a debate (or in the lack of a debate), always deployable, not categorical.

(Veitch 2006: 152)

At one level of analysis, that of explanation, it is pattern, repetition, substance, stability, and so on, that are assumed; at another level, that of the actual moment of decision, it is continuous change, process, that we observe. The patterns that we so readily identify and continually refer to are really no more than momentary haltings of that process, which keeps on changing ceaselessly; in other words, reduction achievements that depend, for their intellectual acceptance, on a certain view of the dialectical relationship between facts and rules, particulars and universals, a view that only exists and is given credence through the action of the human agent that links the two.

So we can see how, for analysis and explanation, focusing both on universals and also on particulars is necessary. In this way we are able to keep in our vision both the big picture of things, the extended horizon of reality where time is arrested and concepts are constructed, related, transferred and used, and where things and patterns appear stable and repeatable, and also the nearer picture where momentary but significant decisions are made and time unfolds in a never-to-be-repeated way. But focussing on both particulars and universals and their relatedness in this way is really to focus not on different accounts of things, as if to differentiate between how they are in themselves and how they appear when viewed through the lens of abstraction, but it is really to focus on different *accounts of change*. 'Rules' and 'facts', 'universals' and 'particulars', appear and come together in the moment of decision, the decision *performed* by the human judge as agent, in a synthesis that is directly connected to that human judge's lived experiences. The change in law and by law that is later represented by this made decision, accounted for by way of *ex post facto* explanation or legal 'justification', is actually experienced by the judge as a continuous process, an unfolding in time of possibilities, events and interactions. It is not a process that can be adequately represented in terms of a shift from one stable position to another stable position; rather, change is fundamental. Therefore, it is not sufficient if we are to take continuous change and process seriously in this way, that we then produce an account of legal change that is represented in terms of decisions that shift the state of affairs from state A to state B (that is, from afar, as abstract concepts). Instead, we need to find a way of understanding and re-presenting change as it is when experienced from within; that is, of re-presenting change in changeful terms, taking seriously the full import of Levi's injunction that the classification changes as the classification is made. So we need now to try and address the difficult problem of how to do this: how can those ideas that we have been contemplating be expressed in law? How would we begin to describe a processual model of legal institutional change and decision-making?

All of the legal and social philosophers whose writings we have been considering here accept the idea that law as a social system is to be regarded in terms of its capacity for reducing differences between human agents. In MacCormick's terms it is the procedure of generating repetitive behaviour through institutional categories and structuring thought: for something to be an instance of institution A implies A-typical behaviour. As we have noted, following Searle and Berger and Luckmann, MacCormick relates types of behaviour to types of situations and types of actors. In this way, a legal institution, say, contract, provides legal persons with a thought framework with corresponding and appropriate choices of action.

Clearly, on the one hand, decision-making implies generalisation and the subsumption of particulars under generic categories which, although not objectively available to institutional actors at every different point in time, are defined socially by context. On the other hand, as we have seen, those same categories and their contents and their meanings are always changing. In this way, therefore, we can see how the legal institution is both a recognisable and *relatively stable framework* or *structure* and also an unfolding, evolving or *continuously changing pattern* in and to which new descriptions are constantly being added. As categories are utilised by institutional actors and drawn upon by human judges as agents so the generalisations change in ways that are not always predictable.

This occurs because although the definitions relevant to those categories are to some extent set by the institution they are not set conclusively: law lacks full control over these definitions. In order for legal institutional action, in terms of established and recognisable recurrent behaviour patterns, to be possible there must be some stability or control exercised over definitional categories, some form of closure of these categories, however impermanent. We can appreciate this when we realise that legal institutions do not exist in a vacuum but are set within a wider social context where change occurs more obviously; in this way, social change affects legal institutions through constant interaction. Changes occur in society that challenge and stretch legal definitional categories to their limits, and beyond. Categories which are clearly helpful in many, even most, contexts and situations appear to be of more limited use in others. In these latter situations potential challenges occur that could not be foreseen and so ideas about rules and definitions and their relevant applications must be revised. To make the point in another way, legal institutional action necessarily presupposes both bounded, rule-attracting behaviour and activity and also the non-rule-like behaviours of those involved in ongoing and evolving non-bounded contextual activities.

Just so, we know what we mean when we refer to theft as a category of acts that correctly attract criminal sanction: what we mean by this is derived from a shared cultural background of understandings and experiences. But what about certain types of white collar theft, different types of tax fraud or theft of intellectual property, patents, and so on? We can see that as we begin to move further and further away from the stable core of shared meanings represented by the models belonging to or utilised by our common cultural background, variations appear to challenge the core of settled meanings and the categories in which these are represented, and these must then be addressed individually to determine their inclusion or exclusion. However, the point is that we are still able to do this and do it through extension of our stable categories, to make reasoned and reasonable decisions regarding these because we can see how it is that we are able to differentiate, mark a distinction and extend the scope of application of our generic categories to include or exclude and thus to alter or modify these. Hart's famous example of the question of what exactly is included and what is excluded in an order banning wheeled vehicles in the park illustrates this clearly; as, indeed, for vastly different reasons, does the question of whether artificial insemination by a donor constitutes adultery and provides grounds for divorce in the case of *MacLennan v. MacLennan* (1958 SLT 12). Here the judge is not simply clarifying the content of relevant categories and sorting out the allocation of particulars to universals but making a value judgement that changes, re-defines, re-creates and re-determines the law at that point. As Taylor (1985) maintains, applying a concept is always a performative and normative act in the sense that it involves a functional determination of how the rules apply in practical situations, an extension of the rules through use of the imagination: every application of a rule in a marginal case noticeably transforms the rule. Thus, institutional concepts themselves throw up marginal cases: by their very nature as incompletely circumscribed entities their edges are blurred.

But we can also see how the control of institutional categories and definitions by law is limited in another way. While it is true that our interaction with the world we live in often throws up situations and events that could not have been foreseen, our ability to interact with our own thoughts about the world and to interact with our interactions can also lead to new distinctions, the awareness of ever newer possibilities and potentials, albeit as they are imagined or described through simile and metaphor. Thus, we are back once again with the recursive application of descriptions and descriptions of descriptions, with our reflexive capacity to usher up new descriptions that are themselves the result of our reflection on our own behaviour and thought, and our thoughts about these, as if these were real, independent entities observed objectively by us from a distance. In such 'worlds within worlds' almost everything could always be otherwise. Does law accommodate and encourage, can law ever permit, such institutional reflexivity? Are the conditions necessary for such reflexivity to occur to be found in law? In

Bańkowski's terms, à la Schauer, and bearing in mind Christodoulidis' arguments about the force of exclusionary reasons, can the curtain be lifted? And, if so, how?

The first thing to notice is that, whatever positivistic claims may be made from time to time to suggest otherwise, even legal institutional categories are only closed temporarily. Human interactions, with events, objects and people, as with oneself, are not individually distinct but intermingle and are woven together with other interactions, current and previous, forever altering. Moreover, we do not ever cease to weave this web of beliefs and habits and actions such that any part of it could be said to be identifiably and individually distinct; rather, we continually struggle to maintain some coherent sense of it all both in spite of and because of its forever changing, reconfiguring nature. Thus, our ability to forever generate new forms and patterns of meaning, new descriptions and configurations and reconstructions is unceasing. We repeatedly generate new patterns. Even our memory of past events is not simply a repetition, but a repetition that is constructed in terms of and constrained by our present sense of what is important or significant. Each adjustment may be miniscule, but every repetition is an adjustment that represents a change. This becomes obvious when we consider how the same thing said at one point in time and then again at a different point in time are two different things. Thus, in every case some change, however small, occurs and the categories are altered and reconfigured. Every decision according to law is a change in law and every case changes the rule; every fact, every inclusion and every exclusion, every time. Repeated applications of a rule do not simply affirm its stable, unchanging correctness of application, but effect a modification, or refinement, even if only by the simple fact of each further application operating to accommodate what is significant in each new case, which must also, in turn, do something new to alter the sense of established expectations. Therefore law must always have an improvisational character, consisting more in terms of a working hypothesis, accepted and utilised by legal institutional actors struggling to make sense of and to act in a coherent way in the world.

So we need first to be able to see through the smokescreen that is presented by the way we use the terms 'particulars' and 'universals', 'rule-determination' and 'rule-application', 'legislation' and 'adjudication', to give an appearance of institutional stability, if we are to begin to uncover any sense of this underlying reality of continuing change. Law and legal institutions are not in states of being but in a perpetual process of becoming: legal institutional categories are always on the threshold of change, modifying and altering to allow new experiences and new facts to be accommodated. We may indeed talk of particulars and universals as if these were 'real things' and abstractions from 'real things' but, as Whitehead rightly notes, ultimately there is no such object that undergoes change, no unchanging subject of change. Instead, there is only change and the choices, actions and decisions of change: reality as such does not change but, in Bergson's terms, change constitutes reality.

What, then, might an idea of legal change mean? How does it make sense to talk in these terms? Is change in law something exacted on law from without, or is it more properly something internal to law? If we accept what has been said so far we can see that far from being characterised in terms of the former, as some conscious creative effort or external application of force, change, as underlying reality, is very much an inherent feature of law as, indeed, it is of all reality. Even the most passive accommodation of new experiences already is and is potential for further change. But the degree to which such change will be institutionally effective is, of course, dependent on the extent to which institutional actors, in particular the agents of institutional decision-making, take up its opportunities for interaction.

So we can see how a process perspective on legal institutional decision-making, in light of all of this, will place strong emphasis on the situational aspects of judicial action and on social relations as the source of structure and order. That is to say, legal institutions are contexts of decision-making structured locally through social interaction, possessing durable institutional force. Within such settings and contexts, human legal institutional actors are always confronted with distinct circumstances and choices. These circumstances condition the situations in as much as they are included or excluded as relevant or not by the human agent. It is precisely this emphasis on perceiving institutional life as continually changing and forever evolving contingently that marks the character of process thought as pertinent to our discussion here. Legal institutional phenomena are not considered as entities, bounded states, but as unfolding processes, happenings, events in which decision-makers make choices from out of the various alternatives presented to them, choosing to actualise certain potentialities and not others, and where the further potential choices and possibilities for actualisation depend on those previous choices made for the range of new possibilities open to choose from. Legal decisions *are* unfolding processes, in which judges interact with unavoidably local conditions through recourse to rules, etc. What, from an external observation point, seems like decision-making controlled by legal rules and other norms is, in fact, experienced internally as a subtle yet dynamic succession of finely tuned actions and interactions in a continuously evolving realisation of what is really happening and being made to happen. That is to say, legal institutions do not exist or operate independently of the human actions and decisions that constitute their working out, but in and through them. We might also say that legal rules and legally relevant facts, universals and particulars, operative facts and evidentiary facts, and so on, do not exist prior to and thus determine the existence of the decision-making event; rather, they appear as a part of the process of engaging with the tensions and the fields of force that characterise it.

On this understanding, legal institutions are indeed sites of human activity and decision: institutional actors draw upon the structure and framework of interrelated legal institutional categories that function to make their behaviour predictable but, in so far as it is within and upon inescapably local concrete conditions that their activities of reflecting upon these and seeking to adapt and apply them takes place, such categories are always unavoidably altering and modifying. Of course, this may be minimal, in the sense of dealing with decisions where the question of rule-application is obvious, not in the least bit complicated or problematic, but it may also be maximal, where such certainties do not hold. Nonetheless, every time that a legal institutional actor acts imaginatively to extend the circumference of application of a rule or institutional category significant change occurs. This is really only another way of saying that change is immanent in legal institutions through the inescapable interaction of institutional actors with their environment, in the accumulation of new experiences. Such actors are inherently reflexive: they are forever drawing new distinctions, creating fresh and lively metaphors, making new connections. There is no escaping this: the world around a judge is not closed off from the potential for new experience and every action and interaction with it and in it is pregnant with creative potential. New meanings, new actions, new decisions, all create a constant need and increasing momentum for creating and recreating, weaving and interweaving webs of beliefs and habits and attitudes.

Certainly, throughout, our use of conceptual abstractions from concrete reality is unavoidable. We could not navigate our way around or begin to act coherently within the world of everyday living without recourse to these useful and necessary aids. How could I possibly eat my breakfast if I did not first accept that at some level of analysis that yellowy-white object that I call an egg has some sort of objective existence. But all that this really implies is that not only is change immanent in institutions, but it is also pushed along by them; in other words, it is institutional change. For instance, in MacCormick's understanding of the dual meaning of institution: law as an institution in a social sense is the locus of forever evolving human actions and interactions; institutions of law in the philosophical sense are ways of creating meaning through the patterns of repeated, reiterated human behaviour, decisions and action. So the use of the term institution can be used in respect of law to encompass both the input and the outcome of human action. In one sense, it is the conceptual tool, the structure and framework of thinking, *for* human action, while, in another sense, in terms of pattern, it is generated *by* it. What MacCormick shows us is how law operates both as an institution to enable us to observe change and an institutionalising activity in which we actively work to make and discover meaning out of the otherwise continuous and somewhat chaotic flow and flux of life, and in all of this judges to some extent have to 'make do' or improvise in the activity of judicial decision-making.

In a sense, this is what the common law doctrines of *ratio decidendi* and precedent are all about. Judges, in making legal determinations, must attempt to negotiate the tensions inherent in the activity of legal decision-making by accommodating, adapting and altering legal understandings both in response to past and in view of future accommodations, adaptations, and alterations. The inevitable 'gap' that then appears to open up between our use of abstract generalisations and the concrete facts of individual cases that we seek to relate these to simply reinforces this view that judges must improvise as they reflect on their own understandings and those of their fellow judges. However, the point is that this description is not a description of the exceptional case, the occasional irksome departure from an otherwise stable system; rather, it is the norm. Change is not an imposition on an otherwise fixed and constant state of affairs, but it takes place all the time that judges and others in legal institutions do what they are trained and paid to do, applying the law as legal professionals in concrete settings. Moreover, none of this should be taken to suggest that because of law's inherent inde-terminacy it is somehow bound to be incoherent. Indeed, quite the opposite, since all of this activity concerning the interrelating of one's thoughts, deci-sions and actions with those of others produces, from concrete situations, precisely those patterns that interrelate over time to bring about an emergent institutionalisation.

Of course, law as a system must respond to changes in its external envir-onment. But how law responds is a complex, evolving, multi-textured affair determined internally by law itself, by its own historically created self-understandings. If there is a significant question to be posed here perhaps it should be set in terms of how it is that particular aspects of law's self-understandings are made to seem relevant in particular and changing contexts over time. For example, changes in society put pressure on legal decision-makers' legal understandings in order to improve the response of the legal system to the problems and social pressures that arise. Societal changes may lead to calls for a better determination of criminal law and its many applications and enforcements through the criminal justice system, but, if anything, it is the legal decision-maker's understanding and appreciation of societal changes that will in the end influence her response.

So, to reiterate, each new decision changes law and, as legal decision-makers act later, they do so in the wake of previous decisions. In turn, this must also generate different understandings of the possibilities of legal decision-making, different opportunities for imagining newer possibilities not previously inti-mated. In other words, when viewed from an external position, the changes represented by new legal decisions may seem like discrete, simply locatable closed or bounded episodes that effect a technical shift from one stable position to another, but, seen from inside the decision-making process, they will be experienced more in terms of the ongoing flow of creative potential, choices arising in and through opportunities for decision-making that could not have been predicted or anticipated before. Decisions, once made, may yet have to be presented as based on legal principles, but each relatively discrete legal decision, taken in respect of its own concrete historical circumstances, all unrepeatable in time, must to some extent alter, adapt or modify those legal principles. To put it another way, the decision in *Re A*, despite Lord Justice Ward's insistence on its 'very unique' character, effects change in the legal situation: it expands the criteria merely by being there.

What all of this amounts to is different ways of making the same point: change is not something external to law, imposed on it from the outside. Change is ongoing, in law as in all else, a fundamental feature, law. Levi has shown through a number of case histories (referred to earlier) how a momentum for change can gradually build up and increase to be continually modified and adapted by those involved in the decision-making process. Not all of the opportunities for decision that opened up could have been anticipated or foreseen, but unfolded gradually, some triggering others and opening up new discursive contexts that would then allow them. Where legislative enactments are made to work in local concrete situations, there is always some adaptation, alteration or modification, some improvisation by the human agent as decision-maker, whether this occurs by way of inclusion or exclusion as the terms and categories of law are imaginatively considered and extended and put into effect.

So change in law should not to be understood merely in terms of deliberate, measured change; that is only a small part of the whole situation, at least under the argument being put forward here. Changes in law as an institution and in its legal institutions occur all the time. There is no need to posit an intentional actor, a calculating, purposeful author of change, in order to account for legal change. Such changes as might arise in this way occur only on the back of, and because of, law's always-already changing nature. But without a recognition of this fundamental character of change at the heart of reality as undergirding, overarching and permeating law we will be unable to appreciate law's underlying processual nature. It is only because law is, at root, one expression of an otherwise ongoing activity in which individuals are forever trying to make sense of new experiences and to actualise new possibilities that we are able to appreciate how the more obvious aspects of planned change also come about.

What is the role of judicial discretion and a judge's deliberation in all of this? It ought to go without saying that judges must be able to see clearly what is transpiring in the facts of the case before them and be able to discover and identify among these the coherent and legally sustainable pattern of persons, events and circumstances that accommodates and reflects what is going on. Significant changes in law often take place when a judge or judges consider the circumstances of the case before them and, holding these together with their own experiences of similar cases, effect an intervention in law by agreeing to distinguish the present case on particular grounds. In such cases, these locally significant facts become amplified in terms of their legal significance and their specific differences become institutionalised depending on the structural context envisaged by the judges. Seen from this perspective, as it were from the inside, judges must be attentive to the nuances of the discursive context appropriate to their deliberations; that is, they must keep in mind how certain legal codes have been shaped historically and how these codes and the practices associated with them have developed and changed over time as a result both of others' and of their own thinking and decisions. In other words, in terms of our previous discussion, judges need to acquire the skills relevant to attuning their thoughts to recognise those subtle legally specific differences and sensitive nuances.

Thus, we can see how change in law or, more correctly, deliberate change in law may come about not so much by the realisation of a conscious desire and plan to effect particular change(s) but as the subtle introduction of new ways of thinking or understanding. Such new ways of talking are, effectively, new forms of legal interpretation; in short, a new language, a new discursive context. We can see something similar happening as a result of the new methods of quality assessment in higher education. Here new ways of assessing and recording allow some but not others of the methods, practices and goals of teaching already in place to be amplified. In this way, they work to reinforce certain interpretative codes that in turn will be more likely to allow other novels ways and aims to be more easily and subtly introduced and to become established. In this way, recursively, over time, a whole new system can be created, almost imperceptibly. Here, again, this is not so much about introducing wholesale change as an interruption to an otherwise stable system; really, it is more about recognising the underlying processual nature of reality and discovering the already-existing ongoing changes. In this way, a changing of the terms of the discussion or debate, even altering the accepted meanings of the same terms, will eventually create a new context of discussion.

What all of this suggests is the constant need to be aware of the resources that decision-makers require to be able to interpret and reinterpret their own experiences and of the availability of a common language to enable them to interrelate their decisions. In this sense, change in law is not simply something imposed on from without, as legislative response to growing political unease or social disquiet, but something effected through the locally significant acts and responses of judicial decision-making. Nor is this simply to understand the power of judges to effect change in law as limited to the exercise of some technical device akin to the declaratory power of the High Court in Scots Law, its institutional power to authorise and thereby effect 'a change in the world by representing it as having been changed' (Searle 1998: 150). This sense of 'declaring' change is precisely the reason why the catch-phrase 'You're fired!' in the popular television series *The Apprentice* has become so captivating for contemporary audiences. By the simple utterance of these words the new state of affairs that they describe is brought about. Likewise, judges' powers to make and deliver decisions in law are powers to permit fresh observations from everyday reality, to draw new distinctions and to see new relations and interrelations, to compel others to restructure their systems of thought, and to re-pattern or re-weave their webs of belief, habit and action. However, from the perspective of the underlying processual nature of reality, and already ongoing change, these so-called 'declaratory powers' are merely institutional interruptions: they may indeed introduce new ways of thinking and speaking and understanding and provide revised templates for judicial decision-making, but it is the local circumstance of actual decision-making situations, real cases whose outcomes must be decided under the pressures of time and lack of resources, that will ultimately provide the authentic basis for understanding change, being the places where these new codes and interpretations are further interpreted and re-interpreted according to the local concrete circumstances of the cases they are made to address and brought to bear upon.

As far as the argument being advanced here is concerned, we might conclude that a major part of the legal theoretical task must include a sense in which legal theorists should give a theoretical priority to the natural, incremental, and relentless aspects of microscopic change that produce change by adaptation, variation, unexpected and unforeseen opportunity. Why? Well, not least because such change reflects the actual becoming of things, the underlying nature of reality. This, then, is what it might mean to observe change from within: to look at the different ways in which all institutional actors (including but not only judges) modify, alter and adapt their webs of habit, thought and acting in response to new experiences in new situations and the many different ways in which decision-makers can be said to influence and thus interrupt the otherwise ongoing flow of institutional activity. Making sense of the process of the institutional becoming of law must inevitably mean a bringing together of several dynamics of the experience of legal decision-making that have hitherto been considered separate; that is, not just the legal but the political, the ethical, the cultural, and other dimensions, too.

Chapter 14

Law as process; legal decision-making as an actual occasion in concrescence

For Whitehead, an actual occasion is a whole, undivided occasion of experience that *becomes* immediately in a quantum of time but which, for the purposes of analysis may be distinguished into several logically successive and mutually related phases of its concrescence. In its initial receptive phase, the present occasion of experience comprises a double inheritance from the past, which Whitehead terms 'conformation of feeling'. But each moment of human subjective experience not only involves a reception of data from the immediate past; it also involves some personal response to what is inherited. And while no control can be exercised over *what* is received, *how* it is responded to will involve some measure of choice. The responsive and integrative phases of the process of concrescence are where the personal decision about this reaction is formed. While no restatement of the previous summary description of Whitehead's philosophical scheme will be presented here, the earlier definitional discussion of nomenclature should be assumed throughout the following analysis. At this point, then, we may attempt some preliminary integration of Law and Process.

The sum total of Whitehead's contribution to thinking about law amounts to no more than a few brief comments on common law, legal systems, legal determinations, legal organisations, legal agencies, and legal contracts, and a slightly longer passage on the foundations of property and contract law. However, this lack of a sustained treatment of the subject of law may be due rather more to the unavailability of any systematic or sufficiently detailed theory of law which it could address than to the inapplicability of his philosophy to law as such. Absent such a theory it is difficult to see how Whitehead could possibly have provided the sort of analysis for law that he does in relation to the history of Western civilisation, and that might, in turn, have confirmed his doctrine of the self-creativity of actual entities and his metaphysical system. Nonetheless, recent developments from a variety of theoretical perspectives, particularly those that can be gathered under the banner of an 'institutional' theory of law, appear to adopt precisely the sort of common strategy that, given their shared emphasis on the nature of law as a normative institution combining norms affecting general conduct with those providing authorisation to officials, may now allow that hitherto unavailable form of access.

In what follows, I aim, first, to recall our earlier discussion of MacCormick's institutional theory of law, noting how this fully worked out theory of law defines and deploys its basic unit of explanation, 'the institutional fact': second, with recourse to a Whiteheadian process-theoretical model (Dibben 2001), to provide a theoretical description of the institutional theory of law and its practical application in terms of the meaning structure of process thought and, in so doing, to explore more fully how a legal decision is created and maintained within the legal decision-making process; and, third, thereby help to extend the application and broaden the appeal of process thought beyond its existing boundaries.

The discussion presented earlier outlined MacCormick's theory of the development of institutional normative order and its relation to the common law practice of decision-making through its interaction with a theory of legal reasoning that stresses the significance of the justifying relationship between reason and decision. However, although this theory highlights the importance of understanding the temporal development of law as normative in a way that affirms its dual aspects as momentary and dynamic, no attempt has yet been made to relate this to any wider theory of process or even to suggest that this might be possible.

This chapter argues that not only is such integration possible, it is desirable and necessary. In order to comprehend more fully the deeper complexities of the process under consideration, to increase our awareness of the likely constitution and structure of the judicial decision-making experience, a more detailed analysis of the interaction of the different types and levels of influence will be attempted. This analysis presents an outline of the basic elements of process described by Whitehead and uses these to explore the way in which a discrete instance of legal judgement is created and maintained within the decision-making process.

In an analysis of trust as process, Dibben suggests that the:

> accuracy of a theory of process to trust development depends, ultimately, on selection of the appropriate unit of analysis. Given the concrescing actual entity as the central concept, or irreducible unit of analysis, in Whitehead's explication of the process of the development of experiential existence … integration is made easier by the establishment of four simplifying conditions:
>
> (1) a purposeful distinction can be made between an actual entity and an actual occasion, whereby (a) the actual occasion is the unit under immediate discussion (that which is in the process of becoming) and (b) the actual entity is the unit which is formed, 'is immortal in the past', and which the actual occasion prehends in its coming into existence;

(2) following from the first condition, that the appropriate units of analysis for the actual occasions in concrescence are selected;

(3) the appropriate actual entities affecting the concrescences are identified and discussed and;

(4) the appropriate eternal objects are identified and discussed.

(Dibben 2001: 5)

Assuming Dibben's simplifying conditions, it should now be possible to outline a proposal for how this model might usefully be employed in law (how the legal system might be understood as a society of societies of actual occasions and how the various phases of the theory of concrescence of an actual entity might be seen to map onto the different phases of judicial decision-making) and submitted for confirmation/refutation by a more extensive study of legal decision-making and the decision-making process.

If the attempt to integrate law within a theory of process can be understood as an attempt to explore how a legal decision is created and maintained within the decision-making system, then the accuracy of applying a theory of process to law will depend on the selection of appropriate units of analysis: identifying the levels of actual occasions and actual entities that can be isolated for analysis and the enduring traits or forms that can be termed eternal objects. That a legal decision can be understood in this way, as an actual occasion of experience affected in its concrescence by a set of actual entities, really follows from what has already been said regarding types of knowledge and complex occasions of experience, made possible through the adoption of a process terminology and structure of meaning. The persistence, regularity and significance of legal decisions across the legal system may then be seen to arise from the creative impulse which determines that an actual occasion in the process of concrescence will, in passing from subject to object, immediately become part of the world of entities affecting future concrescing occasion: law's creativity arises from the continuing creativity of new legal decisions.

Following Dibben, then, we can attempt an integration of a theory of legal reasoning based on MacCormick's institutional theory of law with a process-theoretical model derived mainly from Whitehead's Philosophy of Organism. We can isolate for the purpose of analysis:

a. the following levels of actual occasion:

(i) the current quantum moment of the decision-making process upon which situational cues will act to modify expression;

(ii) confirming/conflicting behaviour towards a decision (universalising/consequences);

(iii) confirming/conflicting action towards decision (coherence/consistency);

(iv) the formed (justified) decision.

b. the following four levels of actual entity:
  (i) previous decisions, including the previous moment of decision in the immediately prior occasion, combining to form a set (S) to affect the concrescence of the actual occasion that is the quantum under discussion;
  (ii) criteria for decision-making as separate actual entities combining to form a set (C) which, along with the actual occasion of level (i), now a complex actual entity, affect the concrescence of the actual occasion that is the confirming/conflicting (consequential balancing) behaviour of each of the universalised features under discussion;
  (iii) the actual occasions of level (ii) now each a set of actual entities which are the cooperative behaviours which combine to affect the concrescence of the actual occasion that is the coherent/consistent action that takes place among the rules;
  (iv) the set of actual entities that are the situational judgements (J) which combine to affect the concrescence of the actual occasion that is the altering justified decision of the judge.
c. enduring and eternal objects:
  (i) justified decisions and precedent, rules, principles and values, may be identified as enduring objects due to their semi-permanent nature;
  (ii) dispositional aspects associated with *habitus* are identified as simple eternal objects or universals being both transtemporal and 'unanalysable into a relationship of component eternal objects' (Whitehead 1933: 240). This affects the level (i) actual occasion, where such eternal objects are prehended by the actual occasion in the absence of the enduring object (rule or precedent).

This attempt to integrate the institutional theory of law and its associated method of legal reasoning within a processual understanding is made in order to explore how a discrete instance of legal judgement is created and maintained throughout the legal decision-making process. The purpose of this section is to explore how a legal decision might arise and how it might be maintained throughout the period of its concrescence. To do this, we rely partly on Whitehead and partly on the conclusion reached earlier that law is a form of tacit knowledge invoked in order to overcome a deficit of explicit knowledge about a situation. That law may be considered to be a type of knowledge in these terms is confirmed by Whitehead: '[knowledge is] conscious discrimination of objects experienced ... derived from, and verified by, direct intuitive observation' (Whitehead 1933: 176).

We have noted that conscious perception may be understood in terms of affirmative judgements that arise in some circumstances in relation to propositional feelings. Here, 'the entertainment the mind gives ... is called a belief ... admitting or receiving ... any proposition for true, upon arguments or proofs that are found to persuade us to receive it as true, without [explicit] knowledge that it is so' (Whitehead 1929: 267). This is the general rule of process that allows us to understand and accept law in terms of the positive expectations that an individual holds towards another's motives and acts in a situation entailing risk and which thus allows some general prediction to be made of it regarding both its capacity for endurance (consequential rules) and its decline (terminative rules). However, Whitehead insists that the 'triumph of consciousness comes with the negative intuitive judgement … produced by the definite exclusiveness of what is really present' (Whitehead 1929: 273). Here, the lack of explicit knowledge and the feeling of absence which cannot be addressed lead to the need for law. In this sense, there is a double deficit with regard to law, both in terms of explicit knowledge and of the implicit knowledge required as a result of this. This double deficiency is experienced by the decision-maker as a strong emotion.

The making of a legal decision is properly a type of knowledge, a complex occasion of experience whose concrescence is affected by a set of actual entities (set S). The justification of this legal decision (its determination as a ruling for this case) is the actual occasion in concrescence emerging from the conscious integration of the situational decision (complex actual entity) with the dispositional threshold that is the result of a simplifying abstraction of individual prehensions of another set of actual entities (set C). We can now attempt to unpack these processes in more detail.

We can explicate the creation of a discrete instance of legal judgement (ie a level (i) actual occasion) in a judge's mind, its continuity over time throughout the period of the decision-making process, and the development of coherence and consistency thresholds (level (ii) actual occasions), by further summarising Dibben's analysis of trust and adapting it to law in terms of Whitehead's description of the three phases of concrescence of an actual occasion. For example, let us suppose that a judge, J, is presently involved in the process of decision-making with respect to the facts of a case, F. According to normal usage, we might say that she has come to (intuited) her decision and now she must justify it. But how does she come to her decision, how does she know that it is valid and how can she be sure that her subsequent accounting for it will actually correspond to her intuited decision? This is really another way of asking how *she* knows that *she* has been making *this* decision in *that* way throughout. How is it accounted for in her experience now? In one sense, the answer is obvious, she remembers. But since it is really memory that is at issue here, then this statement explains very little. Whitehead's answer is that the judge experiences it now with the same subjective form of experiencing that she felt a fraction of a second ago. This is the first phase in the immediacy of the new concrescing occasion, concerned solely with physical prehensions.

Whitehead, as we noted earlier, uses 'feeling' as a way of describing this 'passing from the objectivity of the data to the subjectivity of the actual entity in question'; that is, the 'variously specialized operations' that effect its 'transition into subjectivity' (Whitehead 1929: 41). In other words, the 'feeling' our judge enjoyed in her past moment of decision-making is present in her new moment of decision-making as a datum felt, with a subjective form conformal to the datum. So, if A is the past occasion, and E is the datum felt by A with a subjective form describable as A deciding, then this feeling is felt initially by the new occasion B with the same subjective form of deciding. The feeling enjoyed in the new occasion in this initial phase of concrescence is thus grounded in the experience of causal efficacy; that is, it arises from the data themselves as the past is inherited by the present, rather than as subjective notions read into, or imposed upon, the data of experience. The experienced decision (which MacCormick represents in terms of these evidentiary facts being deemed instances of those operative facts such that certain normative consequences then follow) is continuous throughout the successive occasions of experience within the same decision-making situation. Inasmuch as this feeling is a conscious one, J enjoys a 'subjective perception of the past emotion' (Dibben 2001: 7) towards F as both 'belonging to the past, and ... continued in the present' (Whitehead 1933: 236).

In the event of J hearing a new case involving either a recognised context with unforeseen facts or an unrecognised context with foreseen facts then the enduring object which is this decision of J takes the place of the past occasion A; equally, where both the context and the facts are new and unforeseen then the relevant eternal object takes the place of the past occasion A. In the case of the conformation of a settled decision of J, the process is the same, with the descriptors A, B and E varying accordingly. Thus, the first phase is concerned solely with the conformation of feeling in respect of the actual entity (now datum D) that was the past actual occasion A.

The influence of F occurs in the second, intermediate phase, when unpredictable or uncharacteristic behaviour by F may give rise to the prehension of variations in the situational prompts and so introduce a novel content of positive conceptual prehensions which affect the concrescence of the new actual occasion B. This intermediate phase is 'a ferment of qualitative valuation' where conceptual feelings enter into 'novel relations' with each other and are 'felt with a novel emphasis of subjective form' (Whitehead 1933: 269). In this way, each of the level (i) actual entities (x situational prompts) is understood as an objective datum $O(x)$ felt by A, bringing about B's concrescence.

Now, if A is the past occasion of decision-making (now the actual entity, datum D), and F is the different datum felt by A with subjective form describable as A deciding, then this feeling is, to begin with, felt by the new actual occasion B with a different subjective form of deciding; namely, as correlative to F. That is, it is the subjective form in A, of J, that feels and transforms O to concresce as the new decision-making moment B of J with respect to F.

Clearly, this new decision is also continuous throughout successive occasions of experience within the decision-making situation; that is, J continuously embodies the immediate past decision as a datum in the present and, absent the appearance of additional content from other data, maintains in the present this decision that is a datum from the past. However, the level (i) actual entities felt by B may be felt as a single prehension, arising from the set of actual entities (set S) and taken into account as the objective datum O, through '[t]he transference of the characteristic from the individuals to the group as one … [whereby t]he qualities shared by many individuals are fused into one dominating impression' (Whitehead 1933: 273). Again, inasmuch as this novel feeling of decision is a conscious one, judge J now has a subjective perception of the feeling affected by past feelings (the objective data O(x)/O) toward F. In relation to the concrescence of a new level (iv) actual occasion, or justified decision, the introduction of novel content would be through the level (iv) set of actual entities (set T) that are the past moments of decision.

The ultimate phase in the concrescence of the new actual occasion B is anticipation: 'the self-enjoyment of an occasion of experience is initiated by an enjoyment of the past as alive in itself and is terminated by an enjoyment of itself as alive in the future' (Whitehead 1933: 248–49).

Thus, if D is the future actual occasion that is the decision of J with regard to F, this is affected by the prehension of what is now the level (ii) complex actual entity B* (from the previous level (i) actual occasion B) along with the set of actual entities C as a limiting condition for application. This limiting condition is a dominating impression that arises from the intuitive blending of several distinctive features of members of the set of actual entities (set C) detailed above, though there is no necessary relation between this limiting condition and the complex actual entity B* since they are contemporaries; nonetheless, they do 'originate from a common past and their objective immortality operates within a common future' (Whitehead 1933: 252). The valuation of subjective forms yields both the limiting condition and the type of decision that, depending on their values, affect the concrescence of the level (ii) actual occasion as either a rule-determining or non-rule-determining decision of J applied in respect to F. Significantly, this entire process of the concrescence of consequent and contemporary actual occasions will occur on the part of F also, so that the level (iii) actual occasion is the result action resulting from the combined effect of both J's behaviour towards F and F's influence on J.

For Whitehead, to be an actual entity is to be a self-created, fully formed, fully definite, fully determinate, entity with nothing left unresolved. From the whole mass of possible determinations, each actual occasion decides what it will become: actualising some potentials and excluding or rejecting others, and thus taking up some position in relation to everything, both ideal and actual. It is, by virtue of its decision, a new fact in the world, 'externally free' (Whitehead 1929: 41), but limit*ed* in its freedom by past achievement and limit*ing* by its conditioning of future process. In other words, it is a decision that arises out of previous decisions and provokes future decisions: decision amid potentiality constitutes the very meaning of actuality (Whitehead 1929: 68).

Clearly, the concrescence of an actual occasion in the actual world is limited by the factor of order, the limited possibilities available for synthesis in the data settled and given for it by its antecedent world. In simple terms, one can only create the future out of present circumstances. But order is not the same as mere givenness. The actual world given to an actual occasion for its concrescence also contains elements of disorder. So while the latter certainly gives rise to a satisfaction, it is the former that promotes different levels of intensity in satisfactions relative to the initial objective data. That is, it is through the balance of contrasts, the creative synthesis of conflicting elements in an aesthetic unity, that intensity of satisfaction and value is achieved.

Conclusion

The recollections from personal experience with which I began this book were presented in order to illustrate the type of difficulties involved in any notion of a straightforward application of legal rules to particular facts, events and circumstances. Having defined the problem in terms of the articulation of the relationship between universals and particulars in legal decision-making, I undertook an examination of the case of the conjoined twins, Mary and Jodie, to show how, in attempting to address the situation before it by means of abstract legal representations of those events, law is found to encourage a dualism that results in a shortfall between lived experience and that which can be accounted for by legal representation. The result is an obscuring from view of otherwise relevant information, producing a deficit that is, effectively, a silencing of voices. In this way, and under its compulsion to reach a decision, law can be seen to commit an act of violence on the free flow and expression of opinions and arguments. The critical shortfall that appears is difficult to calculate and impossible to remedy, with attempts to provide justifying reasons for legal decisions forever stumbling on the question of time. It seems like an impossible passage, an unbridgeable gap.

Considering how various attempts have been made to deal with this problem, I suggested that the seeming impossibility of bridging this gap that opens up between theory and practice, rule-determination and rule-application, is in fact symptomatic of a far deeper, underlying problem; that is, while much of contemporary legal theory appears as the expression of a continuing concern to connect legal research with actual judicial decision-making, this effort is misplaced. Instead, although legal theory and legal practice are often considered as if they were two separate but connectable areas, I have argued that an alternative understanding based on the notion of a mutually constitutive process of becoming provides a more adequate and correct way of interpreting the interpenetrating and interrelating aspects of this relationship.

This alternative approach can be traced through the tradition of process thought, in philosophers such as Whitehead, Bergson, Deleuze and Polanyi.

Taken together, their complementary insights are found to offer precisely the sort of alternative means through which a reconfiguration of the problem can be effected and a reconstruction of legal decision-making begun. Informed by attempts from within the field of organization studies to engage in a similar way, I outlined a way of approaching legal decision-making based on Bergson's notion of 'creative evolution'. I then tested this approach using Levi's understanding of the process of legal reasoning, in which he portrays it as proceeding on the basis of a pattern of extending examples. Levi's analysis, and his outlining of the mechanism that drives legal decision-making lends itself well to a process interpretation when taken together with Deleuze and Guattari's metaphor of rhizomic communication.

Having outlined the mutually constitutive nature of the relation between institutions and practices in terms of formal legal contexts, I then focused on the role of the judge as institutional actor and decision-maker. Employing Tsoukas' analysis of the links between individual knowledge, organisational knowledge and human action undertaken within organised contexts, I was able to demonstrate how, while the propositional structure of legal knowledge is fully realised within formal legal contexts in terms of institutions, legal knowledge in terms of practices (that is, as shared traditions in and out of which legal practitioners work), exhibits a narrative structure. In this latter sense, informed by Polanyi's notion of tacit knowledge, it is also possible to demonstrate that legal knowledge is essentially unspecifiable, maintained by anecdote, story and example. Attempts to harness a narrative approach within law can thus be understood to suggest a way of reconceptualising what is involved in the task of legal decision-making as a skill that judges use, a tool to enable them to get at the essential features of the situations before them and of which they are necessarily a part in their role as decision-maker. I explored this further through ideas associated with chaos theory and complexity.

All of this was then brought together to suggest an alternative understanding of law: law's institutional becoming, the becoming of law in institutions. Finally, having negotiated a way through all of this, and with the aid of the process-theoretical approaches mentioned above, I attempted a necessary integration of law and process thought, integrating MacCormick's institutional theory of law within Whitehead's scheme of metaphysical principles, relating his theory of legal reasoning to Whitehead's analysis of the process of concrescence.

Thus, it is now possible to give a presentation of the argument in thoroughly Whiteheadian terms: law as process; legal reasoning as an actual occasion in concrescence. Doing so provides a way of introducing a much-neglected and hitherto relatively unexplored philosophical approach within one of the most complex social processes associated with modern living. Now, in turn, this should potentially open up numerous opportunities for further exploring and meaningfully unpacking many more of the otherwise hidden and inaccessible aspects of law and legal reasoning.

Bibliography

Altman, A. (1986) 'Legal Realism, Critical Legal Studies, and Dworkin', *Philosophy and Public Affairs*, 15(2): 205–36.

Anscombe, G. E. M. (1958) 'On Brute Facts', *Analysis*, 18: 69–72.

Atiyah, P. (1986) 'Form and Substance in Legal Reasoning: The Case of Contract', in D. N. MacCormick and P. Birks (eds) *The Legal Mind: Essays for Tony Honoré*, Oxford: Clarendon Press.

Balter, S. J. (2001) 'The Search for Grounds in Legal Argumentation: A Rhetorical Analysis of Texas vs Johnson', *Argumentation*, 15: 381–95.

Bańkowski, Z. (1991) 'The Institution of Law', *Ratio Juris*, 4(1): 79–85.

——(2000) 'Living In and Out of the Law', in P. Oliver, S. D. Scott and V. Tadros (eds) *Faith in Law*, Oxford: Hart.

——(2001) *Living Lawfully*, Dordrecht: Kluwer.

——(2003) 'Legal Reasoning from the Inside Out', in T. Biernat, K. Palecki, A. Peczenik, C. Wong and M. Zirk-Sadowski (eds) *Stressing Legal Decisions*, Warsaw: Polonia Press.

——(2006) 'In the Judgement Space: The Anxiety of the Encounter', in Z. Bańkowski and J. MacLean (eds) *The Universal and the Particular in Legal Reasoning*, Aldershot: Ashgate.

——(2007) 'Bringing the Outside in: The Ethical Life of Legal Institutions', in T. Gizbert-Studnicki and J. Stelmach (eds) *Law and Legal Cultures in the 21st Century: Unity and Diversity*, Warsaw: Wolters Kluwer Polska.

Barnes, B. (1995) *The Elements of Social Theory*, London: Routledge.

——(2000) *Understanding Agency*, London: Sage.

Battersby, C. (1998) *The Phenomenal Woman*, Cambridge: Polity Press.

Baxandall, M. (1985) *Patterns of Intention: On the Historical Explanation of Pictures*, New Haven, CT: Yale University Press.

Berger, P. and Luckmann, T. (1996) *The Social Construction of Reality*, London: Penguin.

Bergson, H. (1910) *Time and Free Will*, London: Allen & Unwin.

——(1911a) *Creative Evolution*, London: Macmillan.

——(1911b) *La Perception du Changement*, Oxford: Clarendon Press.

——(1911c) 'La Nature de l'Ame', four lectures delivered at London University, reported in *The Times*, 23 October 1911.

——(1912) *An Introduction to Metaphysics*, trans. T. E. Hulme, London: MacMillan.

——(1913) *Laughter: An Essay on the Meaning of the Comic*, London: MacMillan.

——(1946) *The Creative Mind*, New York, NY: Philosophical Library.

Boundas, C. (1993) (ed.) *The Deleuze Reader*, New York, NY: Columbia University Press.

Bourdieu, P. (1990) *The Logic of Practice*, trans. R. Nice, Cambridge: Polity Press.

——(2001) *Practical Reason*, Oxford: Polity Press.

Bratton, M. Q. and Chetwynd, S. B. (2004) 'One Into Two Will Not Go: Conceptualising Conjoined Twins', *Journal of Medical Ethics*, 30: 279–85.

Bruner, J. (1986) *Actual Minds, Possible Worlds*, Cambridge, MA: Harvard University Press.

Bryson, N. (1982) *Vision and Painting*, London: Macmillan Press.

——(1998) 'The Gaze in the Expanded Field', in H. Foster (ed.) *Vision and Visuality*, New York, NY: The New Press.

Chia, R. (1997) '*Essai*: Thirty Years On: From Organizational Structures to the Organization of Thought', *Organization Studies*, 18(4): 685–707.

——(1998) 'From Complexity Science to Complex Thinking: Organization as Simple Location', *Organization*, 5(3): 341–69.

——(1999) 'A "Rhizomic" Model of Organizational Change and Transformation: Perspectives from a Metaphysics of Change', *British Journal of Management*, 10: 209–27.

Christodoulidis, E. A. (1996) 'The Inertia of Institutional Imagination: A Reply to Roberto Unger', *Modern Law Review*, 59(3): 377–97.

——(1999) 'The Irrationality of Merciful Legal Judgement: Exclusionary Reasoning and the Question of the Particular', *Law and Philosophy*, 18: 215–41.

——(2000) 'Truth and Reconciliation as Risks', *Social and Legal Studies*, 9: 179–83.

——(2001) 'Law's Immemorial', in E. A. Christodoulidis and S. Veitch (eds) *Lethe's Law*, Oxford: Hart.

——(2004) 'The Objection that Cannot be Heard: Communication and Legitimacy in the Courtroom', in A Duff, *et al.* (eds) *The Trial on Trial*, Oxford: Hart.

——(2006) 'Eliding the Particular: A Comment on Neil MacCormick's "Particulars and Universals"', in Z. Bańkowski and J. MacLean (eds) *The Universal and the Particular in Legal Reasoning*, Aldershot: Ashgate.

Cooper, R. (1976) 'The Open Field', *Human Relations*, 29(11): 999–1017.

——(1983) 'The Other: A Model of Human Structuring', in G. Morgan (ed.) *Beyond Method*, London: Sage.

——(1992) 'Formal Organization as Representation: Remote Control, Displacement and Abbreviation', in M. Reed and M. Hughes (eds) *Rethinking Organization*, London: Sage.

——(1998) 'Assemblage Notes', in R. Chia (ed.) *Organized Worlds: Explorations in Technology and Organization with Robert Cooper*, London: Routledge.

Deleuze, G. (1988) *Bergsonism*, trans. H. Tomlinson and B. Habberjam, New York, NY: Zone Books.

——(1991) *The Logic of Sense*, trans. Mark Lester, London: Athlone Press.

——and Guattari, F. (1988) *A Thousand Plateaus: Capitalism and Schizophrenia*, trans. Brian Massumi, London: Athlone Press.

Derrida, J. (1992) 'Force of Law: The "Mystical Foundations of Authority"', in D. Cornell *et al.* (eds) *Deconstruction and the Possibility of Justice*, New York, NY: Routledge.

Detmold, M. J. (1984) *The Unity of Law and Morality: A Refutation of Legal Positivism*, London: Routledge.

——(1989) 'Law as Practical Reason', *Cambridge Law Journal*, 48: 436–71.

——(2006) 'The End of Morality: Radical and Descriptive Particularity', in Z. Bańkowski and J. MacLean (eds) *The Universal and the Particular in Legal Reasoning*, Aldershot: Ashgate.

Dibben, M. R. (2001) 'Trust as Process: A Study in the Application of Whiteheadian Thinking to Emotional Experiences', *Concrescence, AJPT.* Online. Available HTTP www.concrescence.org/store/2001/02_dibben.pdf (accessed 23 October 2010).

——and A. Pantelli (2000) 'A Journey Towards the Processual Understanding of Virtual Organisations', *Concrescence, AJPT.* Online. Available HTTP www.concrescence.org/store/2000/01_mrdnp.pdf (accessed 23 October 2010).

Dworkin, R. (1986) *Law's Empire*, London: Fontana.

Fish, S. (1989) *Doing What Comes Naturally: Change, Rhetoric and the Practice of Theory in Literary and Legal Studies*, Oxford: Clarendon Press.

Gadamer, H. G. (1989) *Truth and Method*, 2nd ed., London: Sheed and Ward.

Garlan, E. N. (1941) *Legal Realism and Justice*, New York, NY: Columbia University Press.

Gell-Mann, M. (1994) *The Quark and the Jaguar*, New York, NY: W.H. Freeman.

Gillon, R. (2001) 'Imposed Separation of Conjoined Twins – moral hubris by the English Courts?', *Journal of Medical Ethics*, 27: 3–4.

Griggs, E. L. (ed.) (1971) Collected Letters of Samuel Taylor Coleridge Vol II, Oxford: Oxford University Press.

Günther, K. (1989) 'A Normative Conception of Coherence for a Discourse Theory of Legal Justification', *Ratio Juris*, 2(2): 155–66.

——(1993) *The Sense of Appropriateness*, trans. J Farrell, Albany, NY: SUNY Press.

Habermas, J. (1998) *Between Facts and Norms*, Cambridge, MA: MIT Press.

Hart, H. L. A. (1958) 'Positivism and the Separation of Law and Morals', *Harvard Law Review*, 71: 593–629.

——(1961) *The Concept of Law*, Oxford: Oxford University Press.

Hartshorne, C. (1970) *Creative Synthesis and Philosophic Method*, La Salle, IL: Open Court.

——(1987) *Wisdom as Moderation*, Albany, NY: SUNY Press.

Hosinski, T. E. (1993) *Stubborn Fact and Creative Advance*, Lanham: Rowman & Littlefield.

Jackson, B. (1988) *Law Fact and Narrative Coherence*, Merseyside: Deborah Charles Publications.

——(1990) 'Narrative Theories and Legal Discourse', in C. Nash (ed.) *Narrative in Culture*, London: Routledge.

——(1991) 'Semiotic Scepticism: A Response to Neil MacCormick', *International Journal for the Semiotics of Law*, IV(11): 175–90.

——(1992) 'MacCormick on Logical Justification in Easy Cases: A Semiotic Critique', *International Journal for the Semiotics of Law*, V(14): 203–14.

——(2009) 'Structuralist Semiotics of Law'. Online. Available HTTP http://ivr-enc.info/index.php?title=Structuralist_Semiotics_of_Law (accessed 31 October 2010).

James, W. (1996) *A Pluralistic Universe*, Lincoln, NE: University of Nebraska Press.

Kallinikos, J. (1998) 'Organized Complexity: Posthuman Remarks on the Technologizing of Intelligence', *Organization*, 5(3): 371–96.

Kellert, S. (1993) *In the Wake of Chaos*, Chicago, IL: University of Chicago Press.

Leiter, B. (2003) 'American Legal Realism', in W. Edmundson and M. Golding (eds) *The Blackwell Guide to Philosophy of Law and Legal Theory*, Oxford: Blackwell.

Levi, E. H. (1948) 'An Introduction to Legal Reasoning', *The University of Chicago Law Review*, 15(3): 501–74.

Luhmann, N. (2004) *Law as a Social System*, trans. K. A. Ziegert, Oxford: Oxford University Press.

Lyotard, J.-F. (1984) *The Postmodern Condition*, Manchester: Manchester University Press.

MacCormick, D. N. (1978) *Legal Reasoning and Legal Theory*, Oxford: Oxford University Press.

——(1986) 'Law as Institutional Fact', in N. MacCormick and O. Weinberger (eds) *An Institutional Theory of Law*, Dordrecht: Reidel.

——(1988) 'Institutions, Arrangements and Practical Information', *Ratio Juris*, 1: 73–82.

——(1998) 'Norms, Institutions and Institutional Facts', *Law and Philosophy*, 17: 301–45.

——(2005) *Rhetoric and the Rule of Law*, Oxford: Oxford University Press.

——(2006) 'Particulars and Universals', in Z. Bańkowski and J. MacLean (eds) *The Universal and the Particular in Legal Reasoning*, Aldershot: Ashgate.

——(2007) *Institutions of Law*, Oxford: Oxford University Press.

MacIntyre, A. (1985) *After Virtue: A Study in Moral Theory*, London: Duckworth.

Norrie, A. (1991) *Law, Ideology and Punishment*, Dordrecht; Kluwer.

——(1996) 'The Limits of Justice: Finding Fault in the Criminal Law', *Modern Law Review*, 4: 540.

——(2001) *Crime, Reason and History*, London: Butterworths.

Nussbaum, M. C. (1986) *The Fragility of Goodness*, New York, NY: Cambridge University Press.

——(2001) *Upheavals of Thought: The Intelligence of Emotions*, New York, NY: Routledge.

Parsons, T. and Shils, E. (1951) *Toward a General Theory of Action*, Cambridge, MA: Harvard University Press.

Polanyi, M. (1962) *Personal Knowledge*, Chicago, IL: University of Chicago Press.

——(1966) *The Tacit Dimension*, London: Routledge & Kegan Paul.

——(1969) *Knowing and Being*, ed. M. Grene, Chicago, IL: University of Chicago Press.

——and Prosch, H. (1975) *Meaning*, Chicago, IL: University of Chicago Press.

Popper, K. (1988) *The Open Universe*, London: Hutchinson.

——(1989) *Conjectures and Refutations: The Growth of Scientific Knowledge*, London: Routledge.

Prigogine, I. (1996) *Is Future Given?*, Singapore: World Scientific.

——(1997) *The End of Certainty*, New York, NY: The Free Press.

Raz, J. (1975) *Practical Reason and Norms*, 1st edn, Princeton, NJ: Princeton University Press.

——(1990) *Practical Reason and Norms*, 2nd edn, Princeton, NJ: Princeton University Press.

Reichenbach, H. (1955) *L'avènement de la Philosophie Scientifique*, Paris: Flammarion.

Ricoeur, P. (1984) Time and Narrative, vol. 1, Chicago, IL: University of Chicago Press.

Rose, G. (1992) *The Broken Middle*, Oxford: Blackwell.

Schauer, F. (1991) *Playing by the Rules*, Oxford: Oxford University Press.

Searle, J. (1969) *Speech Acts*, Cambridge: Cambridge University Press.
——(1998) *Mind, Language and Society*, New York, NY: Basic.
Simmonds, N. (1993) 'Judgement and Mercy', *Oxford Journal of Legal Studies*, 13: 52–68.
Singer, J. (1988) 'Legal Realism Now', *California Law Review*, 76: 465.
Smith, S. C. (1995) 'The Redundancy of Reasoning', in Z. Bańkowski, *et al.* (eds) *Informatics and the Foundations of Legal Reasoning*, Dordrecht: Kluwer.
Taylor, C. (1985) *Human Agency and Language*, Cambridge: Cambridge University Press,
——(1993) 'To follow a rule … ', in C. Calhoun *et al.* (eds) *Bourdieu: Critical Perspectives*, Cambridge: Polity Press.
Tolstoy, L. (1948) *War and Peace*, trans. R. Edmonds, Harmondsworth: Penguin.
Toulmin, S. (1990) *Cosmopolis: The Hidden Agenda of Modernity*, Chicago, IL: University of Chicago Press.
Tsoukas, H. (1996) 'The Firm as a Distributed Knowledge System: A Constructionist Approach', *Strategic Management Journal*, 17: 11–25.
——(1998a) 'Chaos, Complexity and Organization Theory', *Organization*, 5(3): 291–313.
——(1998b) 'Forms of Knowledge and Forms of Life in Organized Contexts', in R. Chia (ed.) *In the Realm of Organization: Essays for Robert Cooper*, London: Routledge.
——(2003) 'Do we really Understand Tacit Knowledge?', in M. Easterby-Smith and M. A. Lyles (eds) (2005) *The Blackwell Handbook of Organizational Learning and Knowledge Management*, Oxford: Blackwell.
——and Cummings, S. (1997) 'Marginalization and Recovery: The Emergence of Aristotelian Themes in Organization Studies', *Organization Studies*, 18(4): 655–83.
——and Hatch, M. J. (2001) 'Complex Thinking, Complex Practice: The Case for a Narrative Approach to Organizational Complexity', *Human Relations*, 54(8): 979–1013.
——and Vladimirou, E. (2001) 'What is Organizational Knowledge?', *Journal of Management Studies*, 38(7): 973–93.
Twining, W. and Miers, D. (1991) *How to Do Things with Rules*, 3rd edn, London: Wiedenfeld & Nicholson.
Unger, R. M. (1996) 'Legal Analysis as Institutional Imagination', *Modern Law Review*, 59: 1–23
Veitch, S. (1996) 'Doing Justice to Particulars', in E. A. Christodoulidis (ed.) *Communitarianism and Citizenship*, Aldershot: Ashgate.
——(2006) '"A Very Unique Case": Reflections on Neil MacCormick's Theory of Universalization in Practical Reasoning', in Z. Bańkowski and J. MacLean (eds) *The Universal and the Particular in Legal Reasoning*, Aldershot: Ashgate.
Whitehead, A. N. (1919) *An Enquiry Concerning the Principles of Natural Knowledge*, 2nd edn, Cambridge: Cambridge University Press.
——(1920) *The Concept of Nature*, Cambridge: Cambridge University Press.
——(1925) *Science and the Modern World*, New York, NY: Macmillan.
——(1929) *Process and Reality: An Essay in Cosmology*, New York, NY: Macmillan. Corrected edn (1978), D. R. Griffin and D. W. Sherburne (eds) New York, NY: The Free Press.
——(1933) *Adventures of Ideas*, New York, NY: Macmillan.
——(1938) *Modes of Thought*, New York, NY: Macmillan.
Wittgenstein, L. (1958) *Philosophical Investigations*, trans. G. E. M. Anscombe, Oxford: Blackwell.

Wood, M. (2002) 'Mind the Gap? A Processual Reconsideration of Organizational Knowledge', *Organization*, 9(1): 151–71.

——(2003a) 'The Process of Organizing Knowledge: Exploring the In-between', *Process Studies*, 32(2): 225–43.

——(2003b) 'Journeying form Hippocrates with Bergson and Deleuze', *Organization Studies*, 24(1): 47–68.

Woolgar, S. (1998) *Science: The Very Idea*, Sussex: Ellis Horwood.

Index